THE VAST EXTENT

ON SEEING
AND
NOT SEEING
FURTHER

LAVINIA GREENLAW

faber

First published in the UK in 2024
by Faber & Faber Ltd
The Bindery, 51 Hatton Garden
London EC1N 8HN
This paperback edition first published in 2025

Typeset by Sam Matthews
Printed and bound in the UK by CPI Group (UK) Ltd, Croydon CR0 4YY

A CIP record for this book
is available from the British Library

ISBN 978–0–571–35564–8

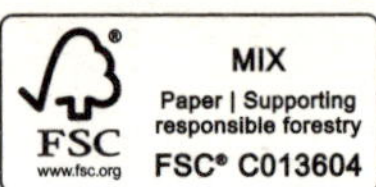

Printed and bound in the UK on FSC® certified paper in line with our continuing
commitment to ethical business practices, sustainability and the environment.
For further information see faber.co.uk/environmental-policy

Our authorised representative in the EU for product safety is
Easy Access System Europe, Mustamäe tee 50, 10621 Tallinn, Estonia
gpsr.requests@easproject.com

4 6 8 10 9 7 5 3

Lavinia Greenlaw has published three novels and six collections of poetry. Her three works of non-fiction are *Some Answers Without Questions*, *The Importance of Music to Girls* and *Questions of Travel: William Morris in Iceland*. Her writing has appeared in *frieze*, the *London Review of Books* and the *New Yorker*, among other publications.

Praise for *The Vast Extent*:

'A remarkable book . . . People will be inspired by it to look again at the world and its mysteries. Nothing is closed, everything is open to fresh enquiry. The seen and the unseen are considered equally in prose that is both scrupulous and visionary.' Celia Paul

'*The Vast Extent* is a work to savour . . . An intriguing, expansive work that accepts the limitations of our vision but enlightens the worlds this artist surveys.' Erica Wagner, *Financial Times*

'Kaleidoscopic . . . bright, mournful.' Brian Dillon, *Guardian*

'Indescribably brilliant . . . [Greenlaw's] truly astonishing range and accomplishments are reflected in this truly astonishing non-fiction book, which she describes as the consolidation of thirty years of work attending to a number of fundamental questions.' Ian Sansom, *Daily Telegraph*

'There is a life's worth of reflection here and a rare pleasure to be had in discovering connections in the writer's thinking, gathered sometimes decades apart. A rewarding and thought-provoking read.' Jessica Traynor, *Irish Times*

Also by Lavinia Greenlaw

poetry
NIGHT PHOTOGRAPH
A WORLD WHERE NEWS TRAVELLED SLOWLY
MINSK
THE CASUAL PERFECT
A DOUBLE SORROW: TROILUS AND CRISEYDE
THE BUILT MOMENT

fiction
IN THE CITY OF LOVE'S SLEEP
MARY GEORGE OF ALLNORTHOVER
AN IRRESPONSIBLE AGE

other works
SOME ANSWERS WITHOUT QUESTIONS
THE IMPORTANCE OF MUSIC TO GIRLS
QUESTIONS OF TRAVEL: WILLIAM MORRIS IN ICELAND
THOUGHTS OF A NIGHT SEA (with Garry Fabian Miller)
AUDIO OBSCURA (with Julian Abrams)
JOY DIVISION (with Michael Bracewell and Glenn Brown)

When I am looking, I am not afraid.

i.m.
Reynold Benedict Lachlan Greenlaw
1966–2021

Contents

. . . the comprehension of our understandings comes
exceeding short of the vast extent of things . . .

John Locke, *An Essay Concerning
Human Understanding* (1689)

One thing beside another (a foreword)

In 1993, I published my first book, *Night Photograph*. The title poem is about being out at sea in the middle of the night and trying to describe the darkness. I've been writing about the difficulties and variables of vision ever since. How do we make sense of what we see? How do we describe what we have never seen before? I'm interested in the things that help us see more clearly (especially interruption and disruption) and those that persuade us to see what's not there. There are times when we want to see more or need to see less, or when we can only see what we expect to.

My way into these questions has been through subjects such as early photography, caves, myopia, bad weather, mountains, microscopes, gilding and the commercial uses of radium. They have in common the kind of arrest that prompts us to pay attention while making us aware of the limits of our attentiveness. It took a long time to find a framework for this. I wanted to keep alive the nature of my practice, which is to travel the question rather than try to answer it, and then to unsettle my subjects so that they tilted a little as in Elizabeth Bishop's '. . . tipping/ of an object toward the light'.[1] My intention has been to draw things to the surface, place them in arrangement while keeping the parts apart, and to leave the reader free to cast their own light and to turn these things over in their own mind as I have in mine.

I've come to think of this form as the exploded essay, and a record of how thought builds and ideas emerge. Each is a series of short texts that cast light on one another rather like the aspects of a poem. They align artworks, myth, strange voyages, scientific scrutiny, reminiscence and a poet's response. I followed all this back through my notebooks and found the moments when something shaped my thinking. I also undertook conversations with scientists, embedded here as moments of live exchange. The parameters of the book are informed by my training in seventeenth-century Netherlandish art and my interest in the Early Modern period in Northern Europe, in particular the formulation of empiricism. I'm engaging with the canon and the writing of history by situating overlooked figures in counterpoint. I've let each essay evolve over several years, waiting for the parts to accumulate, and to reveal and deepen their connections. This has taken a decade and consolidates a thirty-year body of work.

I have approached this in the spirit in which I filled my notebooks, enacting the ways in which these parts align autonomously, leaving me to catch up. My themes often emerge out of the placing of one thing beside another; or by them placing themselves. The consideration of each subject is constrained by it being observed within an arrangement, from a particular aspect and at a specific time. Eventually, I discover a point of connection and within that, the themes in play and the questions I didn't know I was exploring.

Art, science and vision inform one another. My approach has been shaped by growing up in a family of scientists and doctors, and in particular by conversations, from our teenage years onwards, with my younger brother about time and space, meaning and the human scale. He studied physics and philosophy before completing a PhD in astrophysics, and gently showed me that my 'seeing' was qualified by habits of perception of which I was unaware. My brother died recently and this book is dedicated to him as an extension of our lifelong conversation.

1

... Oh what is
this light that
holds us fast? ...
'An Image of Leda', Frank O'Hara[1]

I was about to move house and the move was happening quickly. My new home was just four miles east but I was leaving the part of London where I was born and had lived for most of my life. Although the reasons for moving were happy ones, I hadn't anticipated the level of unsettlement it would bring about. One day, feeling overwhelmed by the detail of it all, I decided that it would be a lot simpler to live in a cave. I was walking past a cinema and went into whatever was showing just to be able to sit in the dark. It was a film about a cave.[2]

The Chauvet Cave was discovered in 1994. It had long ago been sealed off by rockfall, leaving its 32,000-year-old paintings perfectly preserved. The pale walls are covered in bison, horses, rhinoceroses, lions and bears. They are strikingly fluid – a lion's profile is given in a single six-foot-long stroke – but the artist has done even more to bring them alive. The cave is full of outcrops and recesses, the walls ripple and dip, and the animals have been drawn accordingly. One bison has been given eight legs and a rhinoceros six horns to indicate, like a series of frames, that they are moving. Seeking a cave,

I had entered a cinema where I was watching a film about a cave that was a cinema.

The archaeologists and historians mapping and researching the cave had the open mind, and open imagination, that perhaps come from operating so far beyond the ordinary human scale. One said that he dreamt of lions. 'Real lions or painted lions?' 'Both.' He sounded surprised to be asked to make the distinction. Another tried to explain how the world might have been perceived 32,000 years ago, describing an everyday condition of metamorphosis: 'A tree can speak . . . a wall can talk to us, refuse or accept us.'

In the cinema – a place of talking walls – we forget where we are and observe where we aren't. It's a brief but powerful form of exemption like that of entering a cave. The world we find ourselves outside can seem wonderfully clear but this clarity depends on the surrounding darkness. Caught up in the act of watching (so much less strenuous than looking), we dissolve into that darkness by forgetting it exists.

In my cinema cave, I was outside the world as it was now conjured and so safe to accept the presence of lions of any kind. I was in perfect relation to a framed and lit experience that I could explore but didn't have to enter into. I was held fast by the light because it held me in place in the dark.

Yet the cinema is 'cruel/like a miracle' as Frank O'Hara says. It overpowers and obliterates, compels our desires and fools us into 'loving/a shadow and caress-/ing a disguise!'[3] Like all imagery, cinema is a way of testing connection. It's a rehearsal of contact that might be disappointing or disturbing, but is a point of triangulation with the actual, a way of creating a frame, or framework, that we seem to need.

2

Down the one path . . .

'Orpheus, Eurydice, Hermes', Rainer Maria Rilke[4]

To come across a cave where you don't expect it is like discovering a secret. The unexpected rupture draws you in. An unannounced point of access is a chance to see further but only if you are willing to step sideways into the dark.

There is a consistency to walking along any shoreline. We tend to do it in a straight line, from end to end, or one point to the next, channelled between cliffs or dunes on one side and water on the other. A cave is an interruption and a release. As a child wandering along the beach, I would be looking for drama: not so much for something to happen as for something to mean something. I'd always enter a cave but not go so far into it that I couldn't see its entrance. The point was being in the dark but able to see the light, and for the lit world to notice that I was gone and to come looking.

In 1998, I was in Slovenia when my hosts suggested that we visit some caves. They were casual enough about the idea for me to envisage nothing more than a series of the minor recesses I knew from childhood. Almost half of Slovenia sits on karst, bedrock perforated by water. There are around ten thousand caves and I was about to enter one of the largest cave systems of this type not only in the country but in the world.

We walked along a river, which suddenly folded itself away below rock. Then we too were folded away, entering a tunnel just big enough not to feel like one. We joined a group with a guide and I stopped worrying because this was now an organised experience. I didn't want the thrill of exploration. I wanted a brief excursion with someone leading me through every step. As we set off into the mountain, I depended on the guide as proof that wherever we were going had been made safe. I wasn't heading into the dark to look at anything (in which case I would prefer to be alone) but as a test of my ability to enter it and remain there. The tunnel was gently and consistently lit, and in order not to panic I focused on that consistency. Everyone else was relaxed, the guide offhand, nothing was going to happen. I concentrated on fooling my body into accepting where it was – not moving away from the world, just following its reach down a well-made path.

I want to say that we were on that gently descending path for an hour but I've found out since that it was only about four hundred feet long. The slowness was in the time it took for me to adjust to the unfolding scale of this journey and my need to keep remaking the decision that I was not going to turn back, which had the effect in my mind of returning me to the start.

As we passed into a cavern the size of a small church, I looked back at the tunnel to remind myself that I could leave whenever I wanted to. At that moment the guide shut a door that I hadn't noticed behind us. It felt as if the tunnel had rolled itself up and snapped back into the earth. The cavern was gently lit and so I set myself visual distractions, moving from one rock formation to the next and peering closely so as to keep my peripheral vision vague. If I couldn't see a ceiling of rock over my head, there wasn't one.

If there had been painted lions, I might have been able to forget where I was. Instead there were columns and accumulations which looked as if they were being continuously and infinitesimally forced into shape. In even the most eroded form, I insisted on finding something familiar, discerning gods and monsters in the slightest detail. This was a kind of visual making safe – not wanting to be somewhere so unknown that I refused its strangeness.

There is an exact point at which I find a space too small or too crowded to remain there. My body makes a calculation and its decision is absolute. I've climbed an enclosed spiral staircase in a tower without concern only for the walls to contract a couple of inches making it impossible for me to continue. The tunnel had been just large enough and this cavern's spaciousness was a relief, yet I kept turning towards that door because I could only stay if it were possible to leave at any moment.

The guide then turned off the lights. The darkness was so substantial that I felt as if I could lean into it. It was more than air and less than solid, texture or pressure – a form of touch. I felt it on my skin rather than my eyes, and its effect was to make me give up my body. I wasn't anxious anymore but somehow released.

The lights went back on and I waited for the door to be opened, only it wasn't. This was just the start of the journey. We walked on through a series of caves and I found that my fear had been altered by that interval in the dark. My senses had loosened to such an extent that my usual calibrations couldn't be carried out. I no longer knew how large or small a space I was in, or how far I had walked or for how long. It wasn't that this didn't matter. It didn't occur.

We walked under a river. I stood below its bed listening to the force of the water and the river was as clear to me as if I had seen it. We ended up on a precarious path of wooden planks strung high on the wall of the underground canyon that brought that river back above ground. We made our way back towards the light as if through an aperture: reconstituted, redeveloped, re-fixed.

3

> When we know the full extent of any danger, when we can
> accustom our eyes to it, a great deal of apprehension vanishes . . .
> Edmund Burke[5]

As a child, I spent a lot of time lying awake in the dark. Night was a condition I was obliged to accept, as inexorable as weather or a feeling. It meant stillness, silence and self-reliance. It was also a space in which to think. What does a child remember before they can name what they see? Whatever repeats itself: the presences, from a human face to a slant of light, that return in the same form and in the same place, accumulating substance. My earliest memory is of night and two shapes within it: the concentration of detail that was the corner of a picture on the wall beside my bed and the long fall of a curtain. I later moved to a room at the back of the house. Part of a sunken extension, it had small windows close to ground level. Daylight did not press in. There were no cracks or stains to animate, no recess or ornament. Nothing cast shadows or made the curtains ripple. There were no passing headlights, no lighthouse beam, no silhouettes of rattling branches. It was neither cinema nor cave but plain black box.

I played with the dark, not populating it with stories or characters but taking advantage of its freedom from visual laws, conjuring a world – the real world – in which the scale of things was infinitely adjustable and myself within it. I rearranged cities or set up home under a leaf. To invent a game is to furnish emptiness.

Every summer, from eight to sixteen, I was sent to Forest School Camps. The traditions of the camp included cooking on a fire, working in groups called 'clans', gathering every morning at a log circle for 'rally', singing folk songs, whittling and carving wood, and playing the Night Game. For this the entire camp, aged seven to seventy, was divided into two teams identified by the colour of a piece of wool tied around your upper arm. This was your 'life'. The teams then set off after dark to opposite sides of a wood or hill. The objective was to reach the other team's home with that wool, that is your life, intact while taking as many lives as you could. Beyond that, you were on your own. As it was dark, each team had a password by which to identify their comrades but this was quickly dismissed after one or two had yelled it too loudly.

The first time I played, I must have been about ten. The wood was large enough to swallow forty people. As everyone scattered I found myself alone, hearing the game already being played out in bursts of noise – a scuffle or crash, shouts, laughter. I barely registered being caught and having my life taken. What gripped me was being out in the woods after dark and left to my own devices. I wasn't scared because this wasn't night but the Night Game. I had a role and knew the rules: this was only a game and I was sure of its full extent.

I remember bushes like low blue clouds, the tiny hooks that caught at my hair and hands, the shit-stink of unearthed rot, and the mucus veneer on the roots I grabbed as I slid down a steep slope. I remember this wood as every wood. The ground might be hard wax or black squelch or dust. I waded through dead leaves and hid among green ones. I have taken that night and turned its parts into pieces and laid them out as a game in all the woods I've ever known.

I don't know if it was being young that made me unafraid. I don't think so. It was the fact that by imposing the Night Game on the night, we defused it. The dark felt no more dangerous to me than an adventure playground. I was thrilled and alert as I crept and tumbled towards the other side, knowing that in all likelihood someone was going to get me. Whoever I met was the enemy. I imagine the adults operated some restraint but teenagers and children attacked one another with full force. It was easy to break that piece of wool and so take your life, so the fighting part of it was never extensive. As soon as your life was gone, you were left to walk back to your own side. You were a ghost now and could take your time. Nothing could harm you.

4

A sixteenth-century print of Night (Hendrik Goltzius' *Nox*) caught my eye because of its colours: the drab olive and buff of a mind running on empty. It looked as crushingly humdrum as the fifth sleepless night in a row. Night is perched at the front of a chariot being drawn across a cloud. She's naked except for a piece of cloth barely caught on her shoulders. The effect is not erotic but of someone on auto-pilot. Night is inevitable and when you can't sleep, or aren't allowed to, it can feel as if the world is turning while you stand still.

This is the ur-routine – night following day. She seems indifferent to the blazing torch in her hand or the direction of travel. In the back of her charabanc, Sleep is portrayed as a woman slumped on one elbow, still wearing her garland, like a battle-weary teenage girl going home in a cab in the small hours. Goltzius is a better artist than this image suggests but *Nox* is one of a series of prints and his approach seems as routine as the scene feels. It's a worn-out idea, which makes it apt as an image of insomnia. Another night, another day, moving and not moving through the grey perpetual.

Night lived in a cave, as did her son Sleep. She produced oracles while he lay on a couch as the river of forgetfulness flowed past and his children brought him dreams. His first son collected dreams of people, the second those of animals and the third of things. So night and sleep are located in places of suspension and withdrawal where the world arrives in categories of images (like a series of woodcuts).

Consider what night meant in 1600 beyond the lantern in your hand, the fire in the hearth, the candle by your pillow. The darkness that surrounds a light has substance and presence but that is my conception of darkness from a well-lit world. Walk into the dark and it starts to break down. Night would have been both more absolute and more accessible, moonlight less decorative and more of a practical necessity. Was darkness more potent then? Although we now seem to move more safely and swiftly through it, perhaps it increases in power, in mystery, the less of it there is.

5

I talked to the neuroscientist Colin Blakemore[6] about what happens to my perceptions when I enter the dark. The questions I took with me were, I thought, straightforward.

1 What are our eyes and brain trying to do when we look into the dark?

2 How do we physically and mentally compensate for a lack of light?

3 What happens to our sense of space (and what's around us) in the dark? How do we perceive and respond to being in a dark room as opposed to being in open darkness? Would we be able to sense containment and its scale?

4 Why do we find it easier to engage with an image in the dark? Do we better remember what we see when it's isolated?

5 Are there imperatives that drive us to seek the dark?

6 Do we think differently in the dark?

7 What happens when we move from light into dark and vice versa?

I noticed that ahead of answering them, Professor Blakemore took a moment to adapt to my perspective. At one point, he described a question as 'poetic' which provoked defensiveness in me because of what people who use the word usually intend by it. Yet listening back to our conversation, I realised what he meant. His criteria were so different to mine, even when I did my best not to bring poetry into it.

LG: I don't feel as if I stop looking when I'm in absolute darkness.

CB: Some of what you're looking at is non-existent internal events.

We see light that isn't there.* The photopigments in our eyes that react to light and communicate its presence to the brain have to be sensitive to the point of instability. This means that sometimes they react at random and the brain sees light where there is none.

CB: You'll like it because it is poetic: the technical term is dark light.

It pleases me that dark light corrects the thing it names but it is also one of those scientific terms that writes its own poem and so should be left to its own 'poetic' devices. Such terms are irresistible to those looking for a placeholder for meaning – another form of seeing light that isn't there.† Dark light was originally named in German, as *Eigengrau*, 'own grey' or *Eigenlicht*, 'own light'. It is now more usually known as 'visual noise'. We are not seeing darkness when we look at the dark but noise. Nor are we seeing all we see. The brain sets itself limits so as to tune some of this dark light, grey light, own light out. We may be capable of detecting a flash of light as small as one photon but we only register a flash larger than around five.

The obvious thing that happens in the dark is that we rely more on our other senses, particularly on what we can hear.

CB: You start to discover information which is present in your other senses, which you're not normally aware of.

* Our brain can also hear what isn't there. Brain scans taken of people looking at an image of a barking dog showed that the auditory area of the brain had been activated.
† *Dark Light* has been used as an album title by Gary Numan and East 17, and as a book, film and play title. *Eigengrau* is the name of an album by Section 25.

Once I experienced the kind of darkness that made me lose any sense of what I was walking on let alone moving through. I was returning from a pub in Yorkshire down a steep lane with a friend. This was not a place we knew and being city people, we hadn't thought to bring a torch. The sky was cave-dark, as was the surface of the road. I couldn't see where I was putting my feet and so could not believe that there was anything there to meet them. I started to walk with exaggerated steps as if more emphatic movement would force this blackness to take shape. It didn't. Had the darkness been more defined, I might have felt that I could see it or was looking into it, but this was a flattening of vision. I had no sense of dimension.

If you are blind, hearing becomes a way of reading the visual world. John Hull recorded the experience of going blind as a form of spatial collapse. He also described how the sound of rain could recover that space, its activation of acoustics giving him a physical sense of his surroundings. Using the 'regularities and irregularities' of sound, he could build up a visual picture out of the 'drumming staccato' of rain on metal, the 'deeper, duller impact on brick or concrete' and how the 'note being struck' differs from one window pane to another. This way, he could build a picture that extended almost to neighbouring houses.[7]

Even in a cave it takes a while for darkness to become really dark. The photopigments have been bleached and take a while to reset themselves. This is why when you close your eyes, you catch an after-image of whatever you were just looking at. 'Dark adaptation' takes about half an hour, by which time those photopigments are ready to respond. In what first seemed like total darkness, we can now make out furniture, stalactites, a hedgerow, a gilded ceiling or gleam of water. Writing about the 'idea of black', Locke observes how in the absence of light, the eye can still form a clear image – of the mouth of a cave, someone's shadow or an unlit window.

As well as reliance on hearing, sudden darkness prompts a more subtle perceptual adjustment. Although we describe our senses separately, most of the time they are working in synthesis. When a sense is shut down, the others rely more than usual on what the brain already knows and is predicting. If you're in a cave, you hear that dripping sound as moisture falling from a stalactite rather than a tap someone's forgotten to turn off.

LG: In the dark, are we visually active or passive; are we seeing or looking?

CB: I don't know if that translates into a scientific question. If it's in the dark, how can we be seeing anything?

LG: What I mean is, are my eyes actively engaging with the darkness?

CB: This is very poetic.

LG: When we enter the dark, we start to imagine. Is this because of the emphasis our brain is putting on memory? Is the imagination just something thrown together from what we already know to make up for a lapse in perception? Does this help us activate memory and imagination?

CB: Pass on that. I don't think the data exists.

My interest is in what all this tells us about how we receive the world. The scientist is more interested in how we process it.

LG: What about metaphorical darkness? Do you ever feel yourself moving into the unknown or is your work always at a point of logical progression?

CB: The best of science is both things. Very rarely do scientists just take a stab at something without having given any thought to it, without there being any precedent. In the lab you wouldn't say 'Why don't we just put this and that together and see what it does?'

LG: Any more than I would sit down and say I think I'll write a poem.

CB: There's always a background. We're driven by hypotheses. That's the way brains are made to work: what am I looking at — a tree or a person?

If we open up the question of what happens when we can't see, we find within it further questions sitting one inside the other. What is it that we still see? What are the limits of vision? Why are there limits at all?

CB: Science is at its best when the data departs from your expectations but in consistent and meaningful ways, and you suddenly begin to see a different interpretation emerging.

6

For though great light be insufferable to our eyes,
  yet the highest degree of darkness does not at all disease them.
    John Locke[8]

We're used to thinking of light as a tool for knowledge – we are enlightened – but darkness is one too. We test what we know against what we don't. Any insight arrives together with a realisation that the more you know, the more there is to know. The proportion of darkness stays constant to the proportion of light just as we need to sleep and dream as much as we need to act and think. This figurative light and dark translate back into the physical world. The lights go on and the darkness grows. In both senses, we enter the dark less and less, and forget how to move through it, thinking the lit path the safest route when in actuality it exposes us and disables our vision.

Each line of enquiry involves a series of decisions between a number of paths or possibilities and so the aperture closes. Locke says that 'the eye, judging of objects only by its own sight, cannot but be pleased with what it discovers, having less regret for what has escaped it, because it is unknown'.[9] But while we cannot see what we have not seen, we can imagine it.[*] Here, now, where every moment has its signs, cues and images, darkness is precious but it is also disarming in a way we are no longer used to. There's nothing to read and no windows to open.

[*] See 'The imagined image', p. 270, in which a consideration of speculative vision returns us to the starting point of seeing, not seeing further, science and art.

We don't want absolute light — it blinds us — but absolute dark can be something we crave: its restfulness, its insistence on slowness and stillness, and the way it wakens the senses. It is so encompassing that it sensitises us to the present. We can neither look back nor see ahead.

Darkness is present tense, an escape from memory and anticipation and to that extent an escape from ourselves. It gives us a greater sense of space than anything else and yet we do not inhabit it but always feel on the edge of it or about to enter. In this way, it reminds us that we are our starting point and out there is possibility. There is always more to see — and more to see in ourselves — whether we choose to or not.

Solidity, appearance, dullness

1

When J. M. Barrie, the author of *Peter Pan*, was six, his elder brother David died in a skating accident on the eve of his fourteenth birthday. His mother fell into obsessive grief, making it clear that David was irreplaceable. Barrie's response was as logical as it was fantastical: he would become his brother. He perfected David's mannerisms, dressed up in his clothes and sprang his surprise. His mother was horrified. In the rush of such an appearance, the mind responds with involuntary joyful recognition before realising that it has been fooled. She would have been trying to understand that she'd never see David again and yet there he was – and wasn't – in a version close enough to be tormenting.

Regardless of his mother's reaction, this episode seems to have fixed in Barrie the belief that it is possible, through sheer force of imagination, to overcome the difference between yourself and someone else, past and future, life and death. Becoming someone else could be as simple as dressing up. If you put on a pirate's hat then that is who you are. *Peter Pan* is a depiction of childhood that asks questions and offers solutions as a child might for themselves. If you aren't happy in this world, invent another. The imagined world can be as vivid and palpable as the real one, sometimes more so. We enter this story as we would a game, taking up rules we invent as we go along as if they have announced themselves. We want this freedom but also to be told what to do with it. The children accept the strange boy with his torn shadow because he knows the rules. They do not question that if they jump out of the window, they will be able to fly.

There is a time in a child's development when they're able to describe what they see but their vision is not yet regulated by an awareness of physical laws. They've discovered the urge to make sense of things — how the world works — and reach for whatever logic suggests itself. A shadow is a clear shape and so could be perceived as a physical object. Neverland is a child's construction: casual, expedient, spontaneous and built out of what comes to hand — be it an alarm clock or an angry father. It is also unsustainable because it doesn't make sense. Just when the reader, like the children, has put their faith in Peter, Barrie discloses that Peter 'said anything that came into his head'. The great adventure stalls. The children, the Lost Boys, the pirates and even Peter Pan behave in this magical world as they would in the ordinary one. We look around us and see fairies, pirates and crocodiles but sooner or later we argue about the washing-up. Perhaps every world is the same world because we are the same in it.

In the world of *Peter Pan*, time has substance. It lurks in the form of Captain Hook's watch ticking away in the belly of the crocodile who bit off his arm. As the creature slithers through the action we are made to feel, like the pirate, that time has already consumed part of us and is coming for the rest. It's as if the ordinary time of breakfast and school and father coming home from work has been subsumed while the children are in Neverland but even so there it is, ticking away. It's the same in the real world, with the numbers sliding past, hands revolving on a dial, calendars rolling by, but numbers focus us on measurement so we think about how long, short, fast or slow time might be. We rarely think about how it consumes us. Mrs Darling, who sees Peter first, who already knows him, who traps his shadow, has maintained a direct connection to the world of childhood and her child self. She knows what she's lost in growing up, that she has solidified and dulled, and mourns the fact that this will happen to her daughter too.

Childhood becomes crowded with warnings. Children are taught to look but not touch – fire or crocodiles – and that the space beyond the window will not catch them and that they will fall. They're learning that vision provides information intended to stop them in their tracks and that there are many things they can only look at or hear, not touch or taste. Vision is the freest of our senses, the one that can roam furthest, the most instant and uncontrollable. A child's unregulated vision is a form of flight.

> The idea of *solidity* we receive by our touch; and it arises from the resistance which we find in body, to the entrance of any other body into the place it possesses, till it has left it. There is no idea, which we receive more constantly from sensation, than solidity.
> John Locke[1]

We bump into something and are forced to navigate it and so understand that it is there. This extends to things we know we'd be able to touch if we could reach them such as the watch in the crocodile's belly. The imagination works all the harder to come up with the appearance of something when we cannot see it but know where and what it is.

The solidity of an image lends it presence and engages our senses. A shadow is not abstract, nor is it material. While cloud, smoke and fog have some molecular substance, a shadow has none. It is evidence of the interruption of light through which we've learnt to measure time. Peter's shadow is torn off as he slips out of the bedroom window in a rush when Mrs Darling slams it behind him. The shadow is time and he needs it back. If time did not pursue Peter's every step, what would he be resisting? There would be no need to refuse to grow up.

We can hear and smell things that aren't there – music or a scent in the air – but we can't touch or taste them. Vision is more emphatic because of how difficult it is to separate what is seen from what is 'really' there. We may understand that the water on the road is a mirage but still see it. Visual presence is proof of existence. Our shadow holds us in place, in that it is an indication of where we are and when. It also reassures us of our solidity: we interrupt the light and given that such interruption is what reveals the world to us and makes it real, it makes us real too. Without his shadow, Peter wouldn't be able to experience his own presence.

The shadow is, like time, something we can never escape. It reminds us that we're visible even when we cannot see ourselves. Wendy is often depicted as swoony and eager, but she can also be construed as the expression of her mother's inner tension. She's a child under pressure to rehearse the woman she must become. She's not ready to go through the motions of being a mother, and does so ineptly and desperately from her first meeting with Peter to her running the home in Neverland. Why is Wendy keen to play house when she could be fighting pirates? Perhaps she thinks she has to. (Barrie assumed she would.) When she meets Peter, she's entranced and shocked, but falls back on mechanical good manners (becoming her mother's shadow). Peter is pragmatic and invites her to Neverland after she's proved herself useful by sewing his own shadow back on. It's her job, like her mother's, to tidy up and, in this case, to repair the rupture in time.

In a sketch of his mother's life, Barrie depicted her turning away from childhood: 'I see her frocks lengthening . . . and the games given reluctantly up. The horror of my boyhood was that I knew a time would come when I also must give up the games . . . I felt that I must continue playing in secret, and I took this shadow to her, when she told me her own experience, which convinced us both that we were very like each other inside.'[2] This remembered, or perhaps imagined, moment of affinity contrasts with his desperate attempts to become his brother so as to reach her. He writes unthinkingly of the metaphorical as solid matter, taking his secret playing self to his mother in the form of a shadow.

Our own solid selves are mutable but inescapable. Adulthood must have been painful for Barrie, who never seemed fully grown. He was not much more than five feet tall and having endured romantic rejection, turned his desires inwards. His peculiar notes, a sort of third-person diary, record deep humiliation and a revulsion towards intimacy. They also document a recurring nightmare about marriage. His wife Mary endured a husband who was absent in all ways and she eventually divorced him. They had no children.

Barrie met the brothers who inspired *Peter Pan* in 1897, on his daily walk in Kensington Gardens. George and Jack Llewelyn Davies were beautiful boys of four and three, romantically kitted out in red velvet caps. Their brother Peter was in his pram. Barrie courted the children and their mother, wore down their father, offered financial help and inserted himself into the family. He acted as if it were his right to take them over, as if they were already his characters. Two more boys, Michael and Nico, arrived before both parents died of cancer. They made Barrie guardian, having grown dependent on his support.

Home is a fraught construction, and the Darling marriage enacts this. The larger shadow is cast by Mr Darling and the children are eager to escape it. Like his alter ego Captain Hook, he has constructed a kingdom and needs to be reassured that he is its king. Both men are obsessed by humiliation and want to be loved but make themselves unloveable. Mrs Darling must contain him as well as the children and this has eroded her. Barrie says she has 'no proper spirit', but she's also the basis for Mr Darling's dissatisfaction. He cannot know or possess her. Mrs Darling's 'romantic mind' is like boxes one inside the other and 'however many you discover there is always one more'. She has a kiss on the corner of her mouth which no one can claim: 'He got all of her except the innermost box and the kiss. He never knew about the box, and in time he gave up trying for the kiss.' Her mind, the kiss (hers or someone else's) are made tangible and then placed out of reach, intensifying both possibility and failure. Barrie describes Peter Pan as being very like Mrs Darling's unattainable kiss.

If something materialises, it can be grasped and manipulated. Mrs Darling may keep the innermost box of her mind to herself but at night she 'tidies' the minds of her children just as she shuts Peter's shadow in a drawer. We can see this aspect of Mrs Darling's nature, of her relationship with her husband and how she controls her children, because we can see the series of boxes used to describe it. Although her children's minds are not described, they are made visible by her act of tidying them: we see cupboards or drawers because she reaches into them.

Imagery allows us to envisage and comprehend what cannot be seen but it is drawn from ourselves, ready-made out of our histories and associations, our emblems, motifs and subconscious. A completed image has a physicality that makes it into an object. Time solidifies into a watch which we cannot help but listen to. A woman's deepest self is a box within boxes. A shadow lacks substance but is visible and so able to become its own thing, although what it becomes is inanimate – something to be folded (like a child's mind) and kept in a drawer.

We grow up and learn not always to trust what we see and that others see things differently. Peter's vision remains clear because it is without the empathy that is key to this compromise. The fact that his shadow is so easily detached suggests that he can move through the world without affect. For him, this is all a game: 'Peter had seen many tragedies but he had forgotten them all.' He never remembers so everything is new. He has no more attachment to the Darling children than he has to the Lost Boys, whose numbers vary as they 'get killed and so on'. Flying to Neverland isn't fun for long. When the children are on their 'second sea and third night', Michael falters and sinks towards the sea, which Peter observes with animal detachment before swooping down to rescue him. Even then 'it was his cleverness that interested him and not the saving of human life'. Both Wendy and Tinker Bell are brought back from death by a game within a game. When he discovers Tink dying, Peter at first has a child's blank curiosity. He does the same with Wendy. Then he invents a game.

Peter's tragedy, and perhaps Barrie's, is that he cannot construct a world without others even as he cannot relate to them. When Tink almost dies, Peter howls with fear at being left alone. He depends on others to create and enact his world. Without a cast or an audience, there can be no adventure. Peter would have no role, no one to be, and there will be no one left to play the game. Barrie stopped growing when he reached the age at which his brother David died. Was he resisting that moment happening or trapped within it? Like many writers, Barrie only realised later what he was exploring. Having labelled Peter 'the boy who would not grow up', he said that the story's 'true meaning came to me – Desperate attempt to grow up but can't'.[3]

2

In one of my father's notebooks, I found a conversation that he had with his shadow six years before he died and shortly before his dementia started to make itself known. His perceptions were informed by childhood trauma, and by time spent as a naval pilot, a medical student and a doctor who became a psychoanalyst. Unlike his children, he had excellent sight throughout his life. As I read it, I found myself in conversation with this conversation.

The shadow – an experience of solitude

[He was alone but this is not about that.
It's about feeling alone.]

I was sitting in the window with my back to the light so that I could see the newspaper more clearly.

[Turning away from the light in order to see more clearly.]

As I lowered the paper to think about some piece of political nonsense, I was shocked to see an image of myself on the opposite wall of the room.

[He sees it as an image before he makes sense of it as shadow.]

The low winter sun had cast my shadow as a clean-cut silhouette like the old portrait silhouettes whose blank blackness suggested the character of the sitter so vividly.

[No light or colour but vividness. Of character.]

It was definitely me. I could easily recognise that.

[Definitely. Easily. Not words he often used.]

I looked to the left to watch the image change, but I could not obtain a full profile and see it without straining my eye muscles.

[The proof that it is him lies in it changing as he changes.]

I could make the image move.

[He realises that he can control himself.]

Suddenly I had a feeling of existing and of physical reality which was not usually there.

[He realises that he is not usually there.]

This shadow self was so real that I thought I could address it. I was reminded of the day when I met my Scottish cousin Charlie Webster. The moment when we met on the path in front of his house was like meeting an identical twin or another version of oneself.

[The shock of recognition and that what
he is recognising is himself and that he did not know himself.
His father died when he was eighteen months old.
He had no one in whom to see himself.]

This projected image on the wall felt as if it had more substance than I did.

> [We cannot see our own substance.]

It was as though I was looking out from myself to reality outside – over there.

> [Reality is over there, even his real self.]

Mayakovsky's title 'A Cloud in Trousers' came to mind.

> *then the twilight*
> *spun around from the window*
> *and stomped off into nightmarish darkness*
> *frowning,*
> *decemberish.*[4]

And R. S. Thomas's identity difficulties – his autobiography entitled *Neb* meaning 'Nobody' or 'Anybody'. About the birth of his son he said that he was puzzled that 'nobody could give rise to somebody'.

> [His clinical phrase – 'identity difficulties'.]

> *We made a brave foray;*
> *the engagement was furious.*
> *We came back alone.*[5]

I began to talk to this shadow with more substance than myself.

I could feel the interest and pleasure in holding a conversation with this inviting stranger. We could sit down together and exchange views, observations, questions, jokes and laugh over the absurdity of life.

[He is setting a tone and it is that of books and pictures and plays.
It is two men on a bench, waiting.
Two men who meet on a path in the forest.
Two men who play chess in an empty room.
Two men passing in a valley on horseback.
Two men, strangers, pausing in their separate journeys,
passing something back and forth
until it makes them laugh and they feel brave enough to go on.]

I started to talk to myself and observed the response, but then
stopped, the experience was too strange, too unsettling. Who was
the real person and who was the shadow.

[It is one thing to feel an affinity, quite another to be so alike.]

[There is no question mark – as if he assumed
there could be no answer.]

3

LG: I'd like to ask you about the problem of the shadow
being defining but not material.

CB: Nothing is material. It's all just shadows in your
eye. In that sense Plato was right. There are no solid
objects in our understanding except through touch.
We create the apparent solidity from a flat pattern
of variations of light and dark in the eye. That's all
there is.

You cannot invent a shadow. It is evidence of presence just as uninterrupted light is proof of emptiness. In his *Natural History*, Pliny the Elder says that while the Greeks and Egyptians argued over the origin of painting, 'all agree that it began with tracing an outline round a man's shadow'.[6] Pliny goes on to tell the story of the daughter of a potter in Corinth who, when her lover was going away, drew round the shadow of his face on a wall (I wonder what her father, a maker of solid objects, thought of that?). This story is often told because of its pathos. Someone is leaving and all you can capture of them before they go is the way in which their presence altered the light – what we do when we take a photograph.* She was bound by time and place and had to endure separation – but she wanted him still to appear, even when he wasn't there.

A shadow allows us to see clearly. It comes from somewhere and is of something. She was not only a bereft young woman but an artist attempting to intervene as little as possible between image and subject. How did she draw his outline without interrupting it?† She too must have cast a shadow. Her subject was someone she did not want to recast in the conventions of portraiture as a soldier, a king, a shepherd or a god. She wasn't interested in what he might represent but in him. In capturing the most *superficial* thing about him, she felt in contact with his innermost self. As with cut-out silhouettes, there is nothing to distract us in a shadow from the impact of presence.

* See 'Boredom, repetition, fixatives', p. 60, on early photography and constructing memories.
† See 'Seeing clearly, glimpsing, picturing', p. 75, on artists getting out of the way, and in the way, of their images; also 'Becoming, resistance, dissolve', p. 93, on ways in which they try to resist taking full control of an image and how the image itself might resist them.

The tracing of an outline was nothing new. It is what our eyes are doing as they organise visual material, finding the edge. It's where we meet the surface of what we're looking at and so is where vision meets touch. She wanted to sustain a sense of touch through the tracing of an edge. The urge to capture what cannot be grasped or will not remain is central to artistic impulse: the withdrawing, veering, distant, flaring, whispering, blaring, creeping and scuttling aspects of vision – not what I'm looking at but what appears.

4

When that misty vapour was agone
And cleare and faire was the morning.
   'The Complaint of the Black Knight', John Lydgate[7]

In the early days of the internet as a recreational tool, I found myself compelled by live-streams of nothing happening. The drama lay in the possibility that it might and that I had no agency in this. There were webcams trained on otter dens and eagles' nests and I could get stuck staring at a river bank or cliff edge. I was being given the chance to see a remarkable event but only if I kept watching. When confronted with action, we sit back and take it in. When nothing is happening but might, we search for detail, activity, change. The action is ours.

My favourite webcams were trained on the marshes behind Snape Maltings concert hall near the Suffolk town of Aldeburgh. They weren't even live streams but took a single picture once an hour between dawn and dusk. I saved 150 of them over three years. The cameras rarely caught a bird let alone a boat or passer-by. All there was to look at was light and water. The day was often dull. Dullness offers the kind of light we can look into even though much of it is grey. At Snape, this meant the smoky ember grey of winter dusk, the trout grey of overcast summer mornings, the grubby polyester grey of a July afternoon and the pre-fabricated grey of clouds in the autumn doldrums.

This low, flat coastal land has often been called dull. The eighteenth-century poet George Crabbe lived in Aldeburgh and his book-length poem about the town, *The Borough*, is best known as the source of the story of *Peter Grimes*.[8] It is also a meditation on dullness that extends from the landscape to the pattern of the days: 'At the same time the same dull views to see'.

This is the relentlessness of nothing happening. The view is either water or mud. What little movement there is is predictable. In the poem, Crabbe uses the word 'dull' seventeen times.

> Here dull and hopeless he'd lie down and trace
> How sidelong crabs had scrawi'd their crooked race[9]

Peter has nothing to look at except the marks left by a crab in the mud. Not even the crab. The day is long and full of wearying tasks, the birds are tuneless and the piano playing he overhears is mechanical: 'note after note, all dull to them alike'. Dullness acts as a glue in the mind of someone who is 'cold, selfish, dull, inanimate, unkind'. It encourages resistance to disturbance, inertia, drawing in, and a hardening of surface and response. In Crabbe's borough, drunks and children, music and theatre, success and feelings, the days and whatever labours they hold are all dull.

In Aldeburgh's medieval moot hall, you can see Thomas Thurlow's 1855 group portrait, *The Town Worthies*. These pungent, bearded men look a bit like Rembrandt's *The Syndics* (1662) although while the syndics were negotiating religious interests, the Worthies' story is one of more basic squabbles.[10] They divided into two Beach Companies, the Uptowners and Downtowners, gathered at the North and South Look-Outs respectively, and competed to pilot ships to London and elsewhere. They were salvagemen and lifeboatmen too and, along with the semaphore men, were trying to net something of the life that passed by.

The overall impression is of life drained out of everything. Yet dullness is no more neutral a condition than boredom. If you look at a town or a mudflat and call it dull, you are not indifferent. There's a sense of expectation not met and that visual pleasures sought are being denied. Visual dullness is a failure to stimulate and there are times when that's a relief. Crabbe is alert to the consolations of tedium and the melancholy it enables: 'He nursed the feelings these dull scenes produce' and lingered by the sluice to listen to its 'dull, unvaried, sadd'ning sound'. Grimes could have a reliable experience, one that enabled him to have feelings, if only flat ones.

Virginia Woolf described Aldeburgh as a 'miserable, dull sea village'.[11] She was not casual in her use of adjectives and the fact that she required both 'miserable' and 'dull' tells you how oppressive she found the place. A dull setting makes us assume that life is dull, and the mind dulled as Crabbe suggests, yet *The Borough* is a dramatic story of a volatile place where opium, alcohol and sex tamp down the violence for a while. Dullness can be an excuse to seek out what pleasure you can.

I was often at Snape during those webcam years, standing within the landscape that I then sought out on screen. For me, the two were not the same thing. The webcam pictures were crude and juddering whereas the actual view is always beautiful because it is mostly sky with a low foreground of reeds and water. The weather was often not what I'd expect. The webcam recorded a dawn of palest pink and blue with the sun concentrating into a rosy laser beam in February. On a misty April dawn, the river and sky broke up into one another while the reed beds feathered and blurred. Another spring morning was full of such white light that there was nothing for the eye to meet. One March there was snow on the reeds and the next year, a brilliant blue sky laid over with cirrus. In December and January, seven in the morning and four thirty in the afternoon were inky smears. Real dullness was found mid-afternoon midsummer but compensated for by an August dawn in which the sun spilled fire. One April morning, at two minutes to eight, the camera translated the sunrise into a pink stripe that ran down one side of the picture. These optical accidents drew attention to depths of colour which were really there: cobalt in April, cerulean in June, parma-violet in September. The reeds could appear as straw, seaweed, heather or astroturf. One October dawn was a gaseous red swirl as if the camera had been retrained on Mars.

I particularly liked a shot from one November, just before four in the afternoon, in which the low sun blasted the river with light, blackening the reeds and trees. The crude mechanics of the webcam created a series of tiny refractions and if you looked carefully, you could see that the river bank was lined with a strip of rainbow. There was almost always cloud of some kind, usually nimbostratus and stratocumulus – low-level, vaguely defined and associated with drizzle. Despite this, there wasn't much evidence of rain – perhaps an August shower captured as white streaks against luminous greens and on some autumn days, watery smears on the screen. Often, the view was so monotonous that I thought the camera had got stuck. Sometimes it had.

5

Observe the lovely gliding of the clouds, and how their drift and shapes are related to one another, because the eye of the artist must always recognise things by their essence while the common folk see only weird shapes.

Samuel van Hoogstraten (1678)[12]

In 1995, I became the first artist in residence at London's Science Museum. I grew up among scientists and while I respect their work, I'm more interested in what frames and lies behind it. Going into the museum every week for a year meant that I could see past the foreground. The rockets, planes and engines that captured my immediate attention were soon bulky furniture I made my way past in order to reach quieter presences. Among these were the watercolour sketches of Luke Howard who, at the turn of the nineteenth century, classified clouds as cumulus, cirrus, nimbus, etc. In these pictures I saw a drive to be clear as well as the difficulty of fixing the image without investment. To draw a cloud might be a way to escape the similes that inevitably come to mind. Could he really stop his eye from assuming it knew the shape he was attempting to reproduce? The frail, decisive brushstrokes, the way in which he seems to have wanted to make as little impact on the paper as possible, reminded me of what it's like to want to pin down what you see while knowing that your version will inevitably be more crude and more dull. A cloud isn't solid but paper is. Words have solidity too and they can dull what they describe.

Luke Howard was a manufacturing chemist and a scientist who went to some lengths to distinguish what he did from science. After school, he endured 'a laborious apprenticeship' with a chemist. A serious accident, in which he slipped from a ladder and smashed a bottle of arsenic which gashed his wrist so that some of it entered his artery, led to the tedium of convalescence, time he spent researching the properties of pollen using a microscope. He had a factory east of London and the routine of his commute to and from the place each day, which he passed '*sub dio*' (below the open sky), was alleviated by recording the weather. He wrote his renowned 'Essay on Clouds' because it was his turn to present a paper to the philosophical society he belonged to, otherwise he would be fined. He makes it all sound so incidental, so usual, so dull.

Goethe came across this essay and sent Howard a request. He asked him for an account of his life. Howard was told of Goethe's 'prodigious inclination to sing the Praises of Thy Theory of Clouds' but at first thought this a hoax. Perhaps he distrusted such over-excitement. Reassured – 'one of their very celebrated Poets of Weimar (I think)' – Howard sent his life in ten pages 'having neither so much to say as Benjamin Franklin, nor so much to pass over as Julius Caesar'.[13] He told Goethe about the ways in which he had been constrained or distracted from the pure practice of science but did so in the form of celebration. His five children, well-educated but not sent away, were 'a source of affectionate enjoyment'. His Quaker faith was the primary reason for his 'comparative unfruitfulness in Science' but he was committed to playing an active role in the community and to offering charitable aid. Howard raised thousands of pounds for war relief in Europe and travelled there just after the Napoleonic retreat to offer help. On this journey, his scientific impulse led him to record everything from a stork's dance to the design of continental quilts and the process of evaporation at a saltworks.

Unusual weather phenomena fascinated Howard from childhood: 'I settled in my mind one remarkable configuration of the Clouds in full sky, because it was of rare occurrence.' He several times saw the aurora borealis over Britain. When he was eleven, he experienced 'the *haze*' of 1783, later understood to have been volcanic ash 'and very distinctly also the passage and appearances' of a meteor that summer. He was woken in the night by its brightness. But when it came to writing a paper, it was ordinary weather that he chose to investigate.

Howard's first argument against his right to be considered a scientist was the fact that at school he learnt too much Latin and not enough maths. I'm curious about the notion that you can learn too much of a language. Perhaps he found that words leapt too quickly or with too much variety to mind, colouring what he was trying to see clearly. Despite this, he honed his powers of observation: 'My pretensions as a man of science are consequently but slender: being born, however, with observant faculties, I began even here to make use of them, as well as I could without a guide.'[14] Not having a guide can mean getting lost or it can mean, as it did for Howard, a particularly open-minded approach. This is not a case of not knowing what he was doing but of intensive training from an early age – not in science, perhaps, but in scientific method.

The world of industrial chemistry he describes in his letter to Goethe was competitive and dependent on 'using, while we can do it exclusively, the few new facts that turn up in the routine of practice'. His business thrived but he chose not to publish research in chemistry, explaining that he had to '*live* by the practice of Chemistry as an art, and not by exhibiting it as a science'. Keeping industrial secrets was more important than publishing new discoveries. But he also pointed out that 'the Establishment' helped him evolve chemicals and he was consequently able to provide them with better ones. The Establishment was 'for the most part unconscious of [his research's] existence'. He did eventually become a fellow of the Royal Society, 'to which I have sent some Papers'. He called his thinking 'ideas' rather than science.

Howard was keen to learn from new developments but equally keen to announce his limitations, describing the work of Antoine Lavoisier as 'the Sun's rising after a night of moonshine'. As science became more dependent on mathematics, Howard was conscious of what he lacked: 'Chemistry is now betrothed to Mathematics, and is in consequence grown somewhat shy of her former admirers.' He also had the gift of being present while averted, of being a family man, a community leader, a manufacturer and of spending much time in deep thought: 'People say I am weather-wise, but I tell them I am very often otherwise.'

Ten pages is a fair amount for someone who presents themselves as so inconsequential. Over the years, I've returned to this letter and have a stronger sense of Howard as neither dull nor modest. He was confident of the value of his themes and sent Goethe recommendations for further reading. His declaration of his lack of qualifications and his rejection of the name of 'science' were not an admission of his work being secondary to that of scientists who did not have to work, or travel to work, or run a business or devote themselves to charity. He was asserting the worth of a different approach and was confident of the value of his findings. He distrusted the self-importance that comes with achievement but he believed in the achievement.

Goethe, who wrote twelve thousand letters in his lifetime, sent a note promising a full response. He translated Howard's letter but there is no trace of this reply.

Distance, deception, glow of fire

1

For a short while, the highest point of the New York skyline was marked by a girl standing on tiptoe.[*] She was also the brightest point, at night subject to sixty-six incandescent lamps and ten spotlights at a time when the city was largely unelectrified. During the day, the sun detonated her gilded surface.

> The weather had cleared before we went to bed, and as we
> stepped out of our hotel that morning, the sun shone blindingly
> on the snow-covered park, the gold Diana flashed against a
> green-blue sky.
>
> Willa Cather, *My Mortal Enemy* (1926)[1]

Get closer and you would have seen that she was no girl but a thirteen-foot-high goddess holding a bow and arrow, the string tautly drawn. She was Diana, the goddess glimpsed bathing in a forest pool by the hunter Actaeon, whom she turned into a stag to be torn to death by his hounds. At the turn of the twentieth century Diana stood above New York, untouchable and irresistible, drawing the gaze of those who might have been made to feel (like Actaeon) abruptly closer to the ground, their animal selves exposed.

---

[*] This is generally believed to be the case but has been contested as the tower and statue are attributed with various heights.

Distance brings about the refinement of abstraction. Detail falls away and we're left with large shapes: the epic, the emblematic, ideals rather than feelings. Things take on a universal outline that we can all respond to and an image opens up in terms of time as well as space.

Diana was commissioned in the 1890s by the architect Stanford White for his redesigned Madison Square Garden. The largest amphitheatre in America, it was a home for sporting events, dog shows, political conventions and all-round spectaculars. White topped the building with a lavish 300-foot-high tower and asked his friend the sculptor Augustus Saint-Gaudens to create a weathervane to crown what was going to be the highest vantage point in the city. He wanted the extra height so as to trump a recently built skyscraper nearby.

The first Diana was eighteen feet high and too cumbersome to turn in the wind so Saint-Gaudens came up with a version that was not only lighter but more lithe. Although she had drapery attached, intended to billow out behind her, this Diana was scandalously naked. Forty-two feet higher than the Statue of Liberty, she was intensely visible and way out of reach. A 1901 visitors' guide described how at night

the graceful lines of the tower are half-disclosed and half-suggested, and Diana reveals herself to us in the radiance of electric light.[2]

There is a point at which light ceases to expose and starts to deflect. When the original Diana was installed, White marked the occasion with a festival of light. There were 6,600 electric bulbs strung along Madison Square Garden and another 1,400 on the tower. Unlike the goddess in her dappled shade, this Diana was bathed in the brilliance of ten enormous arc-lights.[3] How could anyone have seen anything?

Actaeon makes his way towards Diana because he too has been dazzled and needs to turn away. The day is at its brightest. 'Midday had contracted every shadow' and he wants to rest after a morning's hunting.[4] At such times, light turns our gaze back on us. Who would not be seeking shade? His path is not deliberate. He 'strays with aimless steps through the strange wood'.[5] If he is drawn to anything, it is to a gentle intensification of light – the suggestion of a clearing or water.

When his eyes fall upon the naked goddess, she's bathing in a pool, surrounded by her nymphs, who immediately move to conceal her. Actaeon's gaze is turned back on him in a way that is pre-emptive. In Ovid's version, there is no moment at which he actually catches sight of Diana. Instead he is described as being seen to be about to see: 'the naked nymphs, seeing a man's face'.[6] This inverted action leads to the inversion of himself. He becomes the subject of a desire he barely registers and is torn apart by it.

New York's Diana was designed for distance. She is not the work of antiquity she appears but a glorified weathervane. The emphatic alignment of her gaze, her bow and arrow, and flatly angled arms reflect the need for her to be clear about the direction in which she's facing. Made of beaten copper sheets held together by invisible rivets, she is hollow and, though supported inside by an iron armature, light enough to turn in the wind. Her pose is conventional but precarious: balancing on top of a sphere on one leg, tiptoe.

The city below may not have been brightly lit but it was roaring towards the twentieth century. Its less grand streets were crammed to bursting point. Stephen Crane's novella *Maggie: A Street Girl*, published the same year that Diana appeared, is set on the Bowery:

a dark region where . . . Long streamers of garments fluttered from fire-escapes . . . A thousand odors of cooking food came forth to the street. The building quivered and creaked from the weight of humanity stamping about in its bowels.[7]

Maggie is led astray by a man who dazzles and diminishes her.

She saw the golden glitter of the place where Pete was to take her. An entertainment of many hues and many melodies where she was afraid she might appear small and mouse-colored.[8]

New York is a city where the eye is drawn upwards, and Crane's truck-driver Jimmie

fell into the habit, when starting on a long journey, of fixing his eye on a high and distant object, commanding his horses to begin, and then going into a sort of a trance of observation.[9]

Jimmie's city is crammed with 'places of forgetfulness', bars and theatres, fumy yellow-green interiors, 'interminable rows of cars, pulled by slipping horses', the chink of coin and glass and 'machine-like music', and new electric lights which 'whirring softly, shed a blurred radiance'.[10] Wouldn't the blurred radiance of Diana have been another place of forgetfulness?

O. Henry, in his story of 1904, 'The Lady Higher Up', makes Diana his subject.

The statue of Diana on the tower of the Garden—its constancy shown by its weathercock ways, its innocence by the coating of gold that it has acquired, its devotion to style by its single, graceful flying scarf, its candour and artlessness by its habit of ever drawing the long bow, its metropolitanism by its posture of swift flight to catch a Harlem train—remained poised with its arrow pointed across the upper bay.[11]

Close up, you see that he has a point. She has the efficient modern body of the tennis-playing tomboy. Her toes splay as she steadies herself, her knuckles flare as they grip the string of her drawn bow. The way in which her raised leg turns slightly in, the attention given to her knees, wrists and elbows, suggest the close study of a model and the desire for her to look not only divine but real. Did people think of Diana as a real woman? A real goddess? A real statue? The immediate response to her suggests that she looked too real to be thought of as the real thing. And the fact that she was 'the second' reminded people that she was not after all a divine apparition but the product of a laborious process.

I first came across her in an atrium by a café in the Metropolitan Museum of Art in New York, only it wasn't her but a copy taken later from a test cast. Less than half Diana's eventual size, this version is made from gilded bronze rather than copper. She's more moderate than the real thing and lacks impact. Somehow the eye knows that this is a reproduction of a version. She's a copy of a model for a study of a woman.

The model for Diana, Julia Baird, was not unlike Maggie. Just seventeen and the youngest of seven children with a widowed mother, she'd started earning a living as soon as she could and was already well known among artists as a talented sitter who was able to become whatever was required. She understood that her job was not to appear real but as a realisation. Her authenticity lay in the artist's recognition of what he was looking for. Saint-Gaudens only used Baird for Diana's body. Her head was modelled on that of his mistress Davida Clark, making Diana a concoction of popular and private favourites. She is both component and ideal as if the perfect woman cannot exist but must always be constructed.

The world Diana looked down upon in 1893 was one in which the 'real' was increasingly contrived and invested. That same year Henry James published a story set in London called 'The Real Thing' in which an artist who makes his living as an illustrator is prevailed upon by a genteel but impoverished couple looking for work as models.[12] The couple have long ago learnt that they make an attractive image which can provide a generalised cachet: 'There was something in them for a waistcoat-maker, an hotel-keeper or a soap-vendor.' They are the worn-out original that has been reproduced too many times, the woman's lovely but mask-like face showing 'friction as an exposed surface shows it'. Diana did not survive the city's scrutiny. Her drapery was quickly lost and her surfaces corroded. How exposed she must have been, blasted by all weathers as her light went gradually out. An attempt was made to turn her to more practical use when in 1924 experiments were undergone to see if she would make a good radio aerial. Eventually she was reduced to the company logo for the foundry where she was made and used to advertise kitchens on television. Madison Square Garden ran at a continuous loss until it went bankrupt and passed into the hands of The

New York Insurance Company, who demolished the building and erected a skyscraper in its place. The city was starting to rise and there were new landmarks, new amazements. *The Evening News* of 1911 observed that 'the people stare from one thing to another . . . without so much as a wink at poor little Diana . . .'[13] Had she remained, Diana would soon have been looked down upon by office workers.

Intended for the sky, Diana was ungainly on the ground. She languished in a Brooklyn warehouse for seven years, where she was 'placed flat, face down, and all the weight of the copper rested on the abdomen, which has caused a very deep sinking'.[14] Plans to relocate her on 'a suitable pedestal'[15] at New York University came to nothing and after six years of negotiations, the insurance company issued an ultimatum:

> I have exhausted myself in efforts to have her suitably placed. They have all come to nothing. I don't want to have her dumped, destroyed, melted, or whatever may happen, without giving you a chance to say a final word.[16]

The university failed to make a feasible offer and so the exasperated insurance company agreed to give her to the Pennsylvania Museum of Art in Philadelphia, who paid for her restoration.

In 2013 Diana was regilded, a process that took five months and 180 square feet of gold leaf. Even though she was refinished according to the sculptor's original instructions with 'matting and toning' to make her 'glow not glance', she is shocking — once again a brash insouciant advertisement for high living. She stands in the museum's Great Staircase Hall. The walls, floors and stairs are thundercloud grey and she appears as if suspended, as harsh and captivating as a lightning bolt. As I got closer, I saw that what looked like modelling was shading. Diana was the product of and an advertisement for the Gilded Age, and her colouring had been turned up and her shape defined for studio lighting. She is contoured as if by a spray tan and the actual lines of her limbs are far cruder than they appear. Her hollow heel is impaled on a spike that fixes her to the ball on which she stands. I took photographs and looking at them later, saw once again a finely moulded and graceful figure. How apt that she is so photogenic.

Revised, reproduced, brought down to earth and now on a 'suitable pedestal' at last, she brings into the muted indoor space a supernatural wildness that we can only absorb in glimpses.

The snow lay in clinging folds on the bushes, and outlined
every twig of every tree – a line of white upon a line of black.
Madison Square Garden, new and spacious then, looked
to me so light and fanciful, and Saint Gaudens' Diana . . .
stepped out freely and fearlessly into the grey air.
Willa Cather, *My Mortal Enemy* (1926)[17]

2

I visited Berlin in the year after German reunification, when the Wall was gone but the two sides of the city still looked very different. As I walked through the Brandenburg Gate, out of the west and into the east, the lights went out. In the dark I couldn't take in the breadth of the avenue or the scale of its monuments and museums. Where were the streetlamps? The signs? For the theatres and restaurants and shops and stations? Where were all the lit windows? I followed the only light I could see – a small glow that led me into a side street with a string of tiny lights, like electrified candles, which led me to a bar. I hesitated by the dark door, the dim name. How was I to know that I could enter a place unless it displayed a loud welcome in large bright letters?

Soon after that, I was looking out over Leipzig at night from high up in a tower block. The city was also still low lit and my eye was caught by another small glow: a distant golden cupola. I assumed it belonged to a church or palace but it turned out to crown the façade of an old department store built by a textile merchant in 1904. It is one of the city's renowned *Jugendstijl* buildings.

The stone frontage and red roof of the Ebert department store are the neutral background for the decoration that made this building, like Madison Square Garden, a landmark. Thick swags of gilding line the roof edge and sit like helmets on each dormer window. At ground level there are large gilded reliefs of goddesses and peacocks, and to either side of these, owls. The gilding stands apart as if permanently lit up, which would have been the intended effect. Its imagery makes no narrative sense but appears to be emblems for the sake of emblems, as if once the eye has been drawn it must be satisfied by the apparent significance of what it sees.

The building doesn't bring to mind its era – that of the car, the aeroplane, Einstein and Freud. Images of Leipzig in 1904 show the streets strung with wires and tracks, as if the city itself were becoming a machine and no longer a place in which golden owls and goddesses made people stare. There's a photograph taken in 1920 of the department store with 'seasonal sale' posters filling several windows and giant banners carrying the same slogan hung across three entire floors. Ebert's name is in shiny stand-alone letters, again just beneath the cupola, embedded in darker letters beneath its windows, and repeated three more times above the front doors. Now those windows are glazed in tinted glass within black frames. The place doesn't want to invite passersby to peer in at what – or how or to whom – it is selling. There is a new name on the façade, given just once though also in gold letters: Commerzbank. The gilded ornamentation has been restored and, like Diana in the Philadelphia museum, seems rather loud in its new hushed environment. The effect is one of a building turning inwards while gold oozes out of its walls. A friend in Leipzig mentioned that the bank was accused of 'showing off' when it restored the gilding, and so it promoted the history of the building as if to clarify that oozing gold was all about light and nothing to do with money. Ebert's promotional techniques would be considered too vulgar today when so much is big and bright that cachet lies in the understated, the small glow.

The cupola acted as an advertisement and shop sign that could be seen from a distance and guide people towards the store. Ebert also patented a new kind of sign in which layers of paint and glass created a three-dimensional effect, as if the letters themselves were made of solid glass. I would have had no trouble finding or entering his store. Gilding soon gave way to electric bulbs and neon but Ebert's use of brightness and optical illusion had a similar effect. His signs would have dominated a turn-of-the-century Piccadilly Circus or Times Square.

The world was becoming brighter and busier, and so signs

needed to be bigger and louder to get our attention. Henry James wrote in 1899 in *The Awkward Age* that

> London doesn't love the latent or the lurking, has neither time, nor taste, nor sense for anything less discernible than the red flag in front of the steam-roller. It wants cash over the counter and letters ten feet high.[18]

To spot a bright sign and travel towards it is like approaching something we already know. We recognise its purpose and its invitation almost as if we've been there before. In this, the experience is not unlike the memories we return to so often that the details we fix on simplify and brighten as the rest fades.

3

If radium has unknown dangers, it might seriously injure the therapeutic use of radium.

Charles Norris, Chief Medical Examiner of New York[19]

One of the earliest poems I wrote and didn't throw away was about radium.[20] I'd come across a scientific fable which spoke to everything that interested me most: the difficulties of seeing clearly, our impulse to fix an image, to measure, map and name. It's also a fable about a light in the dark and how this entices us only to draw us deeper into the shadows. We give things names in order to convince ourselves that we understand them, that they are under our control. We name fears and ghosts as well as mountains and stars. If something appears to have magical powers then we want to use them without stopping to think about what this might mean.

Just before the First World War, a chemist who had formulated radium-based paint set up a factory in New Jersey which became the US Radium Corporation. The workers, mostly young women, were well paid and their skills much in demand as the potential of luminous paint became clear. The paint was used in aviation instruments and children's toys while radium itself was promoted as a medicine, 'liquid sunshine' which could keep you young and cure the troubled mind. People drank a bottle of Radithor, or 'radium water', as they now drink coconut water. It was said that a millionaire who drank a bottle a day was so evangelical about it that he sent crates to his mistresses and had it fed to his racehorses. Radium-based paint was also promoted to artists as a way of creating glowing nocturnes — not a depiction of light but actual light!

Radium was very new. It had been discovered by Marie and Pierre Curie in 1898 but wasn't isolated until 1910. Its potential for luminescence comes from a process called 'scintillation'. Radium salts are combined with crystalline phosphorescent zinc sulphide. When the alpha particles in the radium strike the zinc crystals, they cause a flash. There are so many flashes that it looks like continuous light.

In 1920, radium was still extremely hard to come by and Curie's research was threatened. She had freely shared all she knew and had given radium away to be used for medical purposes and now she didn't have the resources to acquire any more of it. At this time, a single gram cost $100,000. Forget gold cupolas and goddesses, this was something far more bright and rare.

An American journalist called Marie Meloney raised enough

money from 'the women of America' to finance the production of a gram and enticed Marie Curie to come to the US to receive it. Curie arrived in 1921 and was presented with a gram of radium in a ceremony at the White House. It was produced by the Standard Chemical Company of Pittsburgh, whom she visited. There's a plaque on the building marking the event and claiming that the company had produced 76 of the 120 grams of radium that then existed in the world.

The dial-factory workers made the luminous paint by mixing glue, water and radium salts. They were given good camel-hair brushes, and were taught how to purse their mouths and sharpen the tip when painting fine lines. One later said: 'I think I pointed mine with my lips about six times to every watch dial. It didn't taste funny. It didn't have any taste . . .'[21] It must have seemed as harmless as it was magical. For fun, they painted their teeth and nails to make them glow in the dark.

Their managers and the company scientist did not touch the radium. They used lead shields, masks and tongs. Reports into the workers' health were done by experts covertly working for the company. When they finally hired someone independent, Cecil Drinker, this is what he found:

Dust samples collected in the workroom from various locations and from chairs not used by the workers were all luminous in the dark room. Their hair, faces, hands, arms, necks, the dresses, the underclothes, even the corsets of the dial painters were luminous. One of the girls showed luminous spots on her legs and thighs. The back of another was luminous almost to the waist . . .[22]

The company rewrote Drinker's report.

When the women started to connect the paint with their illnesses, they were told they had anaemia, diphtheria, syphilis. By 1924, nine of the dial painters who had become ill had died. Their deaths were hushed up by the factory owners and were easily denied because the effects of radiation can take years to manifest.[23]

All kinds of lights were going on. Not far away, the New York that Diana still overlooked now had the movies and neon signs. The night must have seemed less dark when it would have been more so.

One of the company's owners suggested that the problem was that these women were only mortal, or less than mortal. They'd been given a chance to lead a brighter life and their downfall was their own doing:

> We unfortunately gave work to a great many people who
> were physically unfit to procure employment in other lines
> of industry. Cripples and persons similarly incapacitated
> were engaged. What was then considered an act of kindness
> on our part has since been turned against us.[24]

Eventually a lawyer called Leonard Grossman took on the women's cause pro bono and after eight appeals, won a case in 1939. Marie Curie had died of the effects of radium poisoning five years earlier although she'd been in contact with the dial painters and had advised them to tackle their 'anaemia' by 'eating plenty of raw calves' liver'. She had at least been clear about one thing: 'I would be only too happy to give any aid that I could, [but] there is absolutely no means of destroying the substance once it enters the human body.'[25] The chemist who set up the factory died soon after. His body was placed in an X-ray machine and was so radioactive that it exposed the plate before the machine had been switched on.

4

In the British Museum there is a golden ring which, like New York's Diana, is actually gilded copper.[26] It shows a kneeling Eros playing with an iynx-wheel, a magical device spun to attract or reel in (straying) lovers. Iynx was a girl who tried to seduce Zeus, or who made a magic potion to help Io seduce him. As punishment she was turned into a bird, the iynx or wry-neck, which was pinioned to a wheel as a tool of enchantment. Or the wheel was smeared with the bird's entrails. Or it made a sound similar to the bird's call. The iynx is an image of trapped flight and trapped sound: in Ancient Greek *iunx* can mean a hiss or a howl or a cry of joy or pain.

The ring is not pure gold. The cry of the bird, of the girl, is not straightforward. This is not a simple story but whichever way it's told, it speaks of artificial attractions: an added bright-ness, a blurred image (is it a wheel or a bird?), a visual spell.

Iynx/iunx is given, tentatively, as the source for *jinx* – that inescapable whir of trouble. A spinning wheel, like a spinning top, confounds our sight. It stays still but moves so fast that we can't make it out. It draws the eye but prohibits touch, compelling us towards something we are not allowed to grasp, to understand. The iynx is a vortex pulling the loved one towards it by disarming their gaze. It is a form of suspension or anti-gravitational force, like a centrifuge, holding everything in tension.

Eros was born of night and darkness, of the rainbow and the

wind, of an egg or sea foam, of Aphrodite, whom he also conceived. With his bright wings, he was the first glimmer in the black void. Apuleius describes him as 'rampaging through people's houses at night armed with his torch and arrows' creating romantic havoc.[27] He's the light that draws you into the dark rather than guides you through it; the god of not seeing clearly.

When Eros decided to seduce Psyche, he had her taken up by the west wind and wafted to a grove where she found a palace. 'All the walls shimmered with their native gleam of solid gold, so that if the sun refused to shine, the house created its own daylight.'[28] This brings to mind J. G. Ballard's memory of entering a derelict casino in Shanghai as a child, where chandeliers lay among the rubbish on the floor while 'everything gold glimmered in the half light'.[29] Ballard goes on to say that while his imagination transformed the place into a magical cavern, 'it held a deeper meaning for me, the sense that reality itself was a stage set that could be dismantled at any moment, and that no matter how magnificent anything appear, it could be swept aside into the past'.

Eros refused to let Psyche see his face, coming to her in the dark and leaving before she woke. Unable to trust what she could not see, she lit a lamp and held it up to look at him sleeping. Just as she saw this beautiful creature, a drop of oil fell from the lamp onto his skin and he woke and took flight. In Giuseppe Maria Crespi's early eighteenth-century depiction, a warm light falls on Cupid's lower half, his erotic self, while his deeper self remains safe in the shadows. A cold light fixes Psyche in her transgressive but recognisably human act.

Gilding is a way of keeping the lights on. In a church, a temple, a bedroom after dark or an unelectrified city at night, it glows. Eros can conjure rooms of solid gold. He can flit in and out of human lives creating a moment of suspended reality, a brief escape in which laws are set aside and everything is in a spin. Psyche transgressed by wanting to know what she shouldn't – by trying to create her own daylight. When the drop of oil falls on Eros's shoulder, Apuleius berates the lamp rather than Psyche:

> O you rash, reckless lamp . . . doubtless you were invented
> by some lover to ensure that he might possess for longer
> and even at night the object of his desire?[30]

As if love were a desire for more light – which turns out to be another form of darkness.

5

The joy of firelight and the sunken sun.
   'After-glow', Ivor Gurney[31]

The lamp in the window welcomes you whereas the security spotlight makes you pull back. The small light is something you can remain outside even as you come close. It will not consume you like the bleaching slice of light that might be triggered by your step.

The small light in the distance – not a searchlight or a light-house beam, not a light that's looking for you or one you are looking for – can offer direction and purpose. It might be a glow that looks like the end of something, embers rather than flames. You were not there at its making, you've arrived after the event, you are drawn towards it. It is unclear, mysterious, intriguing, promising.

A glow invites the eye rather than deflects or hurts it. As you draw near, its source can be too bright to bear, the thing seen too clearly. Drawn to the glow of fire, we measure ourselves in relation to it. What is the safe distance from a naked girl, a god, an unknown element? If we find a light in the dark, we're sometimes not content just to look at it. We want to touch the golden walls, caress the naked goddess, enter the forcefield, bathe in the glow. This desire for experience, for consuming rather than observing, for taking something in, drives us beyond curiosity. We want to be transformed: to be less permeable, less mortal, less poorly lit. Like Stephen Crane's Maggie, we dread returning home to the dark of the ordinary day where light falls in slabs or looms as a chemical spectre.

> The girl went into the gloomy districts by the river, where the
> tall black factories shut in the street and only occasional broad
> beams of light fell across the pavements from saloons . . .
> She went into the blackness of the final block . . . Afar off
> the lights of the avenues glittered as if from an impossible
> distance . . . At the feet of the tall buildings appeared the
> deathly black hue of the river. Some hidden factory sent up
> a yellow glare, that lit for a moment the waters lapping oilily
> against timbers. The varied sounds of life, made joyous by
> distance and seeming unapproachableness, came faintly and
> died away to a silence.[32]

Or we want a withdrawing light, not a light that's looking for us but light we can look into without giving up the dark.

1

John Ruskin liked to say that he was given no toys as a child. He remembered playing with a set of keys and later being given some wooden bricks, a cart and a ball but otherwise that 'the carpet and what patterns I could find in bed covers, dresses, or wall-papers to be examined, were my chief resources'. He passed his days 'contentedly in tracing the squares and comparing the colours of my carpet; – examining the knots in the wood of the floor, or counting the bricks in the opposite houses'.[1] This sounds like either equanimity or desperation. Ruskin must have felt lacking in agency within his constrained and cushioned existence. He was whipped if he cried, protested or disobeyed (that is revealed himself) and 'soon attained serene and secure methods of life and motion', which would depend upon a closely controlled focus.[2] Was he looking for something he could predict and reveal at will? Or was he simply expending visual energy? In that case he could have been tracing, comparing or examining anything. The carpet or bricks would be irrelevant. Time was there to be passed and nothing needed to happen. He had the energy to get bored and the luxury of curiosity.

While Ruskin was staring at the carpet, Felix Mendelssohn was hurtling through tunnels and staggering into caves. In 1829, the young composer visited Fingal's Cave on the island of Staffa. The trip is said to have been the inspiration for his *Hebrides* (or

Fingal's Cave) Overture. Uninhabited and less than a mile long, Staffa rises out of the sea and then out of itself in one great undulation. I made the trip in a small open boat that swayed perpetually and when I stepped onto the island, I swayed too. At the foot of the cliff where a path leads to the cave, stone lies in heaped discs the size of millstones. The entrance to the cave is topped by compressed and sliced layers of basalt that make it look like a built place at odds with the wild green island above it.

Mendelssohn must have been powerfully drawn to the mythical cave as he had to overcome his difficulty with seasickness to visit it. He was violently ill and left it to his companion Karl Klingemann to record the experience.

> We were put out in boats and lifted by the hissing sea up the pillar stumps to the celebrated Fingal's Cave. A greener roar of waves surely never rushed into a stranger cavern – its many pillars making it look like the inside of an immense organ, black and resounding, and absolutely without purpose, and quite alone, the wide grey sea within and without.[3]

The story is that Mendelssohn wrote the opening phrase of his overture while on Staffa but he included that first fragment in a letter to his sister the day before he visited the island. He'd also made a drawing of 'A view towards the Hebrides' and this first musical sketch does seem to have been just that, a view towards. His initial name for the work was 'The Lonely Isle', placing an emphasis on its remoteness. He is looking into an imagined distance, responding to the idea of a place he has yet to reach. Mendelssohn knew the power of the idea of a place as well as the subjective nature of visual memory.

People have tried to persuade me that my imagination
had exaggerated the vastness of the Swiss mountains, the
unearthly forms of which hover among the recollections of
my childhood, and that a snow mountain is not so imposing
as I fancied. I was almost afraid to find myself disillusioned,
but . . . the old feeling came back as at first, and I saw my
memory had exaggerated nothing of it.[4]

He tells a friend that Scotland was just as he said it would be
and that 'Long before you arrive at a place you hear it talked
of.'[5] At that time, according to Klingemann, Staffa was 'in all
the picture-books'.

On the journey home, Mendelssohn stopped off in Liverpool
where he was evidently bored. Liverpool itself must have
been in a state of excitement because the first passenger railway station in the world was about to open in the city. You
can still travel these tunnels, where your train moves through
regular slices of light. It's rather like being celluloid run
through a projector. Before the railway opened in 1830, you
could run yourself through the projector. The curious could
descend through a ventilation shaft and in the gaslit white-
washed tunnel, 'the whole vista appeared like a succession of
superb arches . . . the intervening spaces being left in comparative darkness'.[6]

Mendelssohn walked the almost finished railway 'just to have
something to do' and persuaded a watchman to let him ride on
a car through a tunnel. This would have been the Wapping
Tunnel, the largest of the three that begin at Edge Hill. It runs
down to the docks, the car descending by gravity.

. . . off we went, at a speed of fifteen miles per hour, there
was no horse and no engine there, the car runs on its
own, gradually working itself up to the wildest speed; this
was because it was going just a bit, quite imperceptibly,
downhill; two lamps were burning up front, the daylight
disappeared, the wind blew out the lamps, and then it was
pitch dark, for the first time in my life I saw *nothing*, and
all the while the car racing faster and faster, and clattering
louder – it was a bit rough on my stomach.[7]

He had been at a loose end and walking the railway with no
evident curiosity when he found himself hurtling through the
dark and seeing '*nothing*'. No wonder he felt seasick again.

I have found no indication that Mendelssohn connected his
journey through the tunnel with his journey into the cave but
they connect themselves. The being *put out* into darkness, sudden momentum, the *hiss and roar*, the *black and resounding* tunnel through the *wide grey sea* of the city. Fingal's Cave, with
its high arch, pillars and clattering acoustic, looks and sounds
like a railway station. It is acoustically extreme. A small note
blossoms within it but what's more interesting is how it shapes
the sound of the sea that crashes in and out of it. The water
comes to such a peculiar arrest that it seems to change form.
It doesn't sound like water at all but like oil drums tumbling
about or engines shunting into a siding. Mendelssohn worked
on his overture in Rome and then revised it several times over
the next few years. He went on renaming the piece, too. *Fingal's
Cave* is generally held to be the name suggested by his publisher
and is perhaps too figurative a title for such an unprogrammatic
work. It is not about Fingal or even a cave, but light and water,

movement and noise. When asked by family to describe the Western Highlands, Mendelssohn replied, 'They are not to be described, only played about.' He did not want to talk about what he was writing because that risked the music becoming a repetition. He did not want to repeat himself.

> How much has passed in the meantime. The most horrible sickness, Staffa, scenery, travels, people; Klingemann can describe them . . . the best I have to report can be found in the above lines of music . . .[8]

The overture was criticised for its 'indirectness' and 'veiled effects'. Similar complaints were made about Turner's painting of Fingal's Cave, a place he'd visited in 1831. The American who bought the work declared it 'indistinct', to which Turner retorted, somewhat in the spirit of Mendelssohn, 'Indistinctness is my forte.' His subject, like Mendelssohn's, was to be 'played about' rather than described. The work was intended as an experience rather than an idea.

Turner did, though, recommend that the surface of this 'indistinct' painting be wiped, suggesting that the varnish might have bloomed during the journey across the Atlantic.[9] His painting, like Mendelssohn's piece, is about the sea and sky as forces in perpetual motion – engine noise. The cave is veiled by mist, spray and, above all, smoke from the chimney of a steamboat, which obscures the view its passengers came out to see. Once you settle in, detail rises – the brittle lurching cliffs, the stiff waves starting to fray, and the coarse lingering smoke – just as if someone has wiped the surface.

You can't look at a cave unless you're inside it. Turner (in his painting) sailed past whereas Mendelssohn seems to linger at the cave's mouth. Both capture the difficulty of this subject and the buffeting nature of this place. Mendelssohn struggled to make his overture sound less built, complaining in 1832 that 'the would-be working out of the movement tastes more of counterpoint than of train-oil, sea-gulls, and salted cod – it should be just the other way around'.[10] It's as if he wanted to punch a hole in a wall and give his audience a blast of rich dockside air, bringing Liverpool just as easily to mind.

When I listen to the overture, I don't hear the gulls or smell the cod but I recognise the visual restlessness of the place. The work's form isn't linear or circular so much as perpetual. There are oblique crescendos which bring to mind water being drawn into the cave only to hit the end with surprising awkwardness, as if not knowing what to do with itself. The lurching unsettlement of the work's perspective, from the smallest oscillation of sound trapped in the wind to veering stormbursts, reflects the instability of the experience of getting to the island and being there. The work is full of airy fragilities: a detonated human presence, unable to fix itself just like the light and water from which the image is made.

Mendelssohn was determined on experience. He wrote to his family from London on that same trip:

> I must not keep a diary for then I should see less of life, and
> that must not be. On the contrary, I want to catch hold of
> whatever offers itself to me. Things roll and whirl round
> me and carry me along in a vortex.[11]

More than catching hold of what offered itself, he allowed himself to be carried in a vortex, and to get closer to whatever rolled and whirled. A painting, a poem, a piece of music are thought to fix something for us. Maybe what they offer is the opposite, an activation out of our fixed present-tense selves. My aim is to have the poem enable the reader to find their own repetition of that gesture and so to enter something that they otherwise might not. It should be a rush into a stranger cavern and so yes, a bit rough on the stomach. This is what makes Mendelssohn's overture and Turner's painting so compelling. They are not description but action, not vision but voyage.

2

When my father left school, he was somewhat at a loss. His results were poor, other than in chemistry, and his only real interest was photography. My pragmatic grandmother took him off to Kodak and asked if they'd give him a job. He was spending his days mixing solutions and mopping up spilt mercury when he heard a radio programme about the French aviator Antoine de Saint-Exupéry. There was a recruitment ad for National Service navy pilots in the *Radio Times*. He was bored enough to take a chance and it led to what were perhaps the happiest years of his life, landing planes on aircraft carriers and flying Spitfires, after which he settled down to the family profession of medicine.

His interest in photography was lifelong. He collected books about its early history and I would leaf through them as if they were family albums. Some portraits felt more intimately present and connected to me than my actual relations, for whom photography was mostly a formal affair. Grandparents and great aunts and uncles assumed their roles in front of the camera as naval officer, mayor, soldier, priest, artist, doctor, actor — in costume and with instruments to hand. I was more drawn to the portraits of the nineteenth-century French photographer known as Nadar: Baudelaire emerging like a larva from the chrysalis of his coat, Doré caught up in a checked scarf, the pudgy hands of Bakunin. I had no idea who they were but could tell that these pictures revealed their true nature. Nadar was taking pictures of close friends in a studio in his home. He wrote of waiting to be guided towards his sitters' habits and ideas,[12] relaxing them into themselves through long conversation. They look a bit bored, as if they've been worn down by the tedium of sitting for him into forgetting that they're about to be portrayed.

As Susan Sontag says, photography offers us 'an unearned relationship with the past'.[13] It looks like something we remember and so becomes it. As a teenager, I was most interested, but took no pleasure, in photos of myself. I would stare at myself, trying to work out what it was that made me feel so at odds with my own presence. Nadar noted the different ways in which men and women sought themselves in his pictures.

> Nine times, I would even say eleven times out of ten, you
> will see that the wife is absorbed by the portraits of her
> husband . . . the husband, no less hypnotized but by his
> own image . . .

Doré's careful scarf and vigorous hair signal that he is ready for anything. Baudelaire peeks out of his coat with truculence, as if to suggest that while he is a small presence, he is nonetheless very much there. How long did Doré take to arrange his scarf? Perhaps Nadar did that for him to semaphore Doré's need to cut a dash.

I have found in men considered serious by everyone, in the most eminent personages, an anxiety, an extreme agitation, almost an agony in regard to the most insignificant details of their appearance . . .[14]

Maybe it was the unnerving experience of being presented through someone else's gaze that caused this agitation. The women I could find in those books did not seem to be themselves. They were cast as milkmaids, allegories and nymphs, celebrities, waifs and guttersnipes, fixed in the performance of someone else's narrative or desire. At least the famous women whom Nadar photographed give as much sense of having been steered towards themselves as the men. Sarah Bernhardt comes across as self-sufficient, purposefully absent while present, whereas George Sand looks wearily amused and deeply tired.

Having to stay still was one of the most difficult things about childhood and we were punished at school for not managing it. Waiting for time to pass but wanting, like Mendelssohn, 'to have something to do', I moved inwards, inventing things to think about. There were many empty hours and I exhausted everything within reach that I could either read or look at. I remember the carpets well. I also remember the time spent with my father in the shed he converted into a dark room, watching images develop and then deciding the moment at which they would be transferred, slippery and dripping and still on the move, to the tray of fixative.

The latticed window* of William Henry Fox Talbot (1800–77) is thought to be the earliest extant photographic negative. It

* See 'Peering and noticing, flits and swerves', p. 142, for both Henry and Constance on train travel.

still looks drenched in chemical solution and brings to mind a shipwreck on the seabed. Any medium is thrilling in its earliest years – when the paint (or the fixative) is still wet: the sonnet in English, early cinema or jazz. You can still sense the uncertainty of the maker, the chance by which the thing succeeded and was sustained. There's a vividness to experimental form (something we've not made or seen before) that's similar to that of the memory of any first experience: the first kiss, dance, sex, heartbreak. These things make such an impression that they shape us.

Like Ruskin, Fox Talbot was a wealthy man with time on his hands. On his honeymoon, comparing his sketches of Lake Como to those of his wife Constance, he realised that he could not draw and took up the idea of the photograph. Constance, who also experimented with photography, was an accomplished artist and in wanting to remove the human hand as instrument, her husband might have been removing hers. He also believed that photography could escape human investment.

> The picture, divested of the ideas which accompany it, and
> considered only in its ultimate nature, is but a succession
> or variety of stronger lights thrown upon one part of the
> paper, and of deeper shadows on another.[15]

But we don't 'see' a succession or variety of light. We see a tree or a child or a window. Everything is familiar, every act of vision a repetition, a memory. Yet we crave unmediated experience – even of the cups on the shelf.

Fox Talbot praised photography's capacity to give him an immediate inventory, in this case of 'Articles of China':

. . . the whole cabinet . . . might be depicted on paper in
little more time than it would take him to make a written
inventory . . . And should a thief afterwards purloin the
treasures . . . [a photograph] would certainly be evidence of
a novel kind . . .[16]

The idea that removing human mediation would make an
image into evidence casts the human as impediment rather than
agency. Yet it is the human experience that we look for in – and
bring to – an image whether it's a family snapshot or a still from
CCTV.

Baudelaire, perhaps feeling pinned down by the friend who
pictured him repeatedly over the decades, thought photography
would make things too palpable, that we would cease to imagine.[17]
But a photograph does not replace the imagination; nor does it
place its subject within our grasp. The clarity and fixity that make
a photographic image seem so 'real' are also what constrain it.
Someone looks like this but also like this and this. The patterns in
a carpet change too if you stare at them for long enough.

3

We no longer need to take photographs simply to document a
place. It is there, online, for us to refer to. Our own records have
become more intimate, less of a survey or journal and more about
the things that felt particular to us: what we did and saw and felt
and remembered. Once I would have gone to Paris and taken
pictures of the Eiffel Tower and the Seine to show myself and
others where I'd been. Now they can easily see these sights for
themselves. My pictures will be of a particular cast of light on the

wrought iron of the tower or a conjunction of shadow on a turn in the river. I'll notice something passing, or that I am passing, and capture it. Perhaps I think I'm the only person to have noticed it.

At seventeen, I went to Paris with friends. This felt like a grown-up trip in that it was one without adults and wanting to show that I could be prepared, I brought along a camera and a map. I chose these from among boxes of junk at home, purely for their style and without checking their usefulness. The map was a small, leather-bound book and the camera looked like something that the person who owned the book might have used. It was also small and leather-bound. I quickly discovered that the map made no sense. I was trying to navigate by street corners that no longer existed. I took all the pictures I could and asked my father to help me print them as soon as I got home. They were a disaster. Wisps of shadow and streaks of light. But I kept them for years because they were my pictures of that trip and when I looked at them, I saw what I remembered.

If I'm asked about my earliest memories, the first that come to mind are not the most acute and I wouldn't mention them in speaking of my childhood. They are of a fire in a building beyond the garden wall, honeysuckle in full bloom, and the flight of a released bird. The fire was something I knew on a scale I had not encountered before. The honeysuckle repeated itself each year and so accumulated in my memory, becoming heavier and more convoluted as each summer passed. It was the flight and not the bird that captivated me. Like the flames and the honeysuckle, it arced, dipped and then surged upwards. These three images not only occurred in the same place (that corner of the garden) but took the same shape. My mind has found in them a common experience just like that of Mendelssohn repeating his journey into the tunnel and the cave. Other visual memories are of things breaking out of pattern and shape: driving with my mother past flooded fields and cresting a humpback bridge to see nothing ahead of us but a sheet of water; great drifts of autumn leaves on the pavement; a rare heavy fall of snow.

We need to give form to our visual impressions (that word 'impression' changes our shape, leaves a dent in our surface). The first stage happens in how we see, which we do largely by remembering what we've seen before. The brain receives data which it tries to make sense of according to what it already knows. In this sense, everything is repeated, everything is remembered. A bird's flight is like a flower is like a flame. I spoke to the neuro-psychiatrist Paul Fletcher about this.[18]

LG: How do we make sense of what we see?

PF: By remembering what we've already seen . . . We have prior experiences that we then use to disambiguate current input.

LG: How do we know that what we're looking at is real?

PF: Generally? I don't think we do. I think we just rely on its reliability.

LG: I suppose my brain is thinking it's a bit like . . . it's a bit . . . just trying to find something.

PF: Yes, and it will usually settle on the best explanation it can.

There is also the danger of seeing so clearly that the world starts to unravel, which happens when we lose the frame of memory. The brain can stop offering explanations. My father developed Alzheimer's and lived increasingly in the present moment which meant that his brain didn't have a place to go, as in the immediate past, in order to make sense of what it now encountered. He relied on the distant past, which cast itself up in ways he often found soothing. He occupied different phases of his life and mixed them freely. He was not in a care home in Oxford but there with his squadron. The weather was usually too poor for them to go up, which made sense of all that waiting around. Flying was the prospect of something to do.

My father was otherwise healthy and strong, had excellent vision and could walk for miles before the disease attacked his motor skills. On each visit, he took me on the same walk, stopping to remark on the same curiosities with the same surprised exclamations. When walking became difficult, he liked to sit at his window which was on the top floor and offered a broad view of the city. What captured his attention was a barber's pole on a corner a few streets away. It was something that never stopped moving and never changed. Perhaps every turn seemed new to him. Nothing was a repetition and so he had lost the capacity for boredom. Or maybe the spinning pole's continuity gave him the experience of building a memory, of time still passing, of something being remembered and moved on from despite it being the same thing. Who knows? He could watch it for hours.

Mark Wallinger's work *Ever Since*[19] is a video of the front of a barber's shop. The red-and-white spiral of the pole appears to be the only thing moving until you notice that the clock at the back of the shop is stuck and is repeating the same two seconds over and over. That clock is for those of us who can still remember and want to go about the work of memory. In order to fix the moment, we depend on time passing. My father had lost his sense of both ever and since, the future and past that frame (and allow us to experience) the present.

When he let go of any attempt at narrative, my father lapsed into a state of undiscriminating wonder. He might be looking at a crack in a windowpane or a stain on a cloth but he would stare at whatever it was with rapt attention.

> I can only note that the past is beautiful because one never realises an emotion at the time. It expands later, and thus we don't have complete emotions about the present, only about the past.
>
> Virginia Woolf[20]

In completing our emotions, we place ourselves outside the past; we are looking in, we can now picture it. My father no longer completed anything – not a sentence, a thought or a feeling – but to him, for that brief period of serenity, everything was beautiful, all was remembered.

Sometimes in order to see clearly, we have to place ourselves in the position of not seeing at all. We have to enter the dark or find some other way to lose focus: to become seasick, as Mendelssohn did or, like Ruskin, to stare at the carpet. We have to fall into the place that Klingemann, in his account of the voyage to Staffa, describes as 'black and resounding, and absolutely without purpose'. We have to 'see *nothing*'. Seeing without purpose is not the same as seeing without point. It is being open-eyed and open-minded, susceptible, alert, alive.

Seeing clearly, glimpsing, picturing

1

On my first trip to Los Angeles, the thing I most wanted to see was a painted mouse – not a cartoon but an illumination in a 450-year-old manuscript held by the Getty Museum in Malibu. It is a strikingly ordinary mouse but its presence on this page (not intended by the manuscript's author) points to a moment of profound artistic tension. The mid-sixteenth century was a time of rupture, of the *Beeldenstorm* (the 'image storm', a phrase that conjures the freeing up of details, a stream of scurrying mice) when religious conflict led to the destruction of religious images. Stained-glass windows were smashed, and paintings and statues destroyed. Artists no longer permitted to depict sacred subjects turned to what was left in the frame: the domestic background or landscape, and all that had until now crept around the edges of the scene. The story had been excised; nothing was happening, and so the image was deprived of words. From the silence of viewers awestruck by the vividness and grandeur of religious art, another kind of silence emerged – that of the disconnect. New genres such as landscape and still life started to appear but had not yet been formulated. Modern science was also taking shape as the microscope and telescope extended vision, although alchemy and witchcraft persisted, and empiricism was far from established.*

* See 'Curiosity, wonder, rupture', p. 221.

This 'model book of calligraphy', around a hundred pages of alphabets, was made for Emperor Ferdinand I in 1561 by the calligrapher Georg Bocskay.[1] Three decades later, the emperor's grandson Rudolf II commissioned an artist from Antwerp called Joris Hoefnagel to decorate it. Rather than add conventional marginalia, he filled the pages with grasshoppers, toads, insects and flowers. They take up as much space and call for as much attention as the text. Bocskay's alphabets become the background to plants and animals that step forward, free from label or commentary. They are seen but not described and this alone makes them appear more lifelike.

Unframed, and barely arranged, these images are intended not to be thought of as pictures but to offer the experience of seeing clearly, that is of seeing something 'real'. Hoefnagel extends this realness into *trompes l'oeil* in which a reed or a flower stem appear to be threaded through the paper when you turn the page.

Hoefnagel, also a mapmaker and poet, was a curious man who documented and demonstrated the world. His artistic talent came to light through a drawing he made of his own hand as if the need to capture what he saw was so immediate that it started with capturing himself. Born into a wealthy merchant family in 1545, he travelled widely and recorded:

> agriculture, wine-presses, water-works, ways of
> living, marriages and weddings, dances, festivities,
> and innumerable other subjects . . . He returned to the
> Netherlands with many curiosities, and many pictures of
> strange animals, trees, and other subjects.[2]

Everything was captured as a system, pattern, category, process. The subjects that couldn't be packed up and brought home were pictured. This is what art from the Low Countries came to be known for. As Diderot observed: 'Wherever one goes in that country, one sees art grappling with nature, and always winning.'[3]

Much of what Hoefnagel adds to the manuscript is as ordinary as his mouse although some of it is exotic, such as the recently imported tomato, and there are a few insects that appear to have been invented. There are the creatures we would barely glance at, the small things that flit rapidly across our vision. Many make themselves known as an irritant: ants, spiders, wasps, mayflies, hoverflies, gnats, craneflies, horseflies. There are garden pears and peas, runner beans and chard, mushrooms and filberts; the kind of flowers that we notice only en masse such as campion, crocus, daisy, violet, periwinkle; and plants that knit themselves into the view – bindweed, milkwort, sneezewort, thyme. There are caterpillars, snails, centipedes, moths, frogs and toads, everything that creeps and lurks in the corner. These are not creatures we want to touch.

Why are we being asked to look at them rather than being told what they are and why they are in these groups? They seem to be arranged according to the properties they share with the calligraphic style on their page: a caterpillar's ridge of fine gold hairs underlines thread-like gold lettering; leggy ascenders are echoed in a crane fly; a mussel would fit exactly within the loops above it; the hard curves of a tomato match heavy embellishments. They aren't categorised or sequenced or given a narrative frame. They've been taken out of context and brought to our attention. This enlargement of their smallness draws us in and we are curious simply because we can't, or don't, usually stop to look at them. We can neither touch nor smell nor eat them. All we can do is look and it is safe now to peer closely and possible for us to take our time. They can't bite or sting or crawl across our hands. We are being given a chance to experience a new kind of observation.

Seeing these things clearly, we stop seeing them at all and focus on their surfaces as a wonder of colour and design. What makes this possible is also what stands between them and us: the artist and the page. The artist has put us in place. Looking at Hoefnagel's mouse, I find myself a little above it and unusually close as if on my hands and knees. I can't get any nearer and I can't move. This mouse lives up to its decorative purpose. It might belong on a greeting card as its sweet face and blurred fur are softly appealing. It is a neat part of a symmetrical whole, its body echoing the shape of the apple, its tail the line of the forget-me-not. Its delicacy reiterates that of the fritillary which, like the apple, picks up the mouse's colouring. I sent a message to the museum asking if it were possible to view the manuscript, and received an apologetic reply to say that the three people authorised to turn the pages would all be away during my visit. They did, though, have a high-resolution digital version which I was welcome to view, as well as a number of drawings I'd asked about, and so I made an appointment.

On the day, I had to work out how to get there. I had no car and the museum is out of the city and up in the hills. I asked the concierge at the hotel and he had an idea. One of the Starlight Tour itineraries included the Getty Museum so why not sign up for that? They picked people up right there at the hotel. He gave me the leaflet. You spent the morning at the museum and the afternoon touring the homes of the famous. It sounded like my perfect day. The bus was full as we set off but with each stop at a film studio or theme park, more people got off. By the time we were on the freeway out to Malibu, it was the driver and me. He dropped me in the car park where I was directed towards a pod-like train that carried me up a hill. The Getty Museum is designed to look like Roman villas but what it brings to mind is a sci-fi idea of a city on another planet, one that's going to be far more civilised than Earth. The creatures Hoefnagel chose are the kind that depend on unlit corners, cracks and gaps. The Getty shone, smooth and seamless. I couldn't imagine finding any ants or snails there, let alone mice.

The curator who welcomed me had prepared everything I wanted to see. 'And how did you get here today, Professor Greenlaw?' she asked. I explained about the Starlight Tour, and she managed to look both amused and impressed. I'd pictured myself peering at small pages from a careful distance. Instead, I was looking at high-res images of such quality that I felt as if I were sinking into them. High-res imagery is a kind of super-sight. The surface of the page dissolves and you can zoom in, out and all over as the focus breaks down pigment and brush-stroke on a level that the artist could not have imagined. You plunge into detail – a whisker or a pupil – and then into the detail of that detail. It was in doing this that I saw Hoefnagel's mouse come to life as it must have done four hundred years ago under a magnifying glass.

The first thing that caught my attention was the skin on the inside of the mouse's ear, which looked vulnerable and tough. I understood what it would be like to touch. Hoefnagel spent time getting this right as well as the shape of the mouse's eyes.

There is a fringe of tiny hairs on the ear and the claws are angled and jointed in a way that is emphatically not human. If Mickey Mouse's outsized white gloves move him away from mouse and towards human, these claws pull this mouse the other way. Enlargement reveals delicate attention but also the cruder mechanics of creating a lifelike image. Light and shadow coagulate. The whorl of the ear is a crude daub and the hairs that catch the light are thick bleaching strokes. The apple, which seems to be the most convincing thing on the page, flattens and dulls as its cut surface has the same dryness as its skin. The pips are meant to be glossy, as if freshly revealed, but now they look like glass. The fritillary and forget-me-not are also exposed as visual shorthand. They give our eyes the right cues but no depth of experience.

I'm comparing the high-res versions with the edition that the Getty Institute published in the exact size of the original, that of a small paperback.[4] The authors have identified everything Hoefnagel drew so that we now know we are looking at alpine squill or the caterpillar of the owlet moth.

Without label or commentary, Hoefnagel's subjects depend upon their visual qualities to convey their nature. This wakes us up, prompting us to seek clues rather than take information from a caption or footnote. But lack of explanation can have the opposite effect. If we're not told what we're looking at, how can we see it clearly? Or are we so conditioned to explanation that without it, when we really are seeing clearly, we feel as if we're not seeing at all?

Perhaps seeing clearly is not a matter of emptying the eye of preconception but of pinpointing the moment when the brain is starting to make sense of what it sees and before it has crowded out fresh information with those preconceptions. Karel van Mander, who wrote on the lives of Dutch artists, said of Hoefnagel that 'In his art, it so happened, Jooris found more than he had looked for.'[5] What if he did not consciously pursue visual knowledge? At the very least we are looking for an edge, a surface, a shape to make sense of.

I wanted to see Hoefnagel's mouse in order to compare it to another far more mouse-like mouse drawn some fifty years later by another Netherlandish artist, Jacques de Gheyn II, who was born around the time of the image storm.[*] Despite his close connection to a number of leading artists, scientists and humanists, de Gheyn is a solitary figure. His peripatetic existence reflects the nature of his art. His development can be plotted along a line of moments of influence and enlightenment from which he moved on, taking something with him. He is glimpsed through his work, emulating, absorbing[†] and changing, reminding us of how constructed, how composite, any artist or art really is. De Gheyn, like Hoefnagel, made works for Rudolf II, including four books: 'one for all the quadrupeds, one for the creeping, one for the flying, and one for the swimming, animals and fishes.'[6] More than any of his contemporaries, he is able to set aside good taste (something much harder to do than we think) and follow nature beyond harmony, giving his field mouse and crab accurate but seemingly disproportionate legs and claws.

Seventeenth-century Netherlandish art is known for its

* Jacques de Gheyn II (1565–1629). Born in Antwerp, de Gheyn lived in Haarlem, Amsterdam, Leiden and from 1603 in The Hague, where his engraving and print publishing seem to have ended. From then on, he concentrated on drawing and painting.
† For artists absorbing their subject, see also Bruegel, swallowing mountains in order to spit them out, 'Black and white and colour', p. 103.

inviting depth of field. When I first looked at the work of de Gheyn, I was struck by an opposite sensation, that of being pushed away. Isolated and treated as a visual phenomenon, a matter of surface and edge, the mouse that we're used to glimpsing is made both more real and more strange. This push and pull stimulates our curiosity – we know this but in the same moment, we don't. It's as if de Gheyn is able to empty his eye and draw without preconception. His sense of surprise reverberates in the finished work so that we too see a mouse, a rose, a frog as if for the first time.

De Gheyn's intent gaze and liking for multiple aspects is that of the scientist turning the sample over and over under the microscope lens, like a wondering child turning an object over in their hands. There is the same desire to grasp: to know *and* to possess. Do I want to possess this mouse? Not really. It looks as if it smells bad and is capable of giving a sharp nip. When I returned to this drawing after twenty years, it had been relabelled *Four Studies of a Diseased Mouse* with reference made to 'this apparently sick mouse, with its swollen eyes and fur standing on end'.[7] I'd taken those details to be true to its wildness, its realness. The stressed fur enacts a response to our scrutiny; the detail of the bones and cartilage of the feet convey the force and tension needed for survival. It makes Hoefnagel's mouse look positively shampooed.

Hoefnagel's pages are full of the opened surfaces that were to become ubiquitous in Dutch naturalism: a quartered pear, a split pod of peas, a walnut in its half shell, a prised mussel. De Gheyn's surfaces remain closed. While the empiricist project would be to crack the object open, de Gheyn resists. He depends upon the surface to express the substance, arresting our eye. Even when drawing a flayed arm for an anatomy lesson, he resists everything but the surface as if capturing the bark of a tree. Undisturbed, his subjects seem to reveal their essence. We glimpse what a mouse might actually be (which makes us more aware of what we expected it to be). But we aren't looking at the mouse in its natural environment. Here it is a specimen.

Seeing clearly isn't a matter of looking at what is there. We need an image, a metaphor, a description. We need to be encouraged to look, to be given a frame and for the thing to be made clear. This is a strenuous process as Francis Bacon knew: 'the nature of things betrays itself more readily under the vexations of art'.[8] De Gheyn 'realised that it was very necessary to work a great deal from life and at the same time from the imagination, so as to learn to understand all the rules of art'.[9] If artistic vision is a matter of vexation and betrayal, then scientific vision is perhaps a kind of erasure. I asked Colin Blakemore what a scientist considers when trying to see clearly.

LG: Is it a problem for you as a scientist? That you need to strip away habits of vision and perception?

CB: That's what most of science is aimed at doing. It's aimed at providing reliable, unbiased mechanisms for interpretation – microscopes, meters, instruments and things that don't have perception layered on them – that literally measure things as they really are . . .

Scientists use the word 'artefact' to describe something erroneous that is interfering with a signal or record. That is, as Professor Blakemore said, 'distorting appropriate interpretation'.

Technology provides data but interpretation, the application of data, depends on the scientist. Technology has given science its instruments but also a way to explain itself that relies less on metaphor. Science – and physics in particular – has become abstract and remote to the extent that many people think it is of no relevance to their lives. Yet we still look to scientific facts to decide an argument and have only recently begun to interrogate the process of fact-making. The scientific image is a resource. It is not a replication of visual experience. It concerns structure and form whereas visual art encompasses the action of the eye animating both the drawing and the viewing experience. Or a scientific image is an artefact, something constructed within the context of technology, culture and belief.

De Gheyn's insistence on what is seen rather than what is known sets him apart from the scientist as much as it does from his more conventional contemporaries. We now prize his drawings (the Getty has several in their collection) and are far more likely to put a frog or a mouse on our walls than a historical scene. But the superior genre of his period was the history painting and he was determined to become a painter, regretting the years wasted on what he saw as lesser work. De Gheyn's paintings are terrible. He seems incapable of drama. He painted Julius Caesar on horseback 'writing and dictating simultaneously to his scribes' (which may sound impressive but is an unusual choice of event when looked at in the context of Caesar's life). It somehow doesn't surprise me that if de Gheyn chose this subject himself, it was the emperor's intellectual feat that drew him. What is notable about the moment – that the man can write and speak at once – cannot be depicted. Caesar and his six scribes are awkward figures. His horse, cut off at the knees, looks directly at us and rolls its eyes. The atmosphere is that of a seminar. The lack of depth that served de Gheyn so well when projecting small creatures out of the page does not work here. The group are in a tent but the perspective is so shallow that some of the scribes appear to be woven into the curtains. This is not to say that de Gheyn was unable to capture human life. His female nudes prefigure and even exceed those of Rembrandt in their accuracy and empathy. His *Four Studies of a Woman* has a conversational feel to it, as if he is as present as his subject rather than being both all-seeing and absent.[10] They seem used to chatting while she does her hair, and he is attentive to every aspect of her form – elbows, ankles and knees as well as her belly and breasts.

The Starlight Tours bus picked me up in the Getty car park and once again I was the sole passenger until we reached the first film studio. By the time we arrived back at the depot, a storm had broken and Los Angeles was beset by heavy rain. The second half of my tour was cancelled and I was put on another bus that sat on a gridlocked freeway for hours before delivering me back to the hotel. I was surprised to feel so dis-appointed that I wasn't going to spend the afternoon visiting celebrity homes. I knew that in reality I would be straining to see a gate, a hedge, a drive, perhaps a roof or window. The only possible pleasure would be that of proximity. I would take a glimpsed detail of these strangers' homes and build a picture out of it: I would picture them. As I sat on that bus in torrential rain, I thought of the mice of Los Angeles erupting out of the background and streaming through the city as their world, which runs beneath, behind and through our own, filled up with rain.

2

The naturalist Gilbert White (1720–93) is famous for *The Natural History of Selborne*, a minute study of the area of Hampshire he lived in all his life, which spanned much of the eighteenth century. Like Ruskin, he saw clearly in part because he enjoyed both comfort and confidence. He looked closely at everything, noting how a bat shielded its face while eating a fly, how it disposed of the wings and how it sipped water while swooping across the surface of a pond. The world around him was there to be scrutinised and he reached into the picture and took what details he wanted to examine back to his room. He preserved specimens in liquid, a practice that began in the age of Hoefnagel and de Gheyn.

> I have procured some of the mice mentioned in my former
> letters, which I have preserved in brandy. From the colour,
> shape, size, and manner of nesting, I make no doubt but
> that the species is nondescript . . .[11]

The subject of our gaze is suspended in the moment of being seen. We can take our time. She's not going to disappear back among the thistles or start to decay any time soon but she is out of reach. We can't hold or touch her or watch her move. We can only note the colour of her fur, the shape of her ears, her claws. White extracted his subject from its surroundings but he also described it in its own context:

> They never enter into houses; are carried into ricks and
> barns with the sheaves; abound in harvest; and build their

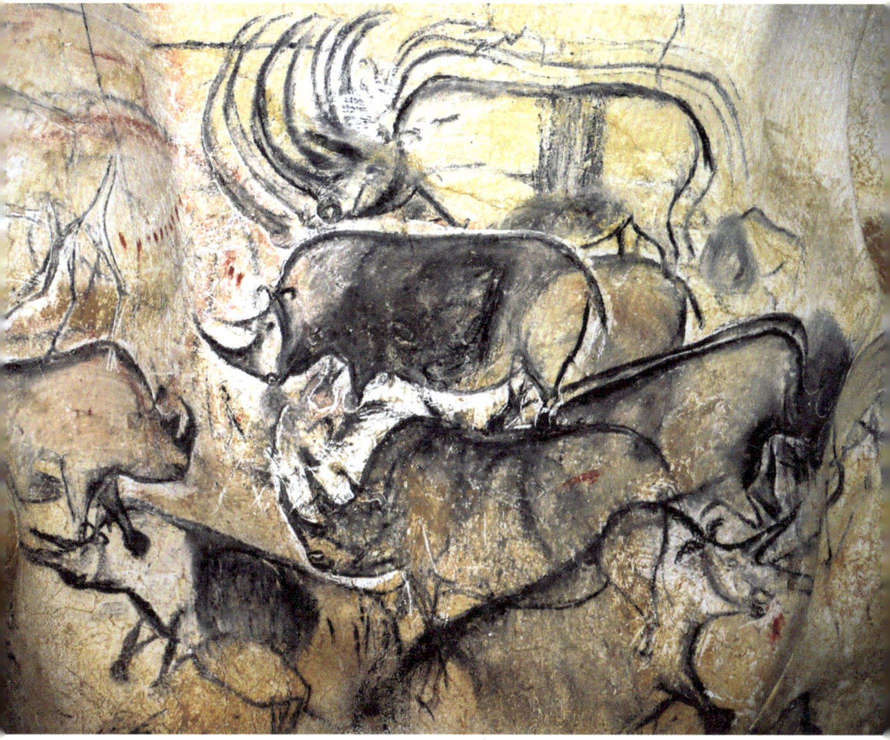

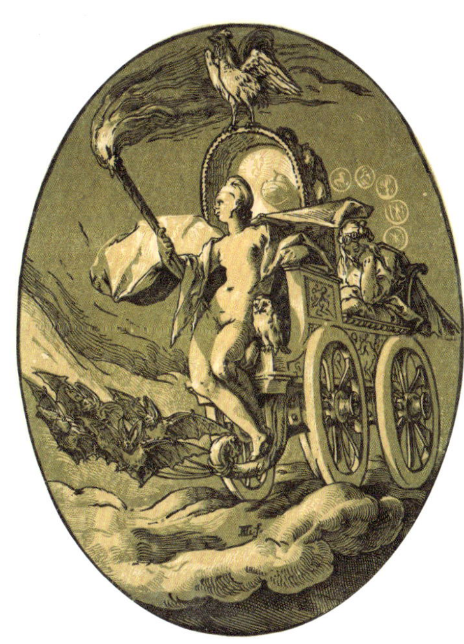

(*above*) Panel of the rhinos, end chamber, Chauvet-Pont d'Arc Cave, France

(*right*) Hendrik Goltzius, *Nox*, *c.*1588/1590

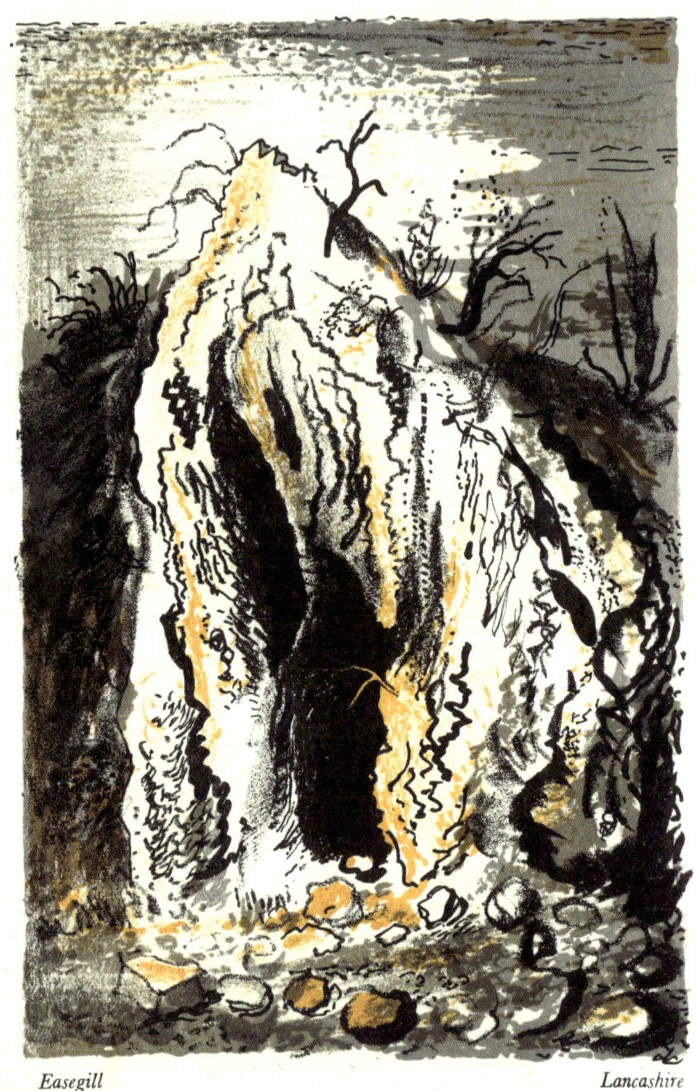

John Piper, *iii*, 1944 (from illustrations and book jackets for *English, Scottish and Welsh Landscapes*)

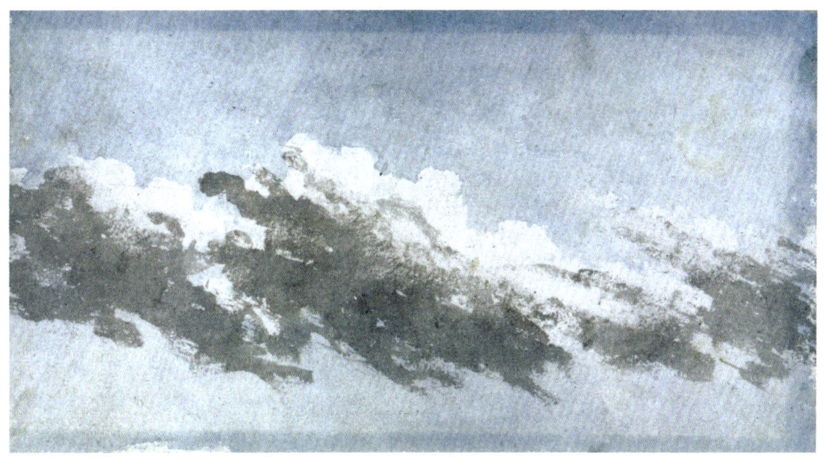

Luke Howard, cloud studies of cumulus and anvil spreading for rain (*top*) and cumulus blowing in high wind (*bottom*), *c.*1803–11

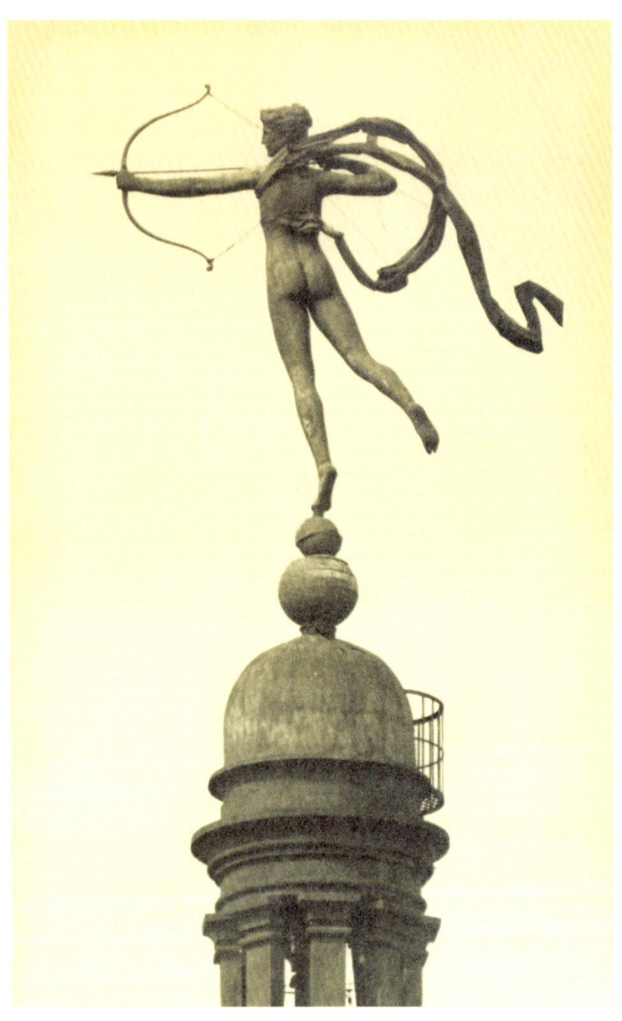

Augustus Saint-Gaudens, *Diana*, 1892–93

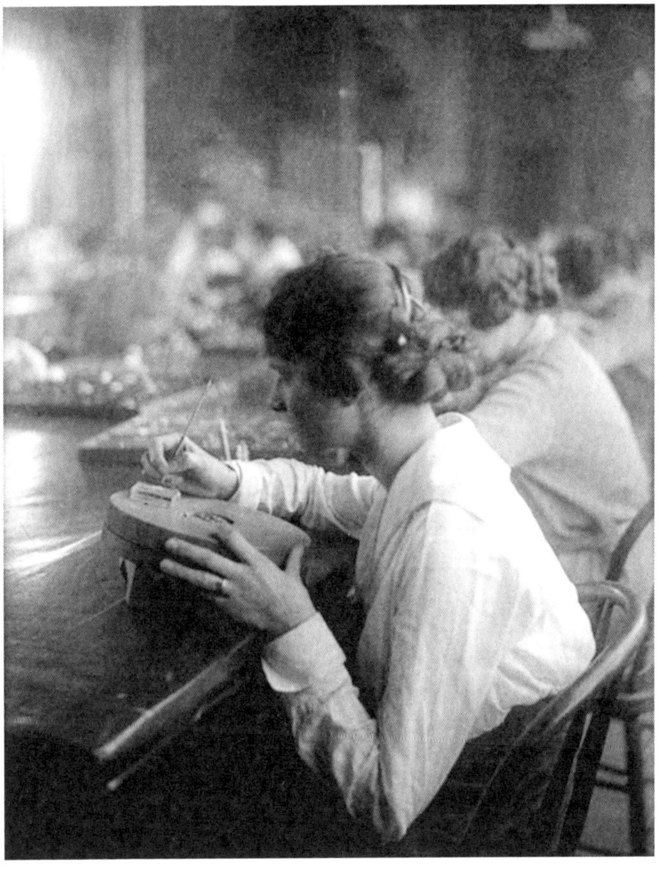

'Radium girls' working in a radium dial factory, undated

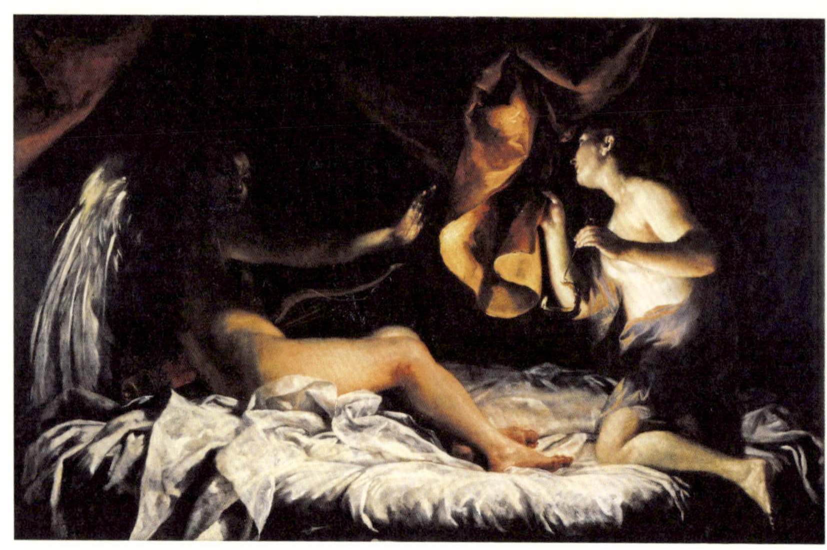

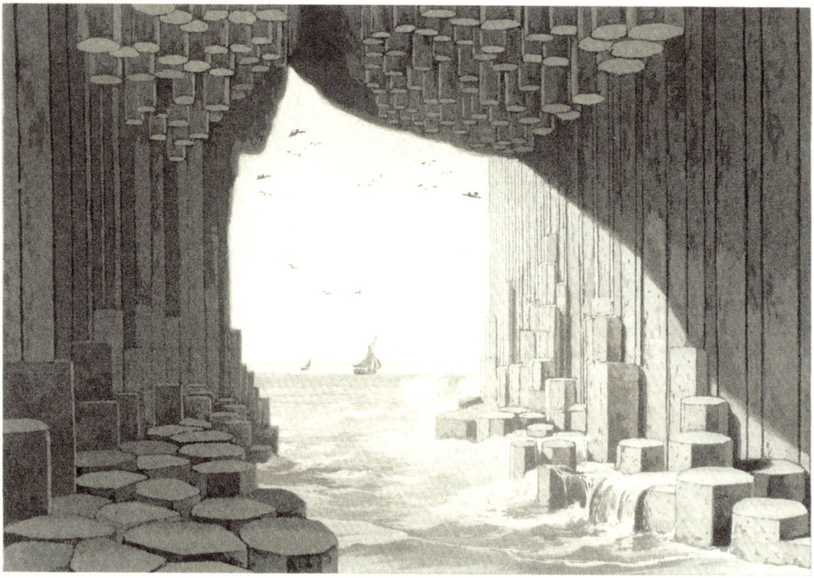

(*top*) Giuseppe Maria Crespi, *Cupid and Psyche*, 1707–9

(*bottom*) William Daniell, from *A Voyage Round Great Britain*, 'In Fingal's Cave, Staffa', 1813

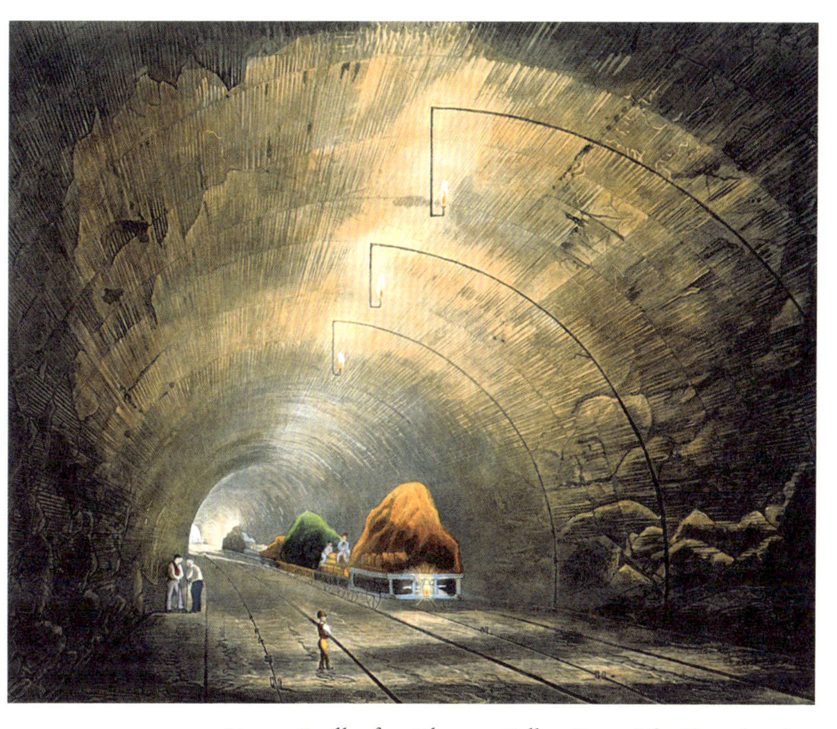

Henry Pyall, after Thomas Talbot Bury, *The Tunnel*, c.1833

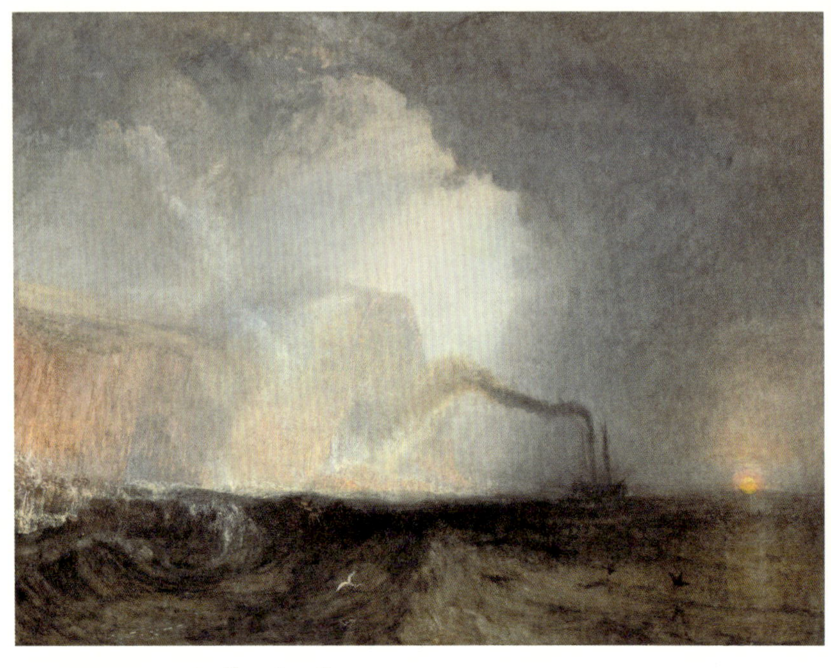

J. M. W. Turner, *Staffa, Fingal's Cave*, 1832

nests amid the straws of the corn above the ground, and
sometimes in thistles. These little round nests are composed
of the blades of grass or wheat.[12]

He admires the artfulness of the mouse in plaiting its nest
from blades of wheat into a perfect sphere and describes the
'aperture so ingeniously closed that there was no discovering
to what part it belonged'. Caught up in observation, White,
the eighteenth-century scientist, does not implicate himself. In
plucking the nest, complete with its babies, from the field, he
thinks primarily of the secrets of its design.

It was so compact and well filled that it would roll across
the table without being discomposed, though it contained
eight little mice that were naked and blind.
    As this nest was perfectly full, how could the dam
come at her litter respectively, so as to administer food to
each? Perhaps she opens different places for that purpose,
adjusting them again when the business is over; but she
could not possibly be contained herself in the ball with
her young, which, moreover, would be daily increasing in
bulk. This . . . elegant instance of the efforts of instinct, was
found in a wheat-field, suspended in the head of a thistle.[13]

White's scientific gaze asks what is this made of and how does
it work? (The illustrator Claire Oldham seems to be asking the
same question, flattening our glimpse between the corn stalks to
emphasise the design that integrates the animal with its environment.) But White's imagination, I might say his empathy, extends
to the mother mouse's difficulty in feeding all eight of her babies

without being able to squeeze herself into the nest. He notes the mouse's habits and lets them lead his eye from the field to the barn. Like de Gheyn, he seems able to inhabit his subject while maintaining an analytical distance. The nest is familiarised by being compared to a cricket ball. You could hold it in your hand. It feels close and real, and we forget the baby mice as we admire its construction, and then it veers away when White explains that it was found suspended in the head of a thistle.

White did not allow his imagination, or his prose, to travel even when he knew that there were remarkable tales to be told:

> neither its extent, nor the clearness of the water, nor the resort of various and curious fowls, nor its picturesque groups of cattle can render this meer so remarkable as the great quantity of coins that were found in its bed about forty years ago. But, as such discoveries more properly belong to the antiquities of this place, I shall suppress all particulars for the present . . .

He wants us to stay focused on the clearness of the water when all we can think about now is the coins, which we cannot see.

3

Beatrix Potter described herself as being descended from 'Lancashire yeomen and weavers; obstinate, hard-headed, matter-of-fact folk . . . Dissenters. Your Mayflower ancestors sailed to America; mine at the same date were sticking it out at home, probably rather enjoying persecution.'[14] Her childhood was comfortable and secure to the point of oppression. She and her brother had a menagerie of rabbits, frogs, bats, snakes, hedgehogs and lizards. Even as an adult, Potter travelled with a frog and walked a rabbit on a lead.

Like White, she brought the subjects of her curiosity into her home. She also shared his impulse to investigate and classify. There is tremendous equality in her attentiveness: she is as interested in the curve of a tap as in a new book of birds. 'Plenty of people can draw,' said the painter John Everett Millais, a family friend, 'but you . . . have observation.' Despite treating animals like toys, Beatrix paid expert scientific attention to nature, in particular to fungi, about which she made key discoveries. She submitted a paper to the Royal Society and attempted to discuss her findings with the experts at Kew Gardens only to be dismissed.

At the same time, she was writing and illustrating stories for the children she knew, based on her pets. This led to greetings cards and eventually *The Tale of Peter Rabbit*, which appeared in 1902 and sold out on publication. Potter was taken aback: 'The public must be fond of rabbits! What an appalling quantity of Peter!' She wrote a book a year, and was entrepreneurial about spin-offs but adamant about authenticity. When her publisher queried the colouration of a frog, she brought it to town in a jar to prove her point.

I first thought the Lady Mouse was holding a magnifying glass even though she looks unable to move let alone examine anything. She sinks under the weight of her crinoline and frills, and the exaggeration of her cap. It's not a magnifying glass but a mirror. She's a comical imposter, overwhelmed by her pretensions to ladyhood, nothing but a tiny detail (it is we who are holding a magnifying glass) in an actual lady's thickly decorated boudoir. Another mouse peeps out from behind her with the same inscrutable expression – her animal shadow.

Potter was not one for mob caps. Described by a friend as 'short, blue-eyed, fresh-coloured face, frizzy hair brushed tightly back, dresses in a tweed skirt pinned at the back with a safety pin', she sounds rather like Mrs Tiggywinkle, the pet hedgehog on whom she had based her famous character. But when the actual hedgehog began to fade, Potter was decisive: 'She has got so dirty & miserable I think it is better not to keep her any longer. I am going away for a few days so it is best to chloroform her first.'

'I began to assert myself at seventy,' Potter said, and she moved contentedly into old age until 1938, when she had a hysterectomy from which she never fully recovered. The Second World War was as remote to her as the First. She insisted that 'not even Hitler can damage the Fells' and that if the Germans invaded, 'I shall not run far. I will retire into the nearest wood.' This might have been like stepping into one of her own pages.

4

Zoe Kourtzi, a professor of Experimental Psychology, talked to me about excitement, predictability and prediction error.

ZK: We don't see discontinuous things, we see continuous things . . . a continuous line.[15]

LG: When I'm looking at the whorl inside the mouse's ear, I'm not seeing the mouse at all. Nor is my mind stopping to look.

ZK: The brain is never in a quiet state, it is always ready and this readiness gets muddled by this past experience.

LG: Over time we learn how to predict what we are going to see and how to navigate the world but in another sense we see less clearly because more of what we see is coming from us and less from outside.

ZK: We interpret not once but twice – what we are seeing and what is going to happen next . . . And when we predict something, our brain shows a lower response to it. When something new happens, the brain has a higher response. This is new information.

LG: So it's the difference between me walking out of the house and saying, 'Oh, it's raining,' and me walking out and seeing a comet. The pleasure and excitement I feel is my brain working to make sense of something new.

ZK: People call this prediction error.

LG: Excitement is a consequence of prediction error?

ZK: If you have a single neurone in a dish and you flash a light at it and you repeat this, the neurone will show a decreasing response: 'I know this, I've seen it before.' People have been surprised because it seems that repetition makes us respond faster and makes it easier for us to respond to a situation but on the other hand it looks as if the brain doesn't care. We get better, we get faster, because we're primed but our brain shows a slower response. It's saying, 'OK, I've figured this out, I'm ready for the next experience.'

If you associate things that are very dissimilar, the brain responds to them as a new thing.

LG: This makes me think of metaphor and how, if something is described in a surprising way, it can be seen freshly. Am I being unrealistic to think that when my brain makes a fresh connection, I will actually feel stimulated?

ZK: No. Definitely.

Becoming, resistance, dissolve

1

When I walked into a gallery full of Eva Hesse's 'test pieces' or 'studiowork' in 2014, I felt as if I'd found something I'd been looking for.[1] It was some time before I was able to say what this was. The curator of this exhibition, Briony Fer, says that 'The studiowork is work without making *work*.'[2] The difference lies in part in emphasis. These pieces are small arrangements of scrap material – card, plaster, cheesecloth, latex and wax. They are almost objects or not quite containers, incipient forms. Hesse placed them in her studio and included them in exhibitions, making them adapt to their surroundings. They could be cast as significant or peripheral depending on where and how they were displayed.

The materials that Hesse used here have strong associations and cultural placement. She resisted all of this by focusing on their latent qualities and not allowing them to become recognisable let alone functional. Although she built these objects with great care, they were often perishable. Making something that is intentionally impermanent can be a romantic act but this doesn't feel at all like that. There is none of the pathos of imminent loss. By not becoming what we expect, they remain at the starting point of material and form, and evade the assumption that they are steps towards something more significant. Hesse was picking up unlikely matter (less than material), drawing out its character and finalising it before it could be named.

Hesse's friend Sol LeWitt said that 'I think in the beginning she was just fooling around.'[3] He was not dismissing her but acknowledging that in order for things to take shape, she sometimes had to abandon intention, she had to play. In the first approach, an artist might grip their tools and hold themself rigid whereas sometimes they just need to play. Play means not thinking of what you're doing as work let alone a work.

> I would like the work to be non-work. This means that it would find its way beyond my preconceptions. What I want of my art I can eventually find. The work must go beyond this.
> Eva Hesse[4]

If a work is going to be realised, it moves from concept towards form, which is drawn from preconception. 'Non-work' suggests a reversal whereas Hesse is saying that it is a 'way beyond'. The test-pieces look activated rather than made. They reach a point of autonomy, and avoid reversal and slip past. They are, in an odd way, seamless. It's not possible to infer anything from their construction. They have become.

They contain no evidence of effort or tension although tension is what they produce. Hesse was investigating the provisional without being provisional about it, which is what a poem can do too. Going through the process of making these things enabled her to form a shape. Many look like empty containers – envelopes, wrapping, packaging – giving the sense that there was this thing that could not be described or grasped and all she could do was offer it containment.

She meets her material.

She is allowing it to happen.

She will not pay attention to where this is taking her.

Each piece lies halfway between conception and idea and although constructed, does not reach a point of construction.

It has an openness that we find increasingly hard to allow.

She is pulling against making just as I pull against language.

Never stable, these pieces test the balance between controlling the work and being controlled by the work.

She had a large upstairs space but liked to work downstairs in a corner. There were no borders between work and home. She entered the frame, sometimes wearing, or placing herself among, her work.

'Life doesn't last, art doesn't last, it doesn't matter.'[5] She is not saying that art or life do not matter but that you should not be deterred from making art by the fact that nothing lasts.

She did not want to know what the end was going to be but she knew where she began.

I had been looking for someone to show me that it is possible to resist completion of the kind that leaves the viewer/reader with nothing to do; that even in resistance, completion is necessary; and that there is a form of completion that is not the completion of an idea.

2

She is standing on the edge of the world. There is no greater darkness than that she is about to fall into. You can see her toes grip and her ankle flex. Her left heel is already over the edge. She is naked and therefore intensely present and seen. Her gaze is somehow impossible to meet as if she is refusing to take anything more in, choosing not to see further. She is about to end her own presence, to separate from her visible self, and she is asking for this to be witnessed by pointing (a knife) at herself. Her hips tilt as she draws her thighs more closely together. The veil draped across them is striking in its uselessness. The artist, Lucas Cranach the Elder (1472–1553), enjoys his skill in depicting a material so diaphanous, and his pleasure is indifferent to the hopelessness that this transparency suggests. Clutching this pathetic scrap of drapery, Lucretia is all the more exposed. Why is she naked? She has been raped and is about to commit suicide in front of her husband and household. Where are her clothes?

The *Lucretia* in Berlin's Gemäldegalerie is a variation on a popular theme, this scene the ending to a worn-out story. Its subject is no longer Lucretia, her body or death but feminine virtue so adamant that a woman would delete herself rather than remain present and compromised.

The princes are at a feast outside the city, boasting of their wives' devotion.[6] Unconvinced by each other's claims, they set out to surprise the women to see how they behave when their husbands are away. They arrived 'as darkness was beginning to close in' (a time when the wife of a prince, so contained and observed, could perhaps dissolve a little).[7] Only Lucretia is at home, spinning wool. One of the princes is overwhelmed by desire for her. He tells himself that she is drawing him towards her (spinning a web). On another night, while her husband is away, he sets out to break her spell, forcing his way in. He demands that she submit to him or be killed but she is 'inflexible and not moved even by the fear of death' so he rapes her. He tries to claim her by breaking her surface.

Lucretia tells her husband what has happened, takes out a knife and kills herself. She does this in public, refusing to disappear into the shadows. Instead, she dissolves into a kind of moral concentrate and her name is all that is required to convey what she represents: 'As soon as life was extinct, those round the death-bed raised a loud cry of woe and called out the name of the deceased.' The use of her name disarms and generalises her self. While the men in the story are known by surname and rank, she is made available by being known only as Lucretia. In Benjamin Britten's opera *Lucretia* (1946), her name is sung often and in ways that contort, erode, extrude, inflame, coil, tear and flatten. Everyone around her is invested in what she represents – so much so that the revenge taken on her rapist's family leads to the downfall of the king and the establishment of the republic of Rome. The rape dissolves into the background just as she dissolves into the story's broader historical ending. In Cranach's depictions, her face is empty. She is already absent. She has unbecome. Where the knife meets her skin, it simply disappears as if she became an image even before she was dead. She is already a picture; there will be no blood.

Another Cranach *Lucretia* was sold in 2020 for five million dollars, more than twice its estimate. On the Christie's auction website, you can get an idea of the work's size by seeing it on a wall in a neutral modern room. There's a window, an armchair and Lucretia, roughly the size of the double-page posters I used to pull from teen magazines, slumping a little over her knife. In the beige room, the painting glows like a rare mineral, which must be part of its power. I imagine it's now hung among other works or at least in a more conventional background but how powerful it looks when so alone, so unexpected and so small.

The painting's new owner will appreciate how old and rare and important it is. Does it ever make them think about rape and suicide?

I wasn't thinking of such things as I kept returning to the Cranach in Berlin. I was drawn by the sensation of direct contact across five hundred years that I felt whenever I looked at her, by the ungiving surface on which she stands, the veil she tries to draw, and the encroaching absolute dark. I felt the recognition of fundamental experience that is the truest connection we can have with an image. The details of its origin dissolve and we arrive in a shared place.

Perhaps the subject, regardless of the context in which we look at it, has something to say: You want me to do this *again*? You can pull up several pages of Cranach's Lucretias; there are more than forty. All those breasts and knives and tilted heads, and the single expression which is that of someone already removed. The museums I go to are full of naked women, many of whom are about to die. Should I unsee them? Or should I witness them? Should I look?

A century after Cranach, Artemisia Gentileschi painted several versions of Lucretia, who was still a popular subject. Gentileschi (like Lucretia) is conventionally known by her first name alone so as to differentiate her from her artist father. This practice has not been applied to fathers and sons such as the Bruegels or indeed the Cranachs. Is this artist to be so casually claimed? Do we feel entitled and able to know her? Gentileschi's work has an explicit historical link to Lucretia's story. The recent growth of interest in her has been threaded on the narrative of her own rape, by a family friend, when she was seventeen. This account is from the eventual trial.

> The weather was wet and I was painting when Agostino
> came by and he grabbed the palette and the brushes that
> I was holding in my hand and he threw them around
> the room.[8]

As if he were attacking her art as well as her body. He had to disarm her, to confiscate the instruments of documentation and expression while the wet weather is blurring the edges of things, loosening vision.

One of Gentileschi's Lucretias was rediscovered a few years ago, having been in private collections for decades. It was most recently in Lyon, where it had been stored for forty years unrecognised. At auction in 2019, it was sold to the Getty Museum for 5.3 million dollars, more than five times its estimate. It is not Lucretia that these collectors and museums are buying but Cranach and Gentileschi. She is easy to reach past – just a woman and a knife – and familiar enough to dissolve equably into an artist's oeuvre or into a collection, even into a wall.[*]

The Getty *Lucretia* raises her arms as if trying to draw a circle around this public private act. Her body is turning away while her hands push back at our gaze. She, too, is wearing something so transparent that it makes her more vulnerable than if she were naked. The knife is broad, shiny and ambiguous. It picks up the reflection of her chemise and the line of her chest, suggesting a looking glass that she is turning away from. It could be already deep in her chest but there is no blood. (There's never any blood.) While Gentileschi's other work, such as *Judith Beheading Holofernes*, is full of spurting gore, her Lucretias are bloodless. This is such an old story that there is no more blood to spill. These ambiguities and refusals are a form of resistance. This Lucretia is not what we expect. She is neither the eroded emblem nor its violently human counterpoint.

We cannot know how Gentileschi perceived her own experience, let alone her own body. We try not to respond only through the lens of ourselves, and are anxious to read an image correctly and in context, to stand beside the artist in their own place and time. Yet the power of the image lies in its autonomy. It lasts because it has gone through a process of dissolution in order to reintegrate in a form that can resist, harden and seal. Its impact on the reader is that of an experience rather than a report. The image is resisting its own history. It refuses further words.

If we can hold experience and emotion apart, we might be able to read the image in two ways at once. The historical context of how the artist would have perceived her experience can

* See also Vuillard's sister dissolving into the wall, 'The body, open, itself', p. 135.

100

encourage us to resist imposing our own. It also reminds us that our own is just as local and contingent. Why do I return to the picture? Is it because of the fame of the artist, their life story, or the age and value of the work? Or is it because this is a woman on the edge of her life? Can my reasons be both?

Gentileschi wrote to one patron that 'a woman's name raises doubts until her work is seen' and that her paintings 'will speak for themselves'. She is speaking for herself, to her patrons and to other artists. These are women resisting dissolution, whatever the pressures and impositions, however they are constructed.

I have told the truth and I always will, because it is true and I am here to confirm it wherever necessary . . . It is true, it is true, it is true.[9]

3

The successful becoming of an image meets – without pause – a point of resistance and then a point of dissolve. It's as if the image discovers its limits and so finds its form and can relax into it.

By limits I mean that which it cannot, or ought not, resolve or express. The recognition of these limits is an understanding of its true direction and emphasis.

Unless there is resistance and dissolve, the artist reconstitutes themselves along the same lines with each work and our gaze does the same.

The desire for something to become is the desire for it to be fixed. If the image is to survive this it has to free itself through a kind of dissolution. If it is encased in narrative or emblem, fact or history, it needs to achieve enough fluidity to escape all that and to meet us, sooner or later, as itself.

The artist who inserts a pause needs to ensure that they do not interrupt this outward flow.

Black and white and colour

1

On his journeys Bruegel did many views from nature so that it was said of him, when he travelled through the Alps, that he had swallowed all the mountains and rocks and spat them out again, after his return, onto his canvases and panels, so closely was he able to follow nature.

Karel van Mander (1604)[1]

In making sketches, Bruegel absorbed what he saw rather than just remembering it. The idea of swallowing what you see and spitting it up again is uncomfortable, revolting even, but it is an indication of the commitment required to take in, contain and reconstitute. Bruegel's mountains shrug off colour and I feel rebuffed too, by their scale, obduracy and indifference. Like Bruegel, I'm a person of the lowlands. Unlike him, I do not know how to see mountains. I'm not able to take them in, let alone contain them.

I would not choose to spend much time among mountains. Life becomes about climbing them or finding a way round. But I was offered space and peace in the Swiss Alps for a couple of months a year at a time when I really needed this. I went and sat in a bare room and spent much of each day wondering how to approach the mountains. There was a local saying that when the weather was really good, you could see the sea. Perhaps this came out of desperation to break free from the mountains' grip. I was far inland and surrounded. After a week or two, I longed for the sea.

I went to this place once in winter, and arrived in darkness and falling snow. I could see nothing but when I came to a streetlamp, I found myself in Narnia. In *The Lion, the Witch and the Wardrobe*, the children reach Narnia through the back of a wardrobe, something I had tried many times. Leaving London in late December felt like trying it again, like struggling through a lot of heavy coats while groping for an exit. The Narnia I knew was emphatically black and white. Had my edition been in colour, the world of the book and its battle between good and evil would have been more open to argument, the danger not as acute, the stakes not so high. It is a place drained of colour as it has been cursed by the White Witch with a perpetual winter. Pauline Baynes' illustrations formed my idea of the place, none more than the images of that lamp-post, and of the child Lucy and Tumnus the faun walking hand in hand through the woods in the dark and snow. In neither scene is there any drama but the black and the white of them weigh heavily.

The White Witch has not only imposed this winter; she turns her enemies to stone. I had arrived in Switzerland feeling to some extent turned to stone by illness, exhaustion and upset, and was pleased to find this black-and-white place where the days would be simple. I didn't much care how, or even if, they passed. In the book, the draining of colour equates with the stopping of time. How do we know spring is coming if we can see no green? The robin who guides the children is a small intense hope of renewal: 'you couldn't have found a robin with a redder chest or a brighter eye.'[2] There are other colours but they are artificial: the gold and scarlet trappings of the queen and her entourage; the green silk ribbon that makes the box of confectionary she conjures look so delicious.

I had visited this valley several times before, in summer, arriving in daylight. On the train, I would watch the mountains grow and accumulate, and adjust myself. As a child, I knew nothing grander than the Welsh hills and the cliffs of Cornwall. Mountains were a feature of fairytale geography, a black-and-white world of heightened senses and choices. They were also a trial: jagged peaks that had to be passed through by any questing knight or runaway princess. I needed to toughen up, to prepare myself. On that December night, I couldn't see the mountains but I felt their pressure. Mountains are an atmosphere and as soon as I breathe their air, my thoughts change. They become organised: complications arrange themselves as sequences, ambivalences harden into strata. I slept badly and had a nightmare that was no less terrifying for being oddly formal. It was a neat dance of imagery and archetype, as if my mind was giving me a presentation on my subconscious. This dream was repeated every night.

Ruskin cheered up when he came to the Alps. He believed that verticality was a stimulus, that 'the spirit of the hills is action, that of the lowlands repose'.[3] In the mountains, you can't get away from what's in front of you whereas in the flatlands you can set things aside, you can *overlook*. I grew up in the shallow dish of London and on the plane of East Anglia. If I reach the edge of the island, my thoughts can keep going towards the horizon but mountains stop them dead.

That winter, I was neither down in the valley nor up among the peaks but tucked under a low roof behind a thick door with small windows set in deep walls. I was being pinned down. Would I float away? I felt small enough to do so. I walked up above the town and looked along the valley to where the mountains thinned into a sketch. To the west, the valley unfolded on such an epic scale that I could only think of it in centuries and histories, the big pictures and big stories, and there was room for them all. It wouldn't have surprised me to see pilgrims on donkeys, Hannibal with his elephants, Charlemagne with his army, or the lion and the witch of Narnia staging their battle. Switzerland, with its sea of mountains, can feel like an island. The mountains that refused to let my mind or eye travel – to let me overlook – cut me off from the rest of the world and I became impervious to its emergencies and events.

The scale of mountains proposes space but living among them collapses it. One afternoon I stood up from my desk and turned to the window. From where I was standing, it was filled with mountain. I couldn't see anything of the valley or sky. The mountain was right there pressing up against the glass.

Even when there was some distance between us, the mountains turned me back on myself. I was living in a state of perpetual interrogation. What was I doing there? Why could I not be more decisive? More clear? Bruegel's response was to swallow the mountains and Ruskin's to analyse their structure and to be galvanised by their challenge. I was too timid to do more than document their light. Their remoteness offers perfect shapes and surfaces. I first saw the Alps when I was sixteen and spent a summer camping beneath a glacier. I was shocked by how grubby, dingy and soggy the glacier was, how roughly put together. I had envisaged a glossy lozenge of pure blue ice.

My memory of that mountain is of a series of parts: the dirty ice, a field of snow, a fall of scree, a frozen stream, a terrifying path. I couldn't see the mountain because I was on it. We make only superficial contact with the small parts of mountains that we can reach.

That black-and-white winter, I worked slowly, spoke little and read fast. I watched the mountains gathering and offering back the light. One afternoon, I was taken high up above the town where I was staying and so could see more of the mountains opposite. (We need to climb one mountain in order to see another.) It was dusk and they were finely drawn in black and white, the absolutes of rock and snow broken up by the stipple and cross-hatch of forest and, lower down, the effortful twisting thread of a road. The black and white of things is a clearer argument, and these mountains were to be read as pattern and surface rather than meaning. They looked like etchings, something scratched into a hard surface. I understood that what I could see was not the mountain but what was *on* the mountain. Even that was barely tolerated and had to cling on. Up there, I also saw what I had been imagining – a pure white peak. It caught the last of the sun and shone like something impervious to human contact.

I like the restfulness of being in a world of snow and one day, the whiteness came down to meet me. It was early morning, the light was dull and the valley was busy with mist and cloud which collected and disintegrated, rose and sank and sailed by. All day I watched these apparitions – some barely a white scrape against a white sky, others as gloomy as unanchored shadows. Even when there was no light in the valley, I could usually find a chink of blue in the sky to remind me that there was life and light somewhere. But what lay behind the mountains was always more mountains. However high I climbed, they were all I could see. Towards the end of my stay, the snow thawed and as I walked, I no longer looked out and up but down. The low sun skimmed the snow's surface, bringing out its grain, and the melting white broke into green, pink and blue. The colours were as pure as the whiteness of that peak. As the landscape softened, the sky hardened into a substance-less blue, the pure depth that D. H. Lawrence strives to describe in 'Bavarian Gentians': 'blue . . . darkened on blueness.'[4]

This is not mountain talk. It's not hard or clear or certain enough. While among them, I became conscious that I not only thought in a provisional way but spoke like that too. Did I want something to drink? If it wasn't too much trouble. A cup of coffee? I don't mind if I do. That is the language of a place where the ground is sinking, the fields blowing away, the coastline crumbling. I landed back in London in early January, with my eyes still full of black and white and blue. The city sky was an orange soup and my car windows were grey. As dirty rain fell, I set off into ill-lit streets full of roadworks. For the hour it took me to get home I felt as if I had gone from a mountain into a cave, and then my eyes adjusted. But the mountain atmosphere stayed with me: depth in my dreams and height in my thoughts, a desire for framework and fixed arrangement, for black and white.

It didn't last. It would have been too much like a perpetual winter. I came back to life just like the statues in Narnia, and was restored to colour. C. S. Lewis describes this as being like a match put to the newspaper in an unlit fire:

And for a second nothing seems to have happened; then
you notice a tiny streak of flame creeping along the edge of
the newspaper . . . Then a tiny streak of gold began to run
along [the lion's] white marble back – then it spread – then
the colour seemed to lick all over him as the flame licks all
over the bit of paper . . . then he opened a great red mouth,
warm and living, and gave a prodigious yawn.

2

I spent almost as much time watching television while I was
growing up as I did on music and books. This probably explains
my tendency to describe everything in monochrome as we
didn't have a colour set until I was seventeen. We didn't have
a set at all in 1969 when I was seven and taken to a neighbour's
house to watch the moon landing. I was too young to be able to
place the moon at a significant distance or to understand why it
was so difficult to get there. The event, for me, was the television: a small, juddering, black-and-white picture trapped inside
a heavy wooden cabinet.

Around this time, a Japanese friend invited me home after
school for tea. We knelt at a low table while her mother served us
tiny portions of beautiful things. Afterwards I was taken to admire
her father's television, the first colour set I'd seen. We didn't watch
it so much as look at it. My lasting impression was of the kind of
colour I've come to associate with migraines – a dull brightness
that makes everything look like old sweet wrappers. The colours I
wanted to take home with me were those of Japanese food: glim-
mering pinks, yellows and greens which made me peer closely at
what was on my plate and not want to disturb it.

Colour was expensive, and could be so flat and crude that it made things seem less real rather than more so. Black and white was authenticating, documentary. Newspapers and textbooks were black and white, and I believed them. Colour was something to be remarked on and to get excited about. As a child I pleaded with my father to drive me round the city at night because I loved the strings of traffic lights and streetlamps, the lemon-jelly lozenges of office windows, the advertisements and theatre signs. In the rain after dark, these colours wobbled and streaked across wet tarmac and pavement. The effect was low-key and introverted, and the city felt taller and deeper. I did, too, in living within it.

The photos I have of myself from that time are mostly black and white, which places a particular kind of distance between us. Even the most spontaneous have an air of careful composition. They appear better made and more lasting than recent prints, which they are. They seem more revealing too, as if colour were distraction, attention-seeking or concealment (in nature it often is). I am not black and white and nor is the world, but setting aside colour allows other aspects of an image to come to the fore.

It surprises me to realise how little colour there is in what I write. I seem to treat it like a separable component, perhaps because I grew up with concurrent experiences of the world as lived in colour and reproduced in black and white. I move colour out of the way or slip past it. In daily life, I am compelled by colour, especially that which is unlikely and difficult to pin down. I try to add colour to my appearance by buying something bright and then usually take fright. But I will cross a room to talk to a stranger about the particular shade of their dress and I have never forgotten the blue of a man's shirt as I sat opposite him and could not meet his eyes.

3

Jacques de Gheyn brought the same analytical approach to a military uniform that he did to a mouse or the muscles in a dissected arm.* He analysed colour and painted what he saw within, rather than on, a surface. Under a magnifying glass, the skin of his frog breaks down into grains of harsh pink, yellow and green whereas viewed from a normal distance, it looks like the tough, damp, elastic skin you'd expect. Karel van Mander recorded how de Gheyn analysed colour and drew up a chart of a hundred squares with corresponding shades, and numbered and learnt them. De Gheyn was freeing colour from form so as to see it more clearly but also as a way of putting it in order. He lived among scientists and perhaps felt that colour needed to be classified like everything else.

The crustaceans in Clara Peeters' *Still Life with Crab, Shrimps and Lobster* (c.1635–40) look thoroughly boiled, their shells tight with heat, their redness evoking both pressure and flavour. Francis Bacon took the crab and lobster as his example when thinking about how the meaning of colour changes according to context: '. . . the changing of a lobster or a crab when cooked from a dark to a red colour has nothing to do with cookery, yet this instance is a not a bad one in investigating the nature of redness . . .'[5]

Peeters was a pioneer of the still-life movement although little is known about her now. There are clues in her pictures – her name on a knife from Antwerp, her reflection in a goblet. A still

* See also Jacques de Gheyn's mouse in 'Seeing clearly, glimpsing, picturing', p. 81, crab in 'Curiosity, wonder, rupture', p. 231, and his studies of death in 'The imagined image', p. 278.

life is outward-looking but intimate. It invites us to pay attention differently because what it represents is more subtle than a history painting. Now, a still life is a study in light, form, texture and colour. The red of the lobster is just that. It stands for itself. The painter is saying, 'There's nothing happening and no one is here, but *look*.' Peeters encoded her arrangements with religious or cultural emblems, but she was also demonstrating her skill. Her use of colour is less analytical than de Gheyn's and more subtle. When looking at his frog, I cannot escape my awareness of his technique. The frog has no context and so is much more explicitly a *subject*. Like his mouse, its presence is tactile because it looks so real. My eyes think it can be touched even though I don't want to touch it.

Red and yellow pull into the foreground and they do so in Peeters' arrangement, grabbing at the light. The table is too small for what it must contain, which is a study in abundance and wealth: the damask cloth, porcelain, generous heap of precious salt, the pile of three cheeses, the lobster too large for its plate.

Colour is seen to carry its own properties. The scientist Antoni van Leeuwenhoek encountered a local belief that you could contract a fever from walking through a meadow of bright red grass because it left its colour on your shoes.[6] Leeuwenhoek went out to collect the grass, to analyse its structure and make sense of its colour. He was a radical empiricist who tried to learn about vision by comparing the eye of a cow with that of a fly, and interrogated every part of himself too: his urine, faeces, sputum, blood, catarrh and sperm. In a world where everything might be revealed in visible form, colour becomes another vehicle or material. The visual fire of bright red might be carried home and into our bodies.

4

There is something strenuous about yellow even in its sunniest form. F. Scott Fitzgerald's *Tender Is the Night* (1925) moves from the baked and rotting colours of the French Riviera to the sterile blue-and-white of the Swiss Alps and the clinic where Dick Diver works. His wife Nicole is on the cusp of a breakdown, a stitch unravelling. Her dress is ochre – a subterranean colour that looks unnaturally exposed. Nicole has a sudden imperative. She must move and move fast so as not to slip into the crack between reality and unreality. She is the one live aspect of this otherwise anaesthetised scene.

> Nicole began to run very suddenly, so suddenly that for a moment Dick did not miss her. Far ahead he saw her yellow dress twisting through the crowd, an ochre stitch along the edge of reality and unreality, and started after her. Secretly she ran and secretly he followed.[7]

Only yellow could twist like that. Writing forty years before Fitzgerald, Charlotte Perkins Gilman focused the story of a breakdown on the volatile nature of this colour in 'The Yellow Wallpaper' (1892):[*]

> The colour is repellent, almost revolting; a smouldering unclean yellow, strangely faded by the slow-turning sunlight.[8]

---

* For more on wallpaper of the kind we don't notice, see 'The body, open, itself', p. 135.

A bleached shade of ochre, one that is equally troubling, draws the eye in Elizabeth Price's 2015 video work, *K*. Price uses high-temperature cool 'K light' to film a machine manufacturing yellow tights. We watch the same flat shape being spun and stretched with efficient magic and then bluntly packaged.

In this diagrammatic light, Price places the machine in tight focus, giving its processes an eerie intimacy in which there is no human presence. That comes in the interjecting footage of Crystal Gayle and her backing singers who, like the machine, are broken down into repeated gestures. These pile up like the packets of tights that the machine spits out: swaying hips, undulating fingers, anguished expressions, silky legs and swooshing hair. The models posed on the packaging look cornered and dazzled. They shield their eyes as if in a place of obliterating brightness.

In the corner of the screen, a flickering disc reprises Price's work *Sunlight*, a composite of fifty years of photographs of the sun also taken using 'K light' so as to remove its glare. Only here the sun is reduced to an emblem or logo. Beneath it, a text is being spelt out, also in yellow, as the words are spoken by a voice as synthetic as this colour. The yellow of *K* is not of the earth. It is lifeless, a simulation just like the professional mourning troupe whose practice this text describes, and it has the intense and troubling resonance of Perkins Gilman's wallpaper.

It is the strangest yellow, that wall-paper! It makes me think
of all the yellow things I ever saw – not beautiful ones like
buttercups, but old foul, bad yellow things.[9]

These mourners follow protocols as intricate and nuanced as any other ancient rite. Yet the description given here is a very modern analysis of the mechanics of impact. The expression of feeling is an act of manufacture. We use the repeated gesture in the form of words, dance and song. Our grief is always a performance. Set to music, these are the gestures of dance. Without music they appear desperate, even agonised. A man spins and drops, and this clip is repeated again and again. He keeps capsizing as if the world has suddenly withdrawn its support. This is just part of his performance but isolated like this, without musical context and unable to move on, he well and truly hits the ground.

Set against the black-and-white noise of the factory machine, dance becomes a process of manufacture. The machine noise is heightened and enriched so as to be musical. When it erupts into actual music, into colour, everything takes shape and makes sense for a moment. It all dances and then it all gives way again. What finally emerges from the machine is just something in outline.

As the voice-over describes how long hair is prized by professional mourners and how it is implemented as a phantom or shadow, we watch Crystal Gayle singing country songs and making country gestures. But the extreme length of her hair upsets the balance. The sexual tips over into the animal. What was most attractive, when kept in proportion, threatens us and even repels.

What do we spin? The yarn, the body. Authenticity and authority are spun until they blur and so appear to take shape. The film's synthesised voice is spun into something that could be heard as biblical or testimonial; it could be a research report, manual or corporate guide: 'Sorrow has increasingly become contingent to all public and social affairs. Any occasion of significance requires its proper acknowledgement.'

The tensions out of which we build perception are made explicit as we try to watch, listen and read at the same time. Text, sound and image compete so that we experience a fraying attentiveness. A loose thread is being pulled. Meanwhile the connections we usually make without thinking are subverted. Music is replaced by the punch-and-clamp rhythms of the machine.

We need shapes to inhabit, and these include clothes and song and dance and people who will stand in the place of our grief, spin and fall down. The text claims that outbreaks of dancing mania occurred when the mechanical loom was invented as if people felt compelled to move faster in order to keep up with this new speed of production. What could be more entrancing than the possibility of moving so fast that you forget yourself? Secretly we run and secretly we follow.

5

The disturbance of light is what makes it palpable, and the photographic artist Garry Fabian Miller is highly attuned to this, as he is to the ways we measure light and measure by it. He speaks of life as an exposure to light and says, 'I cannot create light. I can only expose myself to it by placing myself in its path.' He walks every day within a certain circumference and finds that images 'are given and received'.[10] He speaks of images held within us being released and creating 'an imagined space which perhaps I did see or one day will see', an idea that pinpoints the image as a conflation of memory and possibility.

At the end of a day together, we went up onto the moor behind his house, to a place where the view was unbroken by light from streets or houses. I asked him what time the sun would set and he told me exactly when it would start to dim and how long the sky would take to grow dark. There was no streetlight or house light, just the occasional beams of a car in the distance and the light he described as 'the light that is always there and we'll see more of it the longer we stand here'. He gave up the camera around 1980, wanting a more direct contact with his subject and for the next forty years spent hours of each day in his dark room orchestrating light and colour.

In October 2001, I sat for some hours with him in this darkroom and we began a conversation that continued in the brightness of his studio. He began as usual by waiting five or ten minutes for his eyes to adjust. He spoke of being in the dark as a release of the self: 'I am in some space where I no longer exist perhaps . . . to get away from myself or to be with myself.' This is an uncoupling of the self and awareness allowing the artist to see more clearly and also maybe to see themselves. Fabian Miller's ease in the dark is an interesting counterpoint to his precision in locating himself and measuring light when out on the moor.[*]

I was struck by how his relationship with light was both physical and mutual, and how he saw image-making as a process of giving emotion form: 'What the light and I could do to make visible what I felt.' At that time, he was working on a series called *Thoughts of a Night Sea*. They look like exactly that, the horizon at night, but they are not photographs. He

* See Louise Bourgeois on the freedom of knowing where you are in 'Pattern, machinery, punctuation', p. 160.

was making long exposures using light shone through a blue glass vessel filled with water, and interrupted it with sheets of paper to create strata: 'I make decisions in light and have to imagine what it will be like when dark.' Light and dark are a continuum for him in each moment, each thought. The resulting image has a direct connection to the elements it manifests: 'If you put light with water, what you are going to see is the effect of light on water.'

Night diminishes vision and the sea eludes it. Fabian Miller was simplifying process and in doing so disrupting the habits of vision. As we talked or sat in silence in the dense and comfortable blackness of the dark room, he was steadily focused on the image that was taking shape. To him, light is material and he spoke of 'gathering it in, keeping it out, letting it fall'. These are active verbs. His focus was absolute but open, not expecting but finding, drawing out possibility rather than creating or directing. He remained still except to reach forward and move one of the pieces of paper now and again with the relaxed demeanour of someone deeply attuned to and familiar with the process.

He tends to work in series, or phases, defined by colour, at one point speaking of 'When I stop working in blue and black.' Blue is spacious. A blue image has a horizontal pull that lays ground for us to walk on. A red image is vertical – height and depth and danger. If you ask people to name the first blue thing that comes to mind, they will probably say sea or sky. Neither of these, in Britain at least, is blue all that often. Atmospheric perspective means that blue is the colour of faraway hills, of elsewhere and remoteness. Blue is serene, indifferent. Italo Calvino tells the story of a blue stone that makes a king fall madly in love first with a toad that swallowed it and then with the lake that the stone is thrown into.[11] Blue makes the stone's power relentless. Blue is not easily disturbed.

Fabian Miller was then moving in a new direction, having wanted 'to work with red coming out of black'. This led to his series *Magma*, in which the red is so full that it seems to brim and be about to spill as if tipped towards us.* He said that 'blue is full of nuance . . . red is more raw and of itself and its relation to blackness is what the pictures are being made about.' The *Magma* series is volatile, primordial and recognisable in that we know this is not a place we could inhabit. The elemental fire of this red is our beginning as well as our ending – it is energy and origin on a scale and of a time that precedes and extends beyond us.

He already knew then that the materials he used were no longer being made and would eventually run out. Twenty years later, he spoke of tracking down old Cibachrome machines through small ads, picking up whatever old chemicals and abandoned equipment he could find, but his dark room is now closed. There is a red produced by using Cibachrome that he will never achieve again. 'Now I can almost make anything, I have fifty years skill and experience, but I cannot make the pictures.'[12] The colour has been taken away from him which must be like having a word taken from your vocabulary.

* See Elizabeth Bishop on the 'tipping of an object toward the light' in 'One thing beside another (a foreword)', p. 1.

The body, open, itself

1

I went to see the house and didn't know what to do, how to be or where to put myself. I wanted to enter but the house did not exist – only the space that it had held remained. This space had been made visible. Perhaps it had held the house up as it pushed against the doors and windows, keeping every part in shape.

All our thinking about our houses is of ourselves within them: how they will serve our needs, what we might choose so as to make some welcome and how to stop others from entering. There is the impression a house gives of its inhabitants and the view when we look out. There are established protocols about how a house is approached and what constitutes transgression or overstepping the mark. This house was a solid block of interior space that held onto its interiority by refusing me a way in. It felt more private than any actual room. Its inversion (reversal?) left me unsure where to place myself in relation to it. I loitered in its not quite public or private surroundings, which were part park and part demolition site. It was an extremely cold day and there was nowhere to go to get warm. I had to stay outside. Outside of what? I was outside empty space.

Reading about how Rachel Whiteread constructed *House* (1993) makes it seem to be more about the body, about presence and substance and how in ageing we undertake an accretion of matter more durable and less permeable than the body itself. Our joints, teeth, nails and hair can be reinforced or substituted, our organs too. Our walls are shored up while room by room we become empty, and our doors and windows warp and jam. 'The external interior was gradually sealed up, the last person leaving through the roof.'[1]

The concrete was applied in two layers, the first being the kind used to protect the white cliffs of Dover. Millions of years ago, those cliffs were part of the seabed, our most remote interior. Exposed, their chalk remains white because it is continuing to erode. It forms no surface so it remains an external interior. We cannot remain exposed or we, too, would exist in a state of continual barren erosion. We contrive a surface and not wanting others to think of us as behind a wall, offer this as a version of the interior self – an external interior.

2

The eighteenth-century surgeon John Hunter[*] was 'devoured by a passionate desire to know how things were made and how they worked, and it was typical of the man that he realised the only way to do this was to look and see for himself'.[2] If he had not done so, he would have had to rely on the documentation and drawings of others. Now, we do not need to cut things up because most of the time we can look them up instead. The world has been cut open for us, which affects how we receive it – ready-prepared and less satisfying than we might expect.

[*] John Hunter (1728–93). An exact contemporary of the naturalist Gilbert White, who also claimed the world and prised it open, in 'Seeing clearly, glimpsing, picturing', p. 86.

Hunter's home was filled with animals, dead and alive, there to be observed and experimented on. He seems to have wanted to open anything that was closed to him, from an institution to a corpse. He was impatient with people, rules and politics, and ruthless in getting hold of the subjects he wanted. Charles Byrne, the 'Irish Giant', was so afraid of his body being dissected after his death that he stated a wish to be buried at sea but his coffin was filled with rocks and his skeleton turned up in Hunter's museum. It's an eerie place, both horrifying and hyper-scientific – so many parts of all kinds of bodies sliced, pinned and preserved.

Hunter's time, place, status and gender lent themselves to a confident vision that felt able to let itself in wherever it wanted to go. He did though, advise his students to tread carefully: 'Don't think, try; be patient, be accurate.'[3] This suggests that you should elude your impulse to form an impression and instead attempt an investigation. It will be difficult but you must remain thorough and focused. There are times to move quickly past yourself and times when you need to hold yourself back.

Hunter was a radical surgeon who undertook new and extremely difficult operations. He relished the challenge and was sure of his capacities, including that of detachment. The surgeon has to see a body out of its context and to isolate it as a subject. Otherwise they wouldn't be able to cut it open. The same might be said of the poet and the poem, only in that case it's also about knowing when to make your incision as well as where. In one operation, Hunter successfully cleared an aneurysm in a coachman's leg. Restored to health, the coachman returned to work but a few years later, died of a fever. Hunter somehow managed to acquire the man's leg and set about dissecting it. He was excited to record that the blockage had renewed itself but the veins had found a way to work round it.

Hunter dropped dead at the age of sixty-four during an argument at his hospital over which students he was allowed to admit. His will stated that he wanted two parts of his body to be preserved: an Achilles tendon that had once been operated on, and his heart, which he knew to be diseased. His brother-in-law Everard Home – who is generally remembered as Hunter's far less talented assistant – was given the honour of performing the operation. With their colleagues gathered round, Home opened Hunter's body. He noted the evidence of heart disease and the scarring on the Achilles tendon, and then, giving no explanation, closed the body back up without removing them. He had acknowledged Hunter's wishes but, once the instruments were in his hands and the body at his disposal, refused to comply.

Hunter's body of work was equally vulnerable to this man. Home preyed on Hunter's research, taking possession of his writings and soon presenting papers that won prizes and which plagiarised Hunter's work. One day Home casually admitted that he had burned Hunter's archive. The conservator who had been forced to hand it all over to Home had copied out what he could but much was lost.

Hunter's family were left with little income and despite his renown, his body was interred in the crypt of St Martin in the Fields in London in 1793 along with thousands of others. In 1859, the surgeon Frank Buckland came across a notice that all coffins in the church's vaults would be moved to the catacombs and sealed in, if not claimed by a given deadline. Buckland made it his mission to rescue Hunter's remains.

When we threw the light of our lanterns into the vault (for our work was mostly done by lamp-light) I beheld a sight I shall never forget. The vault was a good-sized room, as full as it could hold with coffins piled one over the other from the very top to the very bottom, and placed in all possible directions, reminding one much of books packed in a box to be sent away.[4]

There were over three thousand coffins being moved from the vaults and two hundred in that room alone. Think of Hunter's desire to regulate the body and of the body regulated in death by being placed in a box, and all those identical boxes. Also the body as a box inside a box, containing many other boxes.* Hunter's coffin was one of the last two they examined. His remains were reinterred in Westminster Abbey.

In an oration given in Hunter's name in 1959, it was said that 'By knowing form he could investigate function; by understanding function he could study impaired function.'[5] The scientist must establish a consistent situation in order to see what should not be happening and ought not be there. For all his calls to action, Hunter stopped to think about the questions that for most people don't even begin to form. Such as how a body changes in the instant of death and so we cannot understand the dead body until we understand those changes. We have to understand the functioning machine before we can evaluate its malfunction, and we have to remember that what we are cutting up is already not itself but only the parts from which it had been made.

* The elusive Mrs Darling in *Peter Pan* is described as a series of boxes within boxes. See 'Solidity, appearance, dullness', p. 26.

3

'How are you?' This question, which we ask of each other all the time, is more of a gesture than a true enquiry. If you stop, like John Berryman in 'Dream Song 207', to address it head on – *How am I?* – a trapdoor opens.

> —How are you —Fine, fine. (I have tears unshed,
> There is here near the bottom of my chest
> a loop of cold, on the right,
> A thing hurts somewhere up left in my head.
> I have a gang of old sins unconfessed.
> I shovel out of sight
>
> a many-ills else) . . .[6]

As we inhabit our bodies, we are forced to imagine them. Berryman's inventory starts with something familiar, unshed tears, and then locates very precisely 'a loop of cold', a sensation that has a definite shape. We don't know how the loop lies in the body but its circular nature suggests something unrelenting. It troubles him, which is why he knows exactly where it is and what shape it takes. The 'thing' that he can't quite locate to the left of his head is more vague, dull perhaps and diffuse. He describes the loop and the thing as physical so that when we get to the unconfessed sins, they seem physical too – a gang, crowded and unruly. And there he is, inside himself, shovelling other 'ills' out of sight in some perpetual act of denial.

Berryman's response to 'How are you?' describes a self doubly in parenthesis: 'I am not going to tell you how I feel' and

'I do not feel myself'. When we experience this kind of dislocation, it can seem as if we no longer inhabit ourselves or that what we inhabit is no longer our self. Language attends to this. We fall ill, a passive act suggesting a loss of ground.

The arrest and interruption caused by illness are part of a broader experience of 'something going wrong with the equipment of the world'[7] which forces us to reconsider the familiar. Illness is an acute version of this: something going wrong with the equipment of the self, an extrapolating dysfunction that means that when we go wrong, our relation with the world does so too.

We live within what Zbigniew Herbert called 'the narrow bed of our flesh' and no more so than when negotiating a fever, depression or a broken bone.[8] The acutely unwell person withdraws into themselves. The world is their body, their pain. Illness can also sharpen our perceptions and its confinements intensify our appreciation of the world. Like Emily Dickinson, we might learn to value the present. 'One earns by measuring the Grave—/Then— measuring the Sun—'[9]

The more conscious we become of how we operate in the world, the more we are aware of our physical presence. We watch it, stage it, record it and know it recorded. In many ways we still measure the world according to ourselves but our relation to our bodies has become estranged even as we investigate, medicate and operate upon them. The more we see of our physical selves, the further back we have to stand so as to take in the view. We can see through our bodies, deep into the earth and far out into space, so maybe we forget that, as Lucretius said, 'All kinds of things in outsides are enclosed.' Yet, when our own boundaries are ruptured, we become more aware of them rather than less. We are reminded that we're more likely to go wrong than not. We forget how full of trouble we are until our containments are breached.

My parents were medical students who met in a dissection room in a London teaching hospital in the 1950s. There are photos of this room in one of the family albums.* The students have very young faces and are wearing old people's clothes. One or two are smoking pipes. The corpse in view looks no more exciting than someone sleeping tucked up under a sheet. As a child, I was disappointed that the corpse didn't look more dead. The day they met, my mother had discovered that the body she was working on had its heart on the right side. The other students were brought over to see this rare case of dextrocardia and my father was captivated by my mother's strangely glassy eyes. She was wearing an early kind of contact lens.

I wonder how it is to be trained to view the body as a place of work when you are young and in love and your own body is wildly deregulating itself. The focus in medicine on function and process might override any unease about the reality of the opened body but what does it do to your relationship with your own – the one body you cannot open? In my childhood, my parents spoke clinically about the body and I learnt to do so too. We thought this made us open-minded when it was as avoidant of the mucky actuality as euphemisms. I learnt to see myself as enclosed within a frail outside, largely transparent, a loose and leaking arrangement that others such as my dissecting, analysing, adventuring family could probe and take apart. I was a web

* See more on photography and family albums in 'Boredom, repetition, fixatives', p. 60.

of function and process, as bland as polite names for private parts. This view of the body can lead you to distrust or dismiss your most urgent responses.

> The body is a flowing stream or burning fire and no two of its moments are ever the same – we can't help but change form.
>   John Berger[10]

John Berger's *A Fortunate Man* is a study of the life of a doctor in 1960s rural England, whom he gave the alias John Sassell. This doctor was evidently wise, kind, dedicated and sensitive, a model for young doctors like my father who were trying to find better ways to go about their work. Sassell's approach involved patience and persistence, enquiring and acting. John Hunter would have approved. Yet, at the end of the book we discover that Sassell killed himself. He must have locked a great deal away and kept that lock in place through the pouring of himself – fire and stream – into the care of others. Or he might have been compelled to repair, reorder, resurface, resolve, that prefix re- suggesting that all of this was being done not for the first time and would need to be done again. Perhaps the fire and stream of his patients, who come across as humble and reticent to the point of subservience, exhausted him in the end.

My father moved from an inner-city practice to become a country doctor in the 1970s. Like Sassell, he developed a deep knowledge of his community and adjusted himself to their vision, reference points and beliefs. Sassell's attention extended to the whole person. Jean Mohr's photographs for the book show Sassell's intent focus when in the direct contact of examination or manipulation. He seems to be listening to what his fingers are telling him, receiving news via the medium of touch of a man's frozen neck, the progress of a pregnancy, a woman's lower-back pain. He is detached in a way that is helpful to the patient, disarming them of their embarrassment and shame.

In order to cure the body, you need to have the confidence to reach inside it, the imagination to do this in theory and the lack of squeamishness to do it in practice. Both of my grandfathers benefited from medical procedures which were as brutal as they were experimental. My mother's father was written up in the *British Medical Journal* of 1902 as one of the first two babies to have an operation shortly after birth to unblock the pyloric sphincter which leads from the stomach to the small intestine. The other baby died.

My father's father had his top lip taken off by a bullet in the First World War, and was one of the early plastic-surgery patients. I have the photographs documenting a procedure in which a graft was developed from his chest and extended into a 'handle' which was then attached to his mouth and used to regenerate his lip. I meet his eyes and can't see him. It's as if he has absented himself while his body is the site of this reconstruction. When the doctors examined the progress of their experiment, did they ask him what it was like to grow an extension of your body from chest to face, a living part that is plugged back in only to be eventually cut off? The procedure took over a year, during which time he attended medical school. No doubt many young men who were there had also been injured or had lost parts of themselves. The replacement parts they were offered were not often as human as my grandfather's handle of his own flesh. There were arms and legs made of wood and metal, metal noses and jaws. Was it more seemly to present a complete form than to impose on other people the sight of a body with something missing?

This grandfather, William, was the son of a Scottish railway-worker in the Highlands and one of five brothers. Bill was the first of the family to go to university and he was reading Classics at Aberdeen when the war broke out. Only two men from his class returned and they both became doctors. All but the youngest of the brothers joined the Gordon Highlanders at the outbreak of the First World War. Robert, who joined illegally, was sent home having already received a medal, signed up again and was killed in the last month of the war. When I went to Ypres and the Somme in 2013, I discovered that his body had first been buried at the roadside and was then reinterred in a military cemetery. All those bodies; all their broken shapes disguised by the unity and consistency of their memorials. I can't decide if the regulation of these simple graves breaks my heart or relieves me of the pain of their individual being. It does focus the mind on scale. I can either think about the endless fields of the dead or I can see one body. If my great-uncle died on a road, the troops were on the move. Who would have stopped to bury him? Perhaps in truth no one did.

I never met Bill because he died of pneumonia at the age of thirty-seven when my father, his youngest child, was eighteen months old. Bill was by then an obstetrician in Bury, Lancashire, and according to a newspaper article about his death, much respected and loved. There are a few photographs in which you can see, if you know to look, a slight tightness in his mouth, but there is often a cigarette in place to distract you. I asked my aunt Isla, who was seven years old when Bill died, if she remembered him. I wanted to hear her talk about his benevolence, like the newspaper. It was sad enough that my father had no father so at least the memory of him ought to be comforting. Isla was cautious but it sounded as if Bill was deeply reserved. I thought again of the young man who went to war with a book of poetry in his pocket and how he must have retreated within himself as his body became a subject. Like Berger's Dr Sassell, like my father, his drive might have been to cure pain so as to better bear his own: the good doctor who does not want to look at himself and so looks harder at others.

4

When I broke my arm, I discovered what it is like to carry part of yourself around. It was past midnight in winter and I was cycling home and lost my balance. I was so surprised that I did nothing to cushion the fall. It seemed to happen very slowly, my body falling sideways, my reflexes seemingly asleep. The ball of my shoulder broke in three places. From that moment, my arm became other. I had the sensation of being attached to something that had nothing to do with me. In the same instant, I stopped being able to see. It was as if I were so busy elsewhere in my body that I forgot to look. I could hear a voice asking if they should call an ambulance and my own voice reassuring them that there was no need. The voice reached out and helped me up and handed me my bike, which I pushed the last mile home with my left hand while my right arm tucked itself against my body. I couldn't see the next person to speak to me, who took my bike and pushed it for me then took my keys and opened my front door. Nor the taxi driver who arrived to take me to hospital or the medical team who moved me through rooms and machines and put pills in my mouth and morphine in my arm. Because I have no visual memory, it is the voices that have stayed with me, that and the occasional touch of a kind hand.

The pain arrived and I spent some weeks lying beside this part of myself as it restored communication with the rest of me. We experience our bodies through the sensations within them. For me, pain is foremost because from youth I have experienced pain that is not easily relieved and which over time has established itself as an alien part. I have felt it as a pulsar, a sink hole, a vice or drill, a spear, bubbling tarmac, a boulder, an anchor. If you have experienced chronic pain, your nerves can become hyper-vigilant. The slightest inflammation triggers a cascade of reactions as the body says *I know what this is*. The mind does this too, developing acuity to the point of prescience as a form of defence.[*] If you grow up in a volatile environment and the bad things happen to people you love, you learn to see as much as you can as quickly as possible. You react almost ahead of the event so as to defend yourself against its impact. You appear not to be present but really you have set off into the future looking desperately for whatever will equip you to escape.

We perceive ourselves as both within and without, and the body as something we have rather than are. Alfred North Whitehead spoke of 'the withness of the body'[11] a phrase that has been taken up by artists in the same way as 'dark light' perhaps because of its making a whole out of something that by

* See also Elizabeth Bishop's childhood in 'Disorder, slippage, glare', p. 238.

definition is in parts.* We cannot become completely ourselves
even though, as Whitehead put it, 'No one ever says, Here am I,
and I have brought my body with me.'[12] If Whitehead had been
a teenage girl, he might have reconsidered. I felt as if I were
hauling myself around for years.

My eyes began to fail when I was twelve. The world had
become fuzzy and contracted, and I hadn't noticed or didn't
care or perhaps even welcomed these new limits. I entered a
phase of rudeness and dependency, tripping over everything
because my eyes were fixed not even on but beyond the horizon.
Glasses were an embarrassment while contact lenses were irri-
tating, easily dislodged and expensive to replace. I would stay
out all night and put my lenses in egg cups that got washed up
or glasses of water that got drunk. Life was hazardous but not
stressful. Once, I was making my way home in the morning,
having lost my lenses again, when I saw a bus and ran to catch
it only to realise that it was a bus shelter. They were the same
grey-green. I also once flagged down a milk-float. If I was in
town, where there were many buses, I got on the first that came
along and then asked what number it was.

My understanding of light begins in fractured auras and
halos, leaky shifting colours, and granulated shapes that might
or might not become clear. I'm never surprised to find out that
something is not what it seems. I expect it. Myopia is why I
became interested in perception as faulty and subjective; and in
why we need to create fixed pictures when they are so evidently
provisional.

* 'The withness of the body' is the title of a poem by Anne Carson and
an album by Laurie Anderson. For a discussion of 'dark light', see 'Caves,
sleep, absence of light', p. 15.

. . . theoretical physics arises from deep-felt need to perfect the
physical world picture in the sense of its unity.

Max von Laue[13]

It's not enough to be able to name the parts of the world. We want to know how they fit together. In pursuing this, we have realised that we are not a natural priority. We've traced connection and reaction, dynamics and symbiotics, and have begun to grasp the extent to which the poor silly humans are in the way. But the desire to perfect the picture extends to ourselves. We want to be reassured that we, too, are unities. It is how we see the body – as a distinct outline among other outlines regardless of how plastic and porous it really is.

If you perfect the picture everything is in place, but when you see your internal organs on a scan, they're moving. The parts are always moving. The impulse to mend the broken form, to set the engine running again, to restore the flow, is a desire for wholeness that is there in a scientist like Hunter's drive to make the world known and visible.

For a long time, the body was believed to be stream and fire and earth and air together. How can we ever see ourselves amidst this flux? Not only do our bodies change but how we see them depends on our mood, the light, the mirror, and what we hope for or fear in our reflection. These days we can watch ourselves having a conversation, an experience that seems to make us either disintegrate or disconnect. When I see myself on screen like this, I can't form an overall impression and simply get on with being present. I cannot take myself in in a general way. I see only parts.

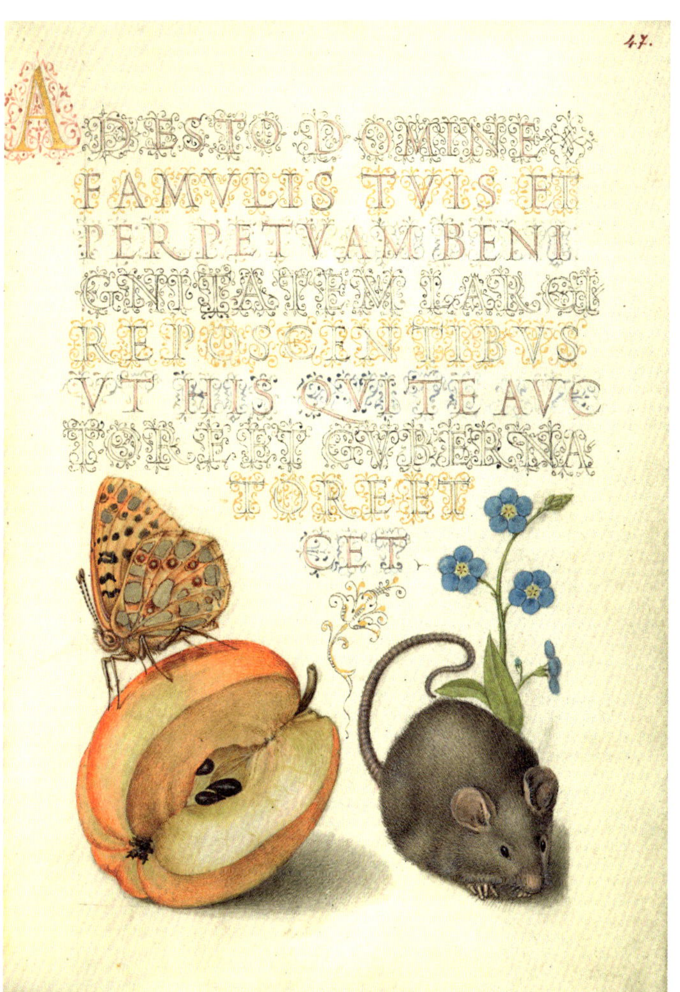

Joris Hoefnagel and Georg Bocskay, *Queen of Spain Fritillary, Apple, Mouse, and Creeping Forget-Me-Not*, 1561–2

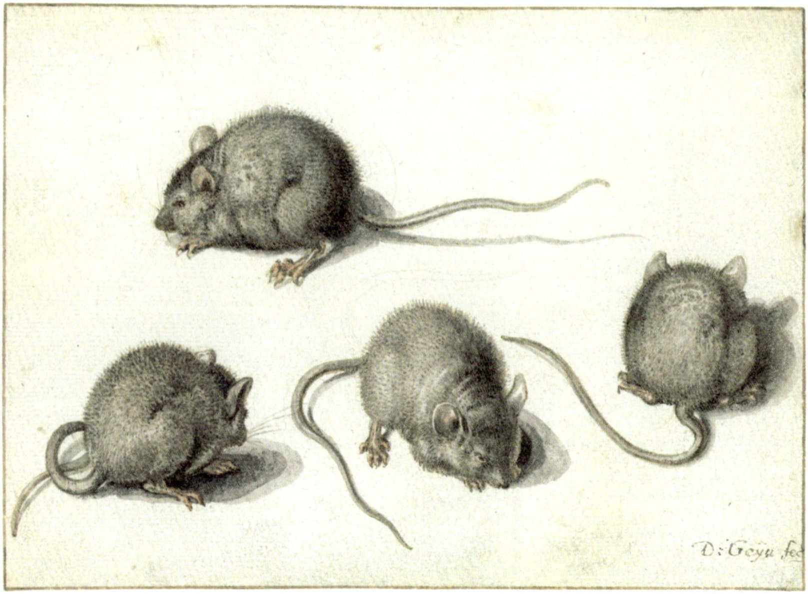

Jacques de Gheyn II,
Four studies of a diseased mouse, *c.*late
sixteenth century

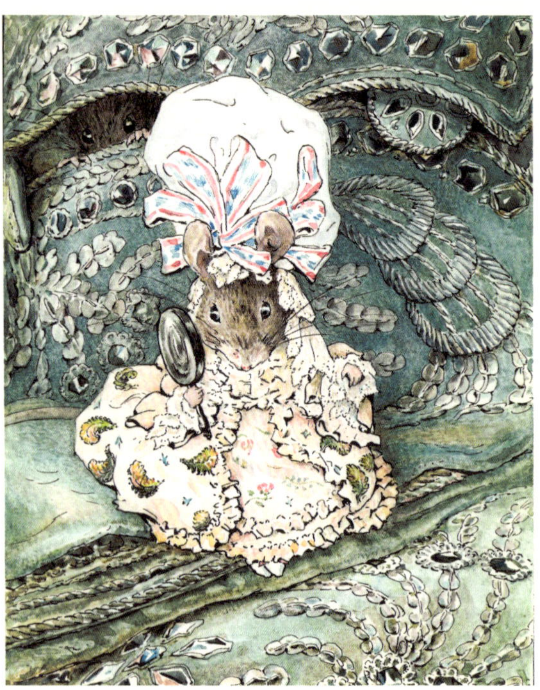

Beatrix Potter, Lady Mouse in mob cap, from *The
Tailor of Gloucester, c.*1902

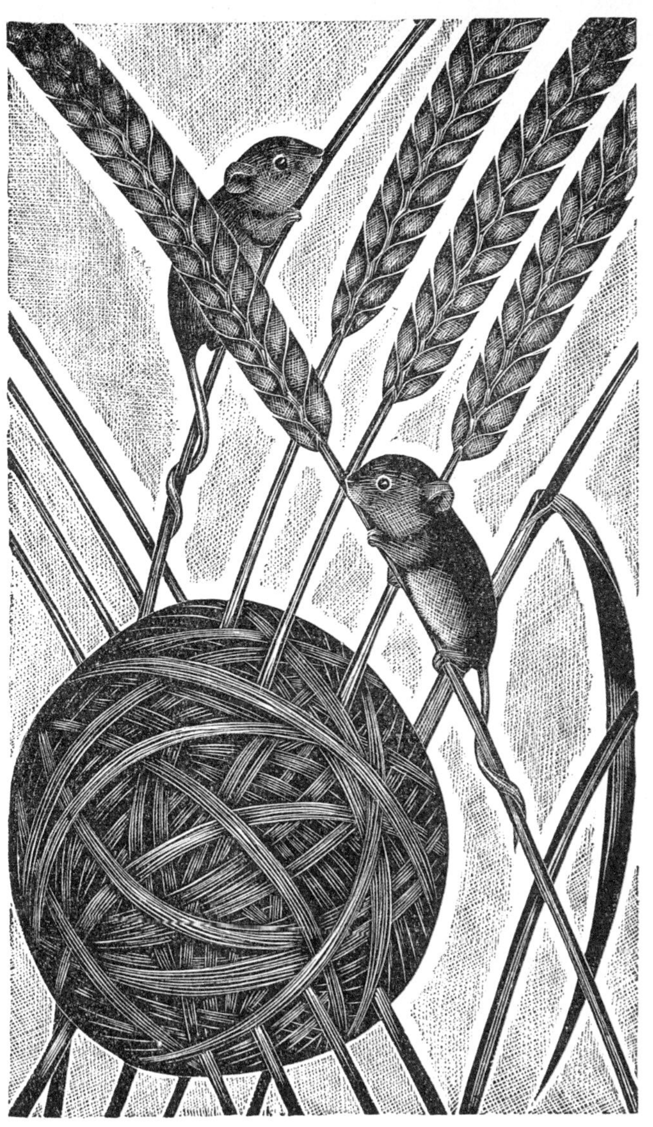

Claire Oldham, *Harvest Mice*, 1947

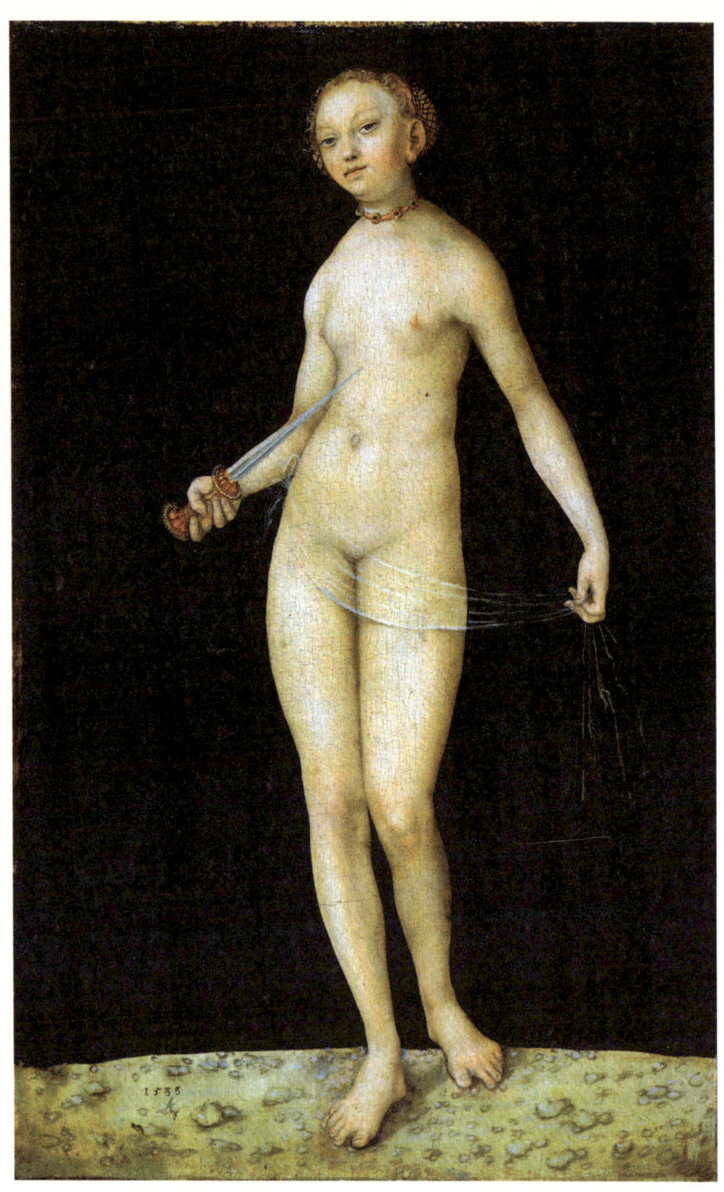

Lucas Cranach the Elder, *Lucretia*, 1533

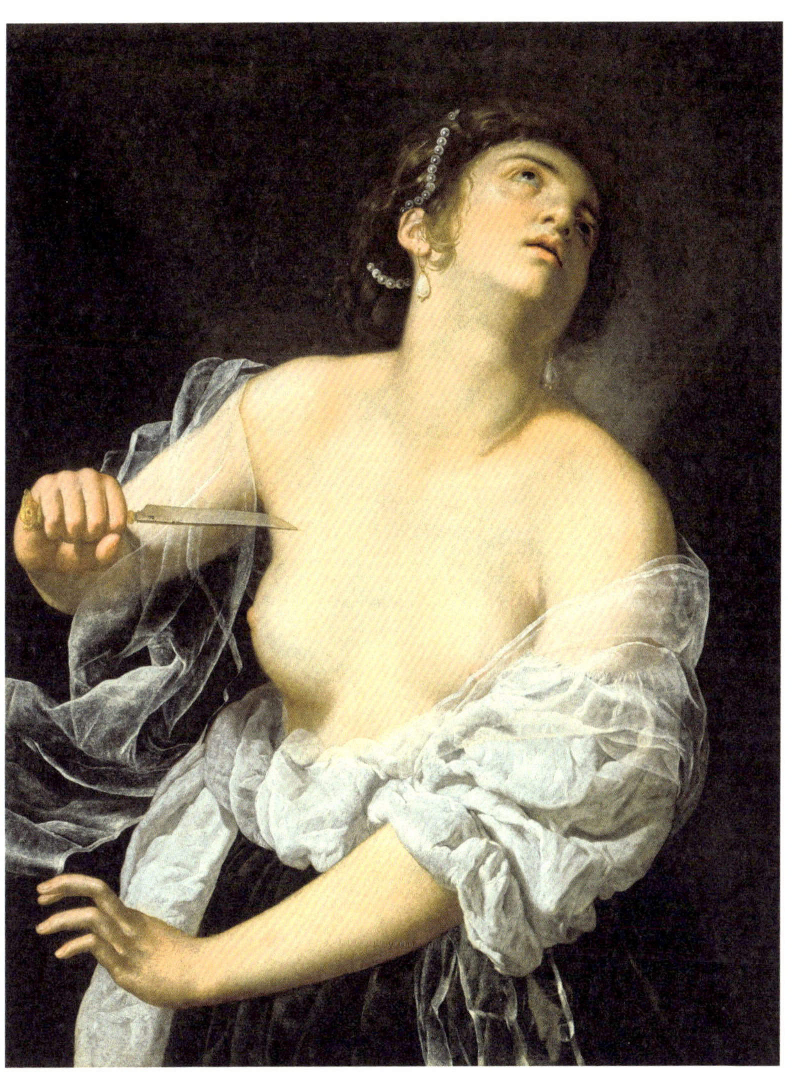

Artemisia Gentileschi, *Lucretia*, c.1627

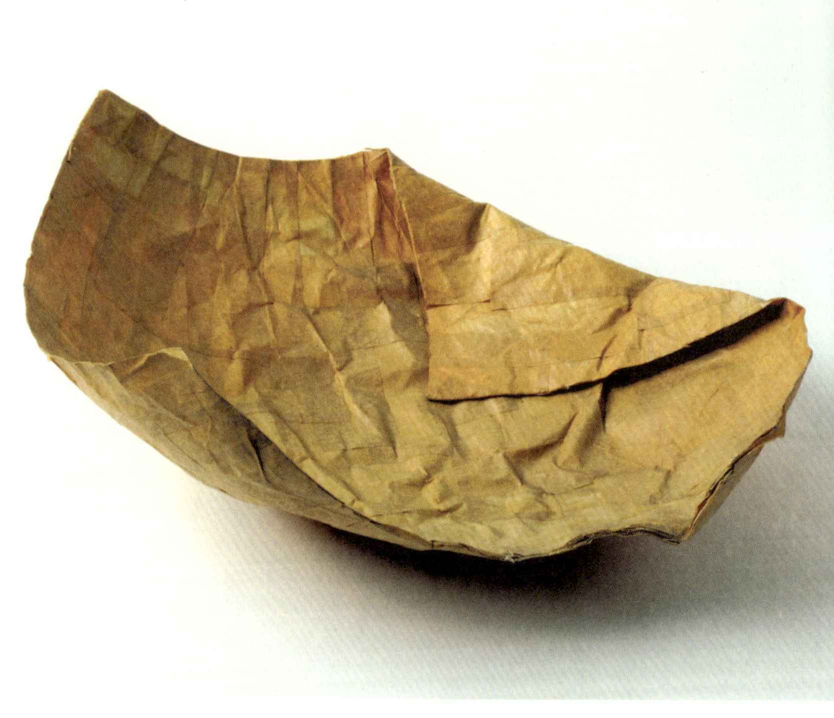

Eva Hesse, No title, 1969, cheesecloth, papier-caché, dimensions: 43 x 35.2 x 16.4 cm / 16⅞ x 13⅞ x 6½ inches. © The Estate of Eva Hesse. Courtesy Hauser & Wirth.

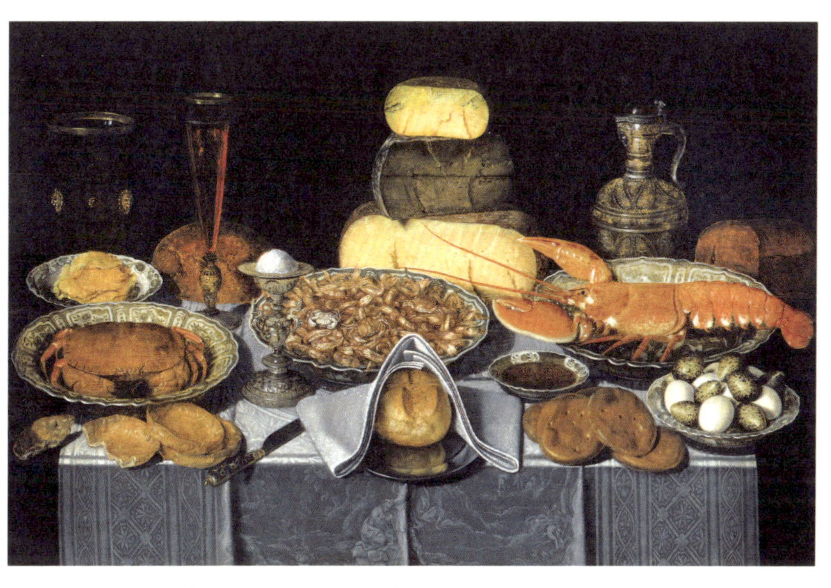

Clara Peeters, *Still Life with Crab, Shrimps and Lobster*, c.1635–40

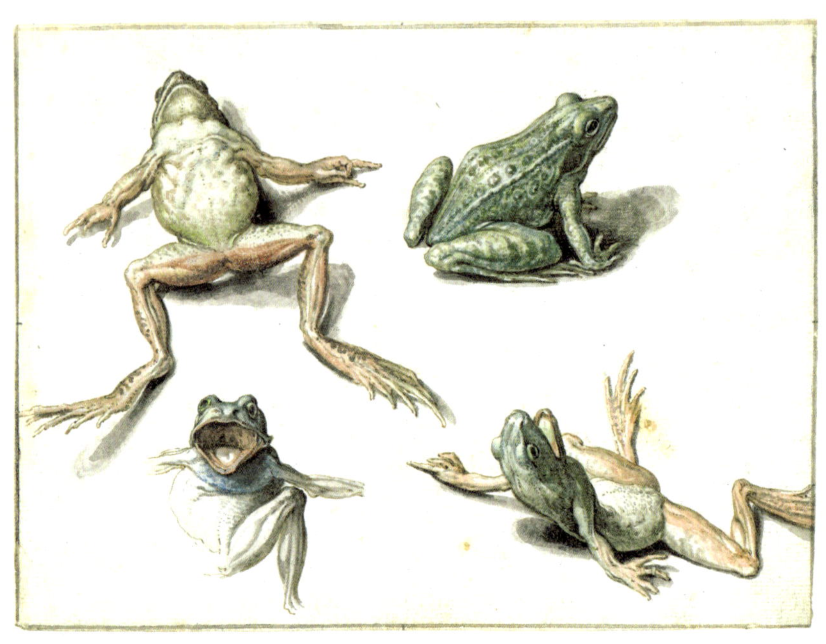

Jacques de Gheyn II, *Four Studies of a Frog*, c.1600

5

What does it mean to describe art as *of* – as opposed to *about* – the body? The American photographer Francesca Woodman built herself into her pictures in a way that was not about dissolving the boundary between artist and work or breaking a surface. Woodman preferred to work indoors and when she took up a residency that marooned her in the woods, declared 'Nature? What am I supposed to do with nature?'[14] She did not shut the door on 'nature's decibels' like Dorothea Tanning, nor did she submit to it.* Photographing birch trees, she sleeved herself in bark so that part of her disappears into the backdrop. In other of her works, she becomes wallpaper and even wall, but the process is never one of mergence or integration, and it is never entire.

One morning in late May, I walked out of the woods to see Francesca Woodman standing in a meadow, holding up her birch sleeves. My mind went straight to her image, not stopping to understand that here were birch branches that looked like arms wearing sleeves which reminded me of a particular Woodman photograph.

In an earlier series, 'Houses', Woodman threaded herself in a similar way into the image. There is something urgent and transgressive about how she places herself, opening space and contriving unexpected dimensions: 'I am interested in the way people relate to space. The best way to do this is to depict their interactions to the boundaries of these spaces.'

Woodman reminds me of Vuillard's sister about to emerge

* See Dorothea Tanning and her doors in 'Staying put, locked doors, wallpaper', p. 181.

from or disappear into yellow wallpaper.[*] The check on her black dress cages her. I thought for a long time that she was trying to disappear, to slip out of the crowded and buttoned-up room of her life. Looking at her next to Woodman, I think of her growing uncontrollably out of the girl she is expected to be and struggling to take, or hold onto, shape.

The desire for contact born of vision is exhilarating. The body wants to enter the picture, plunge into the sea, follow the path, meet softness, draw close to warmth, float in space. The physical object is an invitation to touch and its qualities not so much considered as experienced.

> Now everyone knows that when one sees a wooden statue one feels a mass, which sight has seen, which is not the case with painting.
>
> Philips Angel[15]

The presence of a body proposes touch, which is the most reliable of our senses. There is a painting of Narcissus by Caravaggio in which a strong and beautiful youth props himself above his reflection, his arms outstretched. He completes his own embrace. It looks like a happy ending but it is not how I think of Narcissus, eroded by his unmeetable desire and the impossible reaching towards the self.

In a later, eighteenth-century depiction by Nicolas Bernard Lépicié, Narcissus's body has a heavy softness. He is still the vital and sensual youth who drew everyone towards him but

* This painting was made in 1894, just a year after Charlotte Perkins Gilman's 'The Yellow Wallpaper' was published, see 'Black and white and colour', p. 113.

he can barely move. He is fading into the rocks as he reaches the tip of his finger towards the vaguest of reflections. The ripples in the water suggest that he has just tried to touch his own face, making it disappear. He looks as if he has been doing this forever. These are not the colours of desire; the yellow of the flower he will become has already faded and the bare rocks suggest the tedium and sterility of this pursuit.

We reach towards ourselves only to disappear. Ovid says of Narcissus that 'If he but fail to recognise himself, a long life he may have, beneath the sun.'[16] We wear ourselves out in self-scrutiny, each incidental glimpse of ourselves eroding a little more. I have seen my brain, uterus, bladder, ovaries, bowels, breasts, eyeballs, intestines; my jaw, the ball of my shoulder and the bones of my toes. I was looking at them because something had gone wrong or doctors thought that it might. I had no idea how to read the images I was shown. Is everything as it should be? I didn't even know that there is nothing wrong with my eyes except that they are too large and that is what makes me so short-sighted. It's a matter of scale. Yet such images have no scale. A part of the body in isolation, like the love of Narcissus, is not itself. Has this ability to see inside my body changed my sense of interior and exterior self? Not really. I'm looking at an image which is a measurement of activity or a map in which the focus is on interruption: an unexpected presence, a change of property or flow, a fissure or leak. I am not looking inside myself.

6

Perhaps my father was the first to know that he was soon to die. Dementia had wrecked his brain so that its pathways collapsed, sunk, snapped and frayed. For years, his brain had managed to find new paths, to improvise bridges and diversions, and he remained so physically strong that he could walk for eight miles until the disease attacked his motor skills. Week by week, another impulse or reflex was lost to him. A path petered out. Even when his memory was almost destroyed, his brain was still trying to make sense of things. Once when we were walking in the garden, he heard someone hammering on a roof. He happened to be looking at a pigeon and so he deduced that, 'Someone is trying to hammer the pigeon into the ground.'

His memory broke up into fragments that surfaced more or less at random. When those were gone, he started to struggle even with the present tense. He didn't know where he was and then who we were and then how to speak. Still, his body kept going until completing the process of movement was too much for what was left of his mind.

One day I arrived as he was being helped into bed and I saw that he was going through a change so profound that it was akin to a metamorphosis. He had been a frightened man and then a dreaming child; scared, silly and small, and at times animal. His face had always been animated and crowded with feeling. He might appear amused, suspicious, needy, sheepish, evasive and astute all at once. Now his face cast off all expression, and he looked god-like and characterless. I leant over him and, with tremendous concentration and force, he held my face in his hands and looked into my eyes.

Without character, my father revealed his essential nature. He was simplified and our relationship instantly simplified too. He looked into my eyes with absolute, unqualified love and I was able to meet his love with my own. This was a completion of vision in which one person puts everything into their gaze and the other, everything into receiving it. We held each other's eyes, the same eyes, and he continued to grip my head. He expressed his love by seeing me and I showed mine by offering myself up to be seen. Our difficult history, all its armour, weapons and defences, the rigid versions and redundant positions, the cloaks and curtains and masks and walls, fell away. I saw my father clearly and he saw me, and this could only happen then as he was leaving. Such clarity would be too much to sustain.

They told us to come, that it would be soon, and I was on the next train, clutching my hasty and chaotic luggage, unable to bear that I was not yet beside him. The three of his children on this side of the world met there, and we slept on his floor and sat about the bed and watched him. When I lay down in the dark on the floor and couldn't see him, I listened instead as his breath slowed, paused, thinned and fought its way to the next inhalation. Our vigil was simple. We talked to him but also as if he were not there. We read him poems and told him stories, opened the window to the rain, and placed herbs and incense around his head. Mostly we sat beside him in a kind of readiness.

Late one night, my younger brother suddenly said that he was glad to be there because if not, he would be running through the city dressed as a gorilla. He'd agreed to be part of a team at work who were entering a fancy-dress charity race. Once the outfits they had hired arrived, they realised that they needed to practice running while dressed as gorillas. Seeing the ridiculous outfits made them realise that they didn't want to do it. A colleague had an idea. She would dress up as a banana and they could chase her. This solved everything. There is nothing silly about a gorilla if they're running after a banana. We laughed and laughed, forgetting that the man beside us was dying but knowing how much he would have loved this story, and when two days later, his body had still not given up, I thought what he needed was something to follow, only what could I offer? I didn't have the fancy dress of a religious faith to pull on so that I could lead the way. I could cast no light. He had to travel alone.

Six years later, my brother was diagnosed with terminal cancer and died within four weeks. He had enough time to contemplate his own death but not enough to prepare himself. We had one more conversation before he became too ill. He was an astrophysicist and we talked about stars as we had since our teenage years. He gave me a place in the sky in which to find him. He did not use its name but its number and when I spoke of my haphazard adventures with a telescope, he explained that he was less interested in looking than he was in the stars on paper. It was how the universe arranged itself, how it moved and worked that compelled him. While it was important to me to complete my interest by looking at the moon or a planet or a star, he didn't need to. He was receiving and sharing and setting himself aside.

I sat beside him the day before he died. His body was poisoning itself and he was sinking beneath medication, in and out of consciousness. When he woke, his eyes – green and bright – were a flicker of his absolute self. His words were sliding around and as we told stories of our childhood, he tried to join in. He managed a whole sentence about the dog skidding across the floor after my mother had polished it, and after that we couldn't follow. As his body flooded and swelled, he became more uncomfortable and complained of his *hinges*. I understood this to mean his hips or joints and with the help of a nurse, we tried to get him into a better position. He reached for words but they eluded him until with extreme crispness, he said *Words are a waste* or *Words are waste* or *Words are wasted*. I do not understand why I can't remember exactly. And then he added: *Paper and pen*. I gave him my notebook and he drew a rapid technical sketch which made clear the best angle for his body and where it needed support. We knew then what to do.

I learnt too soon not to trust my eyes. It meant that I did not trust my body.

I wish I could say that my father appeared in that hospital room with two suits, one for a banana and one for a gorilla.

Words are waste / a waste / wasted.

Peering and noticing, flits and swerves

1

Shortly before my aunt Isla died, we visited the National Gallery in London. By then she had lost much of her sight, a limitation she more or less ignored. She was as enthusiastic as ever about looking carefully at interesting things. Isla had a way of peering into me that was both piercing and loving. I was an uneasy child who felt exposed by being seen but when she gave me her attention, I relaxed. She was not just looking, but noticing. She saw me clearly and let me know that she understood what she saw and that it was alright.

Isla was an anaesthetist and so spent much of her time in the confined space of the operating theatre, peering at instrument dials and assessing the weather within the unconscious body on the table. I imagine the rhythm of her attention as a continuous act of adjustment, of expertly bringing what she encountered into equilibrium. This, too, is how I felt when she peered into me – and peering is what best describes it. Peering is an effort: what you are about to look at, into or through is somehow difficult to navigate. It is a way of looking that acknowledges vision as effortful and tentative, an unconfident act. Bound up in this is the assumption that you will not actually see what you are peering at, not properly. When we can't see something clearly in the immediate, we have to stop and look, and in so doing we become conscious of the act of looking; we become *active* observers as opposed to the passive receptors we are as we go about an average day, pounded by images.

When Isla and I arrived in front of one of Philips Koninck's vast panoramic landscapes (*An Extensive Landscape with a Road by a River*, 1655), she walked right up to it and pulled a small telescope out of her bag. She could no longer stand back and take in the sweep of the landscape or travel its distances but she could peer at its detail. I was standing where Koninck intended me to be while Isla stepped in. Seventeenth-century Netherlandish art is known for its depth of field – 'we live in the picture, we walk about in it, we look into its depths'[1] – and Koninck painted as if this was more important than the landscape itself (which was probably invented). I don't look at this road by a river and wonder where it leads. I experience a gently elevated point of view from where I can see for miles.

I wondered what Isla was seeing. If the man on the path in the foreground held a telescope to his eye, the distance that Koninck has worked so hard to assert would collapse. He would see better where he was going but not how to get there. The viewpoint places us mid-air above the river looking down on houses and people but not high enough for it to feel wholly unnatural. We might be looking over the panorama from high on a hill (it's easy to forget when looking at such landscapes that in the Netherlands, there are no hills). These days, our visual experience is all flits and swerves. We are used to inspecting a leaf and then looking down on a forest. We are comfortable whatever our point of view, whereas Koninck would have got no higher than a church tower and would have had to imagine his elevated perspectives.

2

> In a grain of sand, in a drop of water, we discover worlds and inhabitants; besides, our best microscopes only show us the whales and elephants of those worlds; they are still far from reaching the insects.
> Johann Heinrich Lambert[2]

It is hard for us now to imagine the vertigo that must have accompanied the first experience of a microscope. The telescope makes it possible to see further but whatever is in view leaps into the eye and leaves everything else behind. It doesn't bring the world any closer. The microscope is an opposite experience: one of peering so deeply that you sink into your subject. Outlines break down and surfaces give way, losing their smoothness and certainty. Suddenly we could see not just further but through and inside. This was an instrument which could only look at small things that fitted under the lens and in placing them there, we discovered that they contained many other small things; so many that perhaps they weren't so small after all. The invisible loomed and the world slipped free of the human scale. How could we then move through it? When Locke came to write about the view under the microscope, he warned that being able to 'come nearer to the discovery of the texture and motion of the minute parts of corporeal things' would place the viewer 'in quite a different world from other people: nothing would appear the same to him and others'.[3] It is the same world and it is ourselves who are altered. Knowing how much lies beyond our vision contracts our sight. Having broken the surface, we meet the subject of our gaze more tentatively, knowing now how much of it lies beyond us.

> it being very probable, as I elsewhere shew, that fluid bodies are made up of small solid particles variously and strongly mov'd, and may find reason to think there is scarce a surface *in rerum naturâ* perfectly smooth.
>
> Robert Hooke[4]

Robert Hooke devoted himself to the microscope, studying everything from the tip of a needle to a flea. He went to great lengths to see his subjects as completely as possible and, not having a brightly lit and air-conditioned laboratory, was dependent on the weather. He refined a technique of placing the microscope on a table close to a south-facing window and using a 'Globe of Water' to collect and throw the light, or 'an oyly paper' and a 'Good Large Burning Glass' to diffuse its brightness.[5] When the weather was dull, nothing could be looked at.

Both artist and scientist depend upon peering and noticing but also on a readiness to flit and swerve, to move backwards or sideways, take a leap or let go. Like Locke, Samuel van Hoogstraten described seeing further as a kind of alienation, of propelling yourself backwards out of your subject: 'How wonderful a good map is in which one views the world as from another world thanks to the art of drawing.'[6]

Hooke described cork as being made of 'cells', bringing the biological use of the word into the language. On examining thyme seeds under a microscope, he said that 'the Grain affords a very pretty Object for the *Microscope*, namely, a Dish of Lemmons plac'd in a very little room.'[7] In giving us something as familiar as lemons to look at, Hooke softens the strangeness of this enlargement. The looming seeds with their swellings, ridges, cracks, dents and stalks subside into a bowl of fruit. Hooke tries to capture the way they swerve into view under the lens by placing that bowl in 'a very little room' but we're not in the room and for us, there is no visual tension – the lemons remain quite ordinary.

This unboundaried world and the dynamic nature of these new ways of looking must have stimulated the scientist to new lengths of investigation. Antoni van Leeuwenhoek,[*] an autodidact, made his own lenses, the sophistication of which is still admired today. He was not a good scientist in that he refused to share his technical secrets, but he was remarkable in his reach and the ways in which he tried to inhabit his subject. Rather than speculate on or assume the nature of a dragonfly's vision, he dissected one of its eyes, separated and cleaned up the cornea and placed it over a lens. He then looked through it at a nearby church tower. His desire to enter everything he saw was matched by his skill:

> with a small hair pencil and fair rain water, I cleared away
> the many vessels which fill the inside of the tunica cornea,
> or horny coat of the eye, leaving only the tunica cornea
> remaining. This I contrived to place in such a manner, that
> it might not, as it dried, contract in wrinkles . . .[8]

It is easy to forget that he is talking about working on an insect's eye. In describing blood corpuscles under the

* For Leeuwenhoek's investigations of his own body and the colour red, see 'Black and white and colour', p. 112.

microscope, he starts, like Hooke, in a simile but it is not one in which the new scale of things is made ordinary as in seeds being compared to lemons. He refers instead to conditions under which something as tiny as a grain of sand can be ordinarily observed: '. . . as sharp and clean as one can distinguish sand-grains upon a piece of black taffeta silk, with one's eyes, without the help of glasses.'[9]

He could isolate the throat of a flea and the development of the embryo in a dragonfly's egg. In 1680, in a nineteen-page letter (with eight drawings) sent to the Royal Society in London, he documented investigations into yeast, air, rain water and milk; urine, the heart, the circulation and blood; the tracheas of the flea, cockroach and fly; the mating of dragonflies and cockchafers; the spermatozoids of the grasshopper, flea and fly; mites; and the quantity of micro-organisms to be found in a single grain of sand.

At the time some of Leeuwenhoek's ideas, such as looking at the world from the point of view of an insect, must have seemed like a wild unravelling. But he was looking to establish facts and natural laws. We encounter the unknown and then wait for it to fall into place – as if the world is full of blanks ready to be filled by things made visible by our discovery.

3

For five years I lived in a barn that hadn't been occupied before. It was like living indoors and outdoors at the same time. The walls were thick but there was a huge window with a view of the sunset, an ancient pig in a meadow, and a mystical dead tree. When inside, I spent most of my time gazing outwards.

The animal life of the building continued alongside me, and the solidity of the walls and beams was perforated by passageways I could not always detect. A field mouse would appear as if out of the plaster, run along a sill and evaporate. Young swallows would fly in a scatty arc in through the open door and melt away. Sometimes they got distracted and kept flying or perched high up. I would fret about how to rescue them until suddenly they were outside. I went to sleep listening to the white noise of the wasps' nest behind my head, and something substantial and restless moving around low inside or outside or within the walls. My absences encouraged the animals to move back in. Rabbits who had retreated to the meadow romped through the garden, and ran tunnels under, around and probably through the building. The crows who preyed on them took to eviscerating their corpses on my garden table.

All day, hawks hovered and swooped. The crows would gather at dusk, filling the oaks and lining the telegraph wires, growing louder until they returned to their roosts. Then the tawny owls would begin their relaxed hunt, swinging over the meadow. I redirected young moles lost and blinded by daylight. Long-tailed tits built a nest in a clematis just three feet from my front door. When they were feeding their young, I went in and out of the other door so as not to disturb them. This was a problem because some of the bats who lived in the roof used to roost at the top of this door. I learnt to open it carefully as several times there were two or three tiny pipistrelles so fast asleep that they dropped to the ground. I would place them in one of the passageways in the brickwork, and they would dissolve back into the walls like everything else.

At night, if I was sitting quietly, a bat would materialise in the room, bounce round its sonar net and then disappear so instantly that I had not registered its leaving. I would be watching the air, my brain having not caught up with the fact that the bat was no longer there. The movement of these animals made sense to me – all except that of the bats.

When I lived in Florida, in the late nineties, I went to see a colony of bats that had been moved out of a building and into a purpose-made roost. It looked like a miniature version of the houses that are moved around America on the back of a truck. Perhaps its design was chosen to reassure people that the bats were being looked after properly: they had what we would recognise as a home. I wonder what a home designed by a bat would look like. Given how far away we are from being able to conceive of, let alone compare, their perceptions, I suspect it would be something I couldn't make visual sense of and so perhaps wouldn't actually see.

I stood by the fence and waited for the bats to wake up, which I was told they did at dusk. It was a cloudy day and whether or not the sun was setting was unclear. I wasn't looking at the sky but at the bat house, intent on catching the first signs of flight. The light started to dim in a general way and the more I tried to observe this, the harder it was to see. At a certain point, I started to feel rather than hear noise. It was like a growing cloud of interruption, as if each sound each bat made was bouncing round a tiny room. It was coming from the house and already seemed too large to be contained by it. The air started to break up as if grains of light were being snuffed out and these tiny darknesses flitted and swerved. Again, I had the sense that I couldn't see them because however long I watched for (and there were thousands of bats and so they came in waves

over several minutes), I was unable to get any sense of pattern,
rhythm or form.

4

What happens to vision when we start to move through the
world at previously unimagined speeds, when we are carried
along or even swept off our feet? We lose sight of things. In
two hundred years we've become attuned to moving at speeds
of seventy miles per hour and to reading the world accordingly. What a shock it must have been to travel all your life on
foot or on horseback and then to board a train. For me, looking
out of a train window offers a space to think in by occupying
my eyes. In 1838, William Henry Fox Talbot[*] noted after his
first railway journey, when he travelled at the dizzying speed
of thirty miles per hour, that he 'wanted to go no faster than
that'.[10] For all his enthusiasm for innovation, he didn't want to
feel out of control. Constance Fox Talbot was more concerned
about everyone else.

> The weather today was particularly fine, and we quite
> enjoyed our journey, (although it was by railway) for the
> train travelled slowly through Elvanfoot, and its pretty
> environs to Carstairs – On leaving the latter place we were
> 20 minutes or more behind time which ~~they~~ we recovered
> before we reached Edinburgh – And this was the only part
> which frightened us a little for in going so quickly, the
> carriages swayed more than I ever felt them to do before.

* See William Henry Fox Talbot's early photographic experiments in
'Boredom, repetition, fixatives', p. 68.

I cannot help feeling daily more anxious about those
who travel by railway, though the dangers are happily
diminished since the breaking up of the frost . . .'[11]

Accelerating through the dark has become so ordinary to
us that we don't think about how poignantly the act mirrors
the ephemeral nature of time. We're projecting light which we
then travel into only for that light to go out. It's as if we're
moving over and over again towards the next moment, which
we never actually enter. There's a lack of contact, of gravity
and substance in driving after dark. In the last century, Virginia
Woolf recorded a drive in the Sussex countryside at night
during which her senses were so scattered that she described
herself as having four separate selves, each responding differently: 'While they are thus busied, I said to myself: Gone, gone;
over, over; past and done with, past and done with. I feel life
left behind even as the road is left behind. We have been over
that stretch, and are already forgotten. There, windows were
lit by our lamps for a second; the light is out now. Others come
behind us.' Woolf concludes by saying that now she can envisage Sussex five hundred years into the future, as if moving at
unusual speed through the dark gives new momentum to the
imagination, which it does.[*]

Around the time that Woolf was flitting around Sussex in the
dark, Henri Matisse was also getting accustomed to travelling

---

[*] Compare this to Woolf's account of being outside in the dark when
returning to a house where she spent holidays as a child in 'Invisible, unseen'
(p. 264) and encountering her own absence, making her feel like a ghost.
Memory presents time as a maze in which we are directed and constrained
whereas this experience of acceleration through the dark is one of space, and
therefore time, falling open.

by car – although he insisted on being driven at walking pace because he wanted to keep what he called 'a sense of the trees'. We think we know how fast we can or should go and, unless our interest lies in trees, probably get a visceral thrill from going a little faster. Four years after moving to a village, I was out at night in a car in the lanes, crammed in with friends while a boy (it was always a boy) who had only just learnt to drive, drove faster. We lurched and swerved and turned the music up. Our youth and the music made us invincible. The countryside darkness was then something I wanted to break open, to find my way out of, and this pointless driving around, with no place to go, was a way of doing that. One night, the boy took us to the top of a multi-storey car park and drove full pelt down the switchback of the exit ramp. As we ricocheted downwards, all I could see was concrete swerving past and falling away.

Richard Gregory writes about the psychology of seeing and how 'If the observer is walking, or running . . . he or she has a lot of information from the limbs, signalling movement in rela-tion to the ground. But when carried along in a car, or an air-craft, the situation is very different – the feet are off the ground, and the only source of information is the eyes'.[12] We are taught to read the road and also taught to believe in it. We learn its language of signs, its colour codes, and what to expect from one another while on it. We are also taught about the dangers, and how to drive as if expecting them at any time. We assume some-one is watching over the road (traffic wardens, highway patrols, council surveillance) so that we can confidently accelerate into the dark trusting that no sharp corner or sudden junction will go unannounced, that we will have plenty of warning. A good road is ordinary, predictable, a laying out of what we have come to expect. It has been made so that we have to think about it as little as possible.

Driving in the dark is an act of trust but we are accustomed to it. Our eyes have learnt how to read the rapidly shifting content of the pool of light into which we perpetually accelerate even though it is frequently complicated by other lights or things that flash past while sending vital messages about what's to come. At night, speed is both more abstract and more acute. Our sense of movement depends upon the continuous feedback, encouragement and warnings of symbols and signals, patterns of light and how long it takes for the world to slip through the beams of our headlamps.

I learnt to drive in the city, so it took time to get used to the countryside after dark where you travel the reach of your headlamp beams as if they are laying the ground. Whatever appears – trees, tarmac, hedgerows and fences – is a little bleached out as if the light unfolding in front of the car were tissue paper. You fix your gaze ahead while the world rolls past in your peripheral vision. You're not thinking about the walls of shadow on either side but the scattering of reflective markers and white lines. Now and then something catches the eye – an interruption to the side of the road. There might be a barn owl on a fence spotting roadkill, a small affronted ghost.

At night, on the road, your brain is making a series of rapid judgements about the size, shape and movement of any approaching object. It works constantly to read what you can't quite make out: it was an owl, a deer, a fox; those lights are from an oncoming vehicle and the small light wobbling along the hedgerow is someone's torch. You know right away when something doesn't make sense. One night I was driving down an unlit lane when a ball of green light appeared beside my window. It remained there for a second and then bounced in front of the windscreen and disappeared. I could feel my brain whirring to make sense of it, riffling through a process of elimination, but it was too large to be an insect, too solidly and synthetically green, and it didn't flit so much as hover and bounce. To this day, I have no idea what it was. I try not to succumb to the fact that I was near a place famous for UFOs.

When you drive through the night, you do not enter it. You not only drive through the hours but through darkness and the possibility of sleep. You are not where you are either as you do not remain in the places you pass. Nor are you moving. You sit still, watching chains of light: the white stream flowing past you on the motorway and the red stream that carries you onwards. On main roads there are occasional infusions of light – approaching a junction or on a hazardous stretch – but these are now being minimised because lighting the road can make it harder to see.

In daytime, a broad view of the landscape means you can pace yourself and get an idea of where you are according to landmarks – at night, you can't. You could be passing through mountains and not know the difference between a deep tunnel and a steep drop as the lights carry you on. The journey, bereft of its sights, becomes just time that is passing.

You are not looking at what's out there but for what will keep you moving. The road at night is also a series of signs: the next turning, the next town, eventual cities, other roads to come, traffic warnings, speed restrictions, lane closures, graphic signifiers for black ice or spilt cargoes which might be anything from sheet plastic to cattle, kitchen units to sugar beet.

The brighter the interior of the car, the harder it is to see the dark, so dashboards and screens dim themselves. You dim yourself too. Still and not still, you make tiny repetitive movements as you adjust the gears, the steering wheel, the pedals, the headlights, the radio, the air. You must remain alert and responsive but in ways which seem as reflexive as scratching an itch. You flick your head from rear view to wing mirror and then to check the blind spot. You are continually shifting and yet if the road is clear and this is all it takes, and all goes smoothly, you feel as if you haven't moved at all. You might have been thinking, dreaming, listening to music or the radio or talking to your passengers. You probably weren't thinking about driving at all.

5

If we had a keen vision and feeling of all ordinary human life, it would be like hearing the grass grow and the squirrel's heartbeat, and we should die of that roar which lies on the other side of silence. As it is, the quickest of us walk about well wadded with stupidity.

George Eliot[13]

We fail to take in much of what we see. We peer at what we cannot quite see, and what we notice is often not what we choose to or expect. There is nothing more vivid than a sudden coalescence that confounds understanding and detonates memory so that you feel both recognition and bewilderment for the moment before it falls into place. The boredom and repetition of life – journeys, making and remaking works of art, pouring tea – can be what fixes something for us but sometimes, there is a moment in which the shape that is made is so perfect that you never forget it.

> Another time, I remember, I was sitting there just behind the new painting, and Marcel Duchamp was in a chair facing me. I finished my tea, and Duchamp got up from his chair and took my teacup from me with the most extraordinary grace – with a gesture so elegant that I've never forgotten it.
> Georgia O'Keeffe[14]

When I decided to work in sound, I wanted to explore things that we notice but which withhold themselves so that we have to move towards them. When we encounter something incomplete, volatile and potent, we don't just receive it, we respond. We complete it ourselves. The work I made was an immersive installation called *Audio Obscura*, to be experienced in a busy railway station. In a station, we are forced into proximity but tend to assume that we are neither overlooked nor overheard. The intimacy of a phone conversation can overpower the presence of those around us. Moving through a crowd chatting to a friend does the same. Listening to music can absorb us to the point at which we are unguarded about what our face, or body, might express. *Audio Obscura* was also an exploration of the ways in which sound affects vision, and how it can activate or dissolve our boundaries (or those boundaries that we assume we have or imagine we have). Deep tones and sudden acoustic drops can make the world appear to be slowing down as if under water.

Stations are places of meeting, parting, anticipating, escaping. Everyone is waiting for something to happen or moving between events. They might be there for minutes or hours, every day or just this one time. Their thoughts are more than usually elsewhere. Many will be preoccupied by a displaced kind of listening or looking through their phone. Most of us don't scrutinise those around us or listen to their conversations yet find our attention captured by details that we remember whether we want to or not. Things catch our attention because they raise a question and fail to answer it. Why is that child crying or that woman laughing? What did they mean? Why are that couple not speaking? Who is he kissing?

People, even when they're with someone else, look contemplative and I became interested not in what they were thinking but in what they might want to say or might not know that they wanted to say. The camera obscura, or 'dark room', was a once-popular entertainment and artist's tool which used a small aperture and mirrors to project a reflection of the passing world. It was in part what led to early photography as people strove to fix the images it produced. The fragile, shifting but acute images of the camera obscura draw you in. In *Audio Obscura*, the idea was translated into what I've called 'dark listening' with its connotations of depths and shadows, the impalpable and the unreachable. We enter interior lives and discover, somewhere between what is heard and what is seen, what cannot be said. We're conscious of this as transgression but unable to contain our curiosity. And we in turn become less self-aware: caught up in the act of listening, we give ourselves away. The darkness is the undeveloped image of our thoughts.

Audio Obscura is situated in tension with our compulsion to construct narratives, to impose meaning, and to seek symmetry and conclusion. The voices within it hover between speech and thought. They are concentrated fragments of interior worlds which sensitise us to boundaries we depend upon yet break. They glance off one another, meet and diverge as a bigger picture coheres and dissolves like the reflections inside the camera obscura. These stories are neither revealed nor concluded. The experience is not one of being told something but of becoming conscious of what we do with what we notice and how, in the act of dark listening, unconscious aspects of perception are brought to light in ourselves.

6

Peering as intentional scrutiny can be transgressive. The gaze is an invitation that we find ourselves taking as a command. We have to respond, even if it is by turning away. In Judith Leyster's *Man Offering Money to a Young Woman* (1631), she is made visible by the light she needs in order to do her work. He is leaning into that light in order to capture her, his hand on her arm wants to turn her away from the light and towards his shadow. If she moved in the other direction, there is no other light, just bare, dark, space. You can hardly make out the floor from the wall. His eyes are lowered, he is not looking at her face but her body, which is covered from head to toe in virginal white and blue. Her eyes are also lowered as she resists this disturbance by looking ever more intently at her work. We cannot see what she is making or mending – that's not the point. She needs something to do, to be able to offer him a reason for not turning towards him. The cool flame pulls her towards him, its empty light tugging at her equally pale blouse. Neither are looking at the money in his hand.

Learning that there are things you do not want to see.

Rather than see, you will stop noticing.

Some you will have already seen but you want to un-see them now.

Some you see coming and don't look up.

If you don't look around you, you might not have to see.

Tell yourself that you probably got it wrong. You are not see-ing clearly. Make this habit so strong that you never believe your eyes.

Pattern, machinery, punctuation

1

Over the course of a year (2001–2), I went out to meet each solstice and equinox. The rites and symbolism associated with these moments remind us that the sun's presence and predictability is a matter of life or death but they also give us pattern. This can be confused with meaning: our eyes seek out pattern and when we find it, life feels not only more predictable but more purposeful. The world grows friendly when we understand its machinery as if our insight is somehow reciprocated.

> Once I was beset by anxiety. I couldn't tell right from left or orient myself. I could have cried out with terror at being lost. But I pushed the fear away – by studying the sky, determining where the moon would come out, where the sun would appear in the morning. I saw myself in relationship to the stars. I began weeping, and I knew that I was all right.
>
> Louise Bourgeois[1]

I cannot hold in my head the shifting arrangement of sun, moon and earth. I have to watch it happening. To be in a place where planetary alignments become visible, where a beam of light will hit a stone or a river surge over itself at the exact time predicted, is consoling. It places me, as Louise Bourgeois puts it, in relationship. As a child I sought significance, investing trees and stones with magical powers, and believing myself in deep and secret relationship to it all. I wanted to make a story out of everything I saw whereas now I just want to experience landscape and light. I have grown up with an empty frame – the picture emptied of divine presences – and what is left is light. I like close contact with unsettled weather, and to be somewhere which claims my attention to the extent that there is none left for myself.

Maeshowe is a neolithic burial chamber built on Orkney around 2700 BCE. Sunk into the earth, it looks much smaller than it is: a dome on a raised bank surrounded by a ditch that might be a small moat. I'd come a long way to see it and could hardly make it out. When I climbed onto its top, which is only twenty-four feet high, I could see how much bigger and more important it was than anything else around. Orkney is a bare island with a few low trees, which makes the standing stones some of its highest constructions. I could see the edge of the island which, five thousand years ago, must have seemed like the edge of the world. For the builders of Maeshowe, solstices and equinoxes were not just interesting astronomical alignments; they marked the passage of the sun which was their clock, calendar and life source.

I was at Maeshowe for the winter solstice when, as the sun sets, a beam of light should travel along a passageway and into the chamber where it hits the back wall and illuminates the space. That year, the odds of this happening, with the sun unobscured at just the right moment, were given as fifty-fifty. A driving wind and flurries of snow meant that I kept my head down and barely glimpsed the sun, which rose around nine, moved in and out of the clouds, and set before three. You enter

Maeshowe through a tunnel that faces south-west. It was longer than I expected and so low that I had to double over and scuttle. Arriving in the chamber, crouched down, face to the floor, made its impact all the more remarkable. The first thing I did was look up as if into the sky. The chamber is about sixteen feet square and has three side chambers. It's built out of huge tightly aligned stones, some weighing as much as thirty tonnes. I was barely below ground but felt as deep inside the earth as when I walked under a river.* After a while, the absolute stillness became difficult to bear.

The timing of the beam entering the chamber can be predicted to the minute but however much we know about the sun and when to expect it where, we can do nothing about the weather. Alongside the handful of others who had arrived in the chamber, I waited for the cloud to move. We lined up on either side, trying not to lose sight of the entrance while not getting in each other's way. The well-dressed Dutch tourists stood considerately at the back and got the poorest view. A group of young men rolled in straight from the pub. A photographer arrived and set his tripod up in the middle of the floor so that no one could see anything. He was impervious to all the muttering and someone had to ask him straight out to move it. The guide checked the webcam and chatted to a friend about his holiday. The rest of us were tense, embarrassed and already disappointed.

I knelt on the floor, growing stiff and cold as we waited. Just before the predicted moment arrived, a diffident couple in their fifties moved to the centre of the floor and rummaged beneath

* For an account of walking under a river, see 'Caves, sleep, absence of light', p. 9.

their kagouls. I thought they were going to bring out sandwiches and a flask but the man produced a bodhrán, crouched in front of the stone by the back wall and began to drum. The light shifted and a faint beam formed in the tunnel. I want to say that a flicker appeared in the chamber but I'm not sure. My memory is of seeing a piece of light, almost animate, form, move and disappear. I was now staring at the back wall, waiting for the light to re-form and reach it. It mattered terribly to me that I see this happen. If the light did not hit the wall, the solstice had not passed, the year could not move, time would stop. The light failed. The guide shrugged and packed up his things. We waited for a while as if the moment had not passed and then one by one we scuttled back through the tunnel and out into the darkening day.

The winter solstice is not an ending but a beginning: the arrival of new light, and a time of transformation and rebirth. When we emerged from the chamber, the world had indeed been transformed – by a blizzard. This extreme combination of night and snow, light and dark, made sense of why people would go to such lengths to worship and take control of the sun; to go underground and make the sun come to them. That night I waited at Orkney airport as snow piled up against the windows and plane after plane was cancelled. I remember a man with a giant broom sweeping the runway but surely I've invented him. I was surprised by the fact that he was using an actual broom. He moved back and forth like someone under a curse, doomed to keep sweeping as the snow moved instantly to re-cover whatever surface he cleared. Had I been trying to clear a surface in my desire to witness the beam of light hit the chamber stone? To sweep away the accretions, variables and detritus of vision and see only the pattern, machinery and punctuations of light?

I returned to Orkney twenty years later in summer and was there for the festival of Lughnasa. A gathering at one of the groups of standing stones had been advertised and I went along. Only when I arrived did I realise that I had had a pre-conception of what it would be like: hundreds of people, some in druid's cloaks, and a solemn and arcane ceremony. Lughnasa celebrates the harvest to come, appeasing the god Lugh so that the crops will be protected. We would dance, and wear flowers and berries. It was cold and I wore my waterproofs. Rain swept across the path. As I walked towards the stones, I saw a handful of people who looked as if they didn't know each other and had been drawn together by a problem such as a lost dog. They seemed keen to be off but held there by politeness. I, too, succumbed to good manners and despite a strong impulse to walk straight past and keep walking, I complied when a woman hurried over to gather me in.

There were ten of us and the circle we formed lacked conviction. Even the stones looked uncertain of what they were doing there. Only the rain showed any confidence and the organisers started by saying that they would cut things short rather than keep everyone out in it for too long. We all said it was fine and they read the declarations in a muted hurry. If someone in a cloak with a flaming torch in one hand and a skull in the other had roared the words at us, we would have been happy to stay there for hours. But they read the invocations too gently and did not demand that we become ceremonious. At the centre of the circle was a large supermarket bag. After some words were said, a horn was taken from it and a young man blew a few hesitant notes. He filled the horn with mead and passed it round with honey-cake. We weren't at a pagan ceremony, we were at a particularly awkward picnic. I wanted it to be a success but I also wanted to go home.

The next day, I went back to Maeshowe. From being a neglected place you could wander up to, it has become a proper tourist site. It's now fenced off and can only be visited in a group on a bus from the nearby visitors' centre. The fence and the tour were there to manage numbers. People want more than ever to go to such sites, to see for themselves something so ancient and invested. This time I wouldn't be allowed to climb on the roof. There were maybe twenty people inside the chamber, too many for me, and I had to keep to the edge near the exit tunnel. The guide explained that the chamber would have been sealed from the inside during certain rituals. I did not stay long.

Despite the appearance it gives of having sat undisturbed for millennia, Maeshowe has been broken into, plundered and emptied out several times. Drawings from the nineteenth century show it standing twelve feet higher than it does now, its roof rising in a cone that then collapses in on itself. A concrete roof was added in 1910 when the mound passed into the care of the state and the outside was reshaped into what we see today. Norse invaders broke in and left runes on the chamber walls that are the equivalent of the graffiti found everywhere from village bus stops to Fingal's Cave – initials, dates, innuendo. This seems to happen less now as we have other ways of punctuating where we are, of saying *I was here,* and carry them with us rather than leave them behind. The graffiti in Maeshowe reminded me of a wall I came across in Chatham Dockyard. It was at the back of a building and was covered in names, initials and dates going back two hundred years. 'A Lawson' is in cursive with loops and flourishes, and doubly underlined. He was patient, skilful and proud, and must have been there some time. Other inscriptions look as if they were on tombstones, complete with chiselled serifs. Those who had less time, energy or interest left shallow, messy initials. The first letter of 'H.S.' is deeply scored whereas the 'S' seems abandoned as if he had been urgently called away. 'FREDY' is a gangling scrawl. In 1851, 'G. Bucket' added his neat precise lettering, two branches above and the name of his ship or regiment, 'Royal'. The style of lettering becomes simpler and more fluid by 1923, and more functional in 1941. In 1834, S. Plant gave full details, 'Nive India Peninsula, York and Lancaster'. Nearby there is the 'Reg. J. Jones will not make old bones'. I wonder if he was right or if by saying so, by inscribing himself into the wall, he kept himself safe. The Vikings carving themselves into the chamber at Maeshowe were far from home and had stumbled on that still, safe place where everything stops. Like the Chatham sailors, they were perhaps waiting for weather to pass, for the sea to calm, for the next step to be decided on. Things would start moving again soon enough.

2

I live on an island of moderate landscape. It contains much beauty and variety but is formed on a minor scale. I can move through it quickly and in relative safety – there are no lions or bears. Forests, rivers, marshes and mountains look manageable. There is flood and fire but earthquakes are gentle (I've felt them twice, a shudder deep in the body that I did not recognise and so thought I'd imagined). I'm not particularly adventurous and

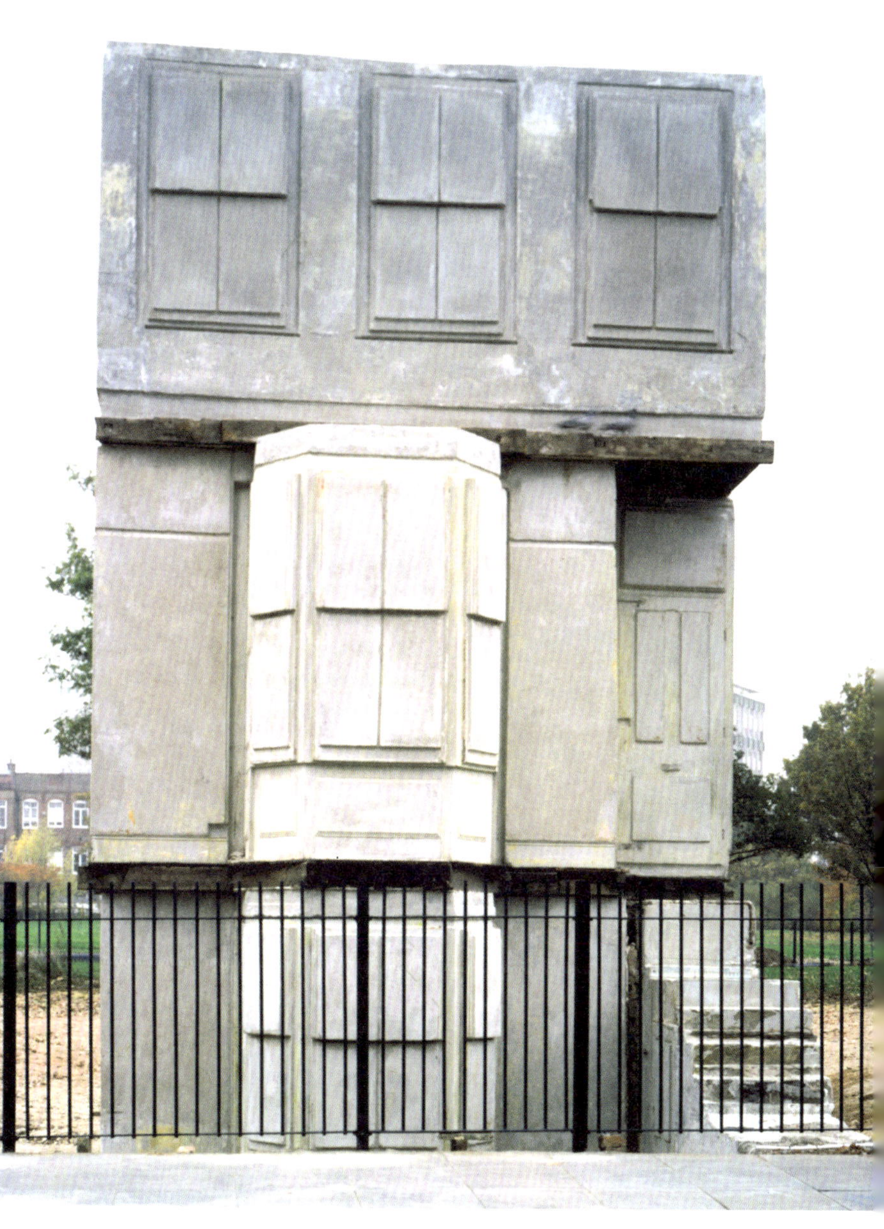

Rachel Whiteread, *House*, 1993. 193 Grove Road, London E3. Destroyed 1993.
© Rachel Whiteread. Photo: Sue Omerod. Courtesy of the artist and Gagosian.

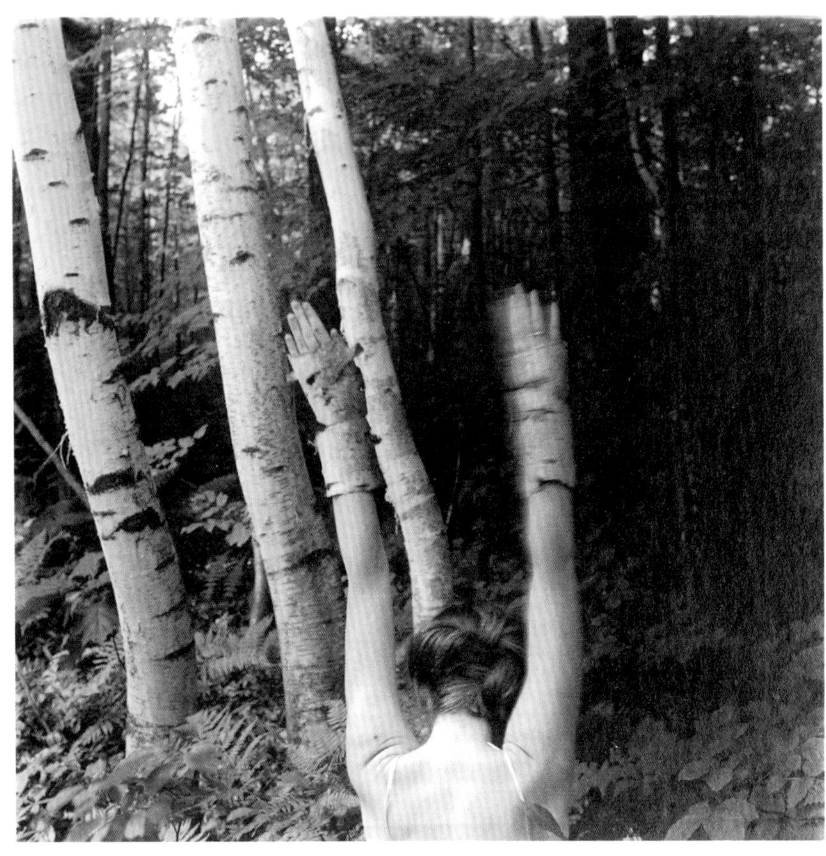

Francesca Woodman, *Untitled* (MacDowell Colony, Peterborough, New Hampshire), 1980

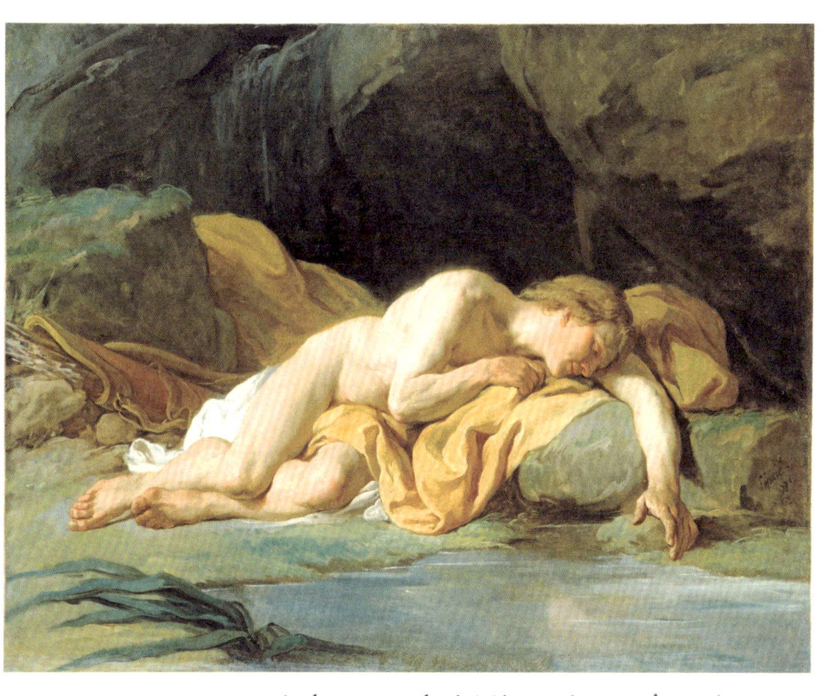

Nicolas-Bernard Lépicié, *Narcissus*, eighteenth century

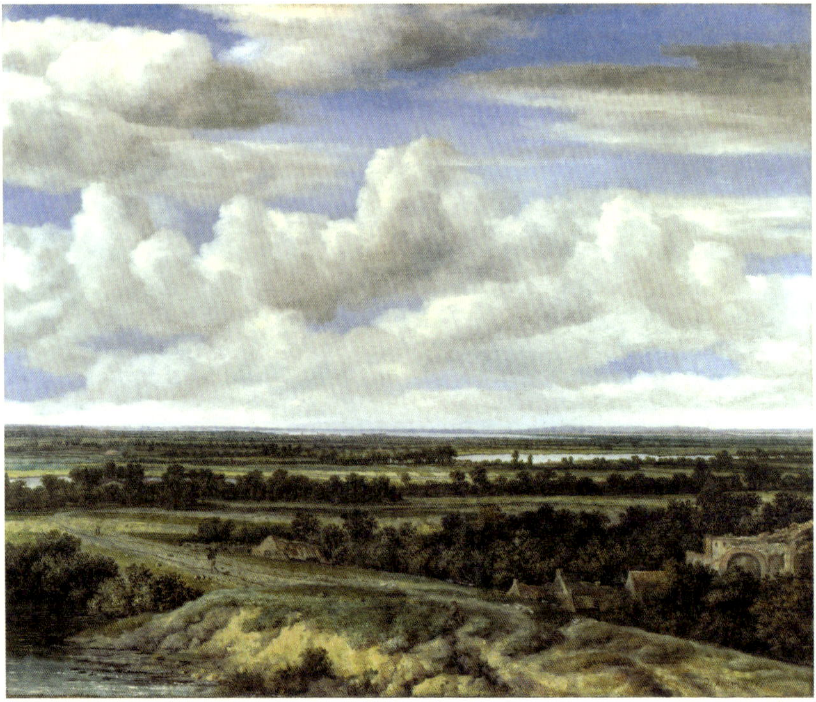

Philips Koninck,
*An Extensive Landscape with
a Road by a River*, 1655

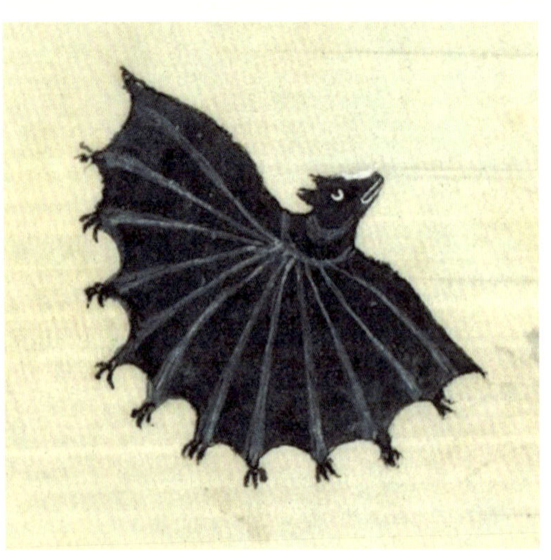

Simon d'Orliens, medieval illumination of a bat
from *The Art of Falconry*, 1241

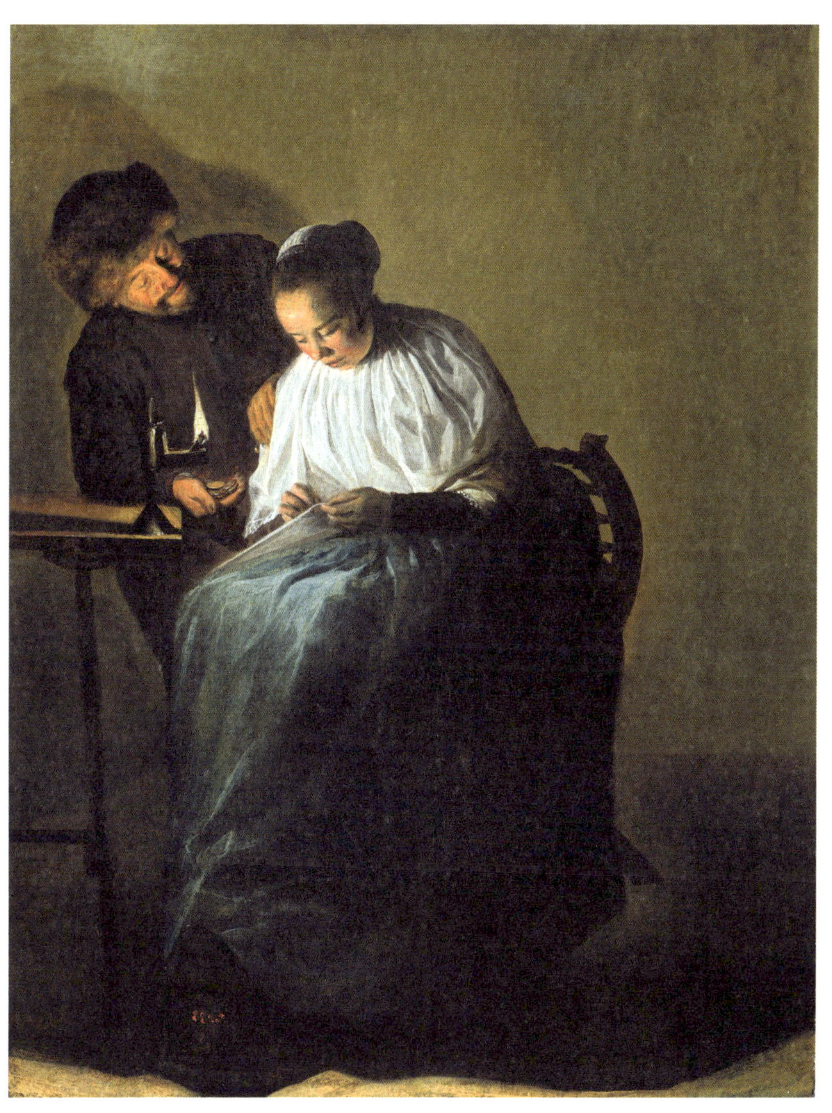

Judith Leyster, *Man Offering Money to a Young Woman*, 1631

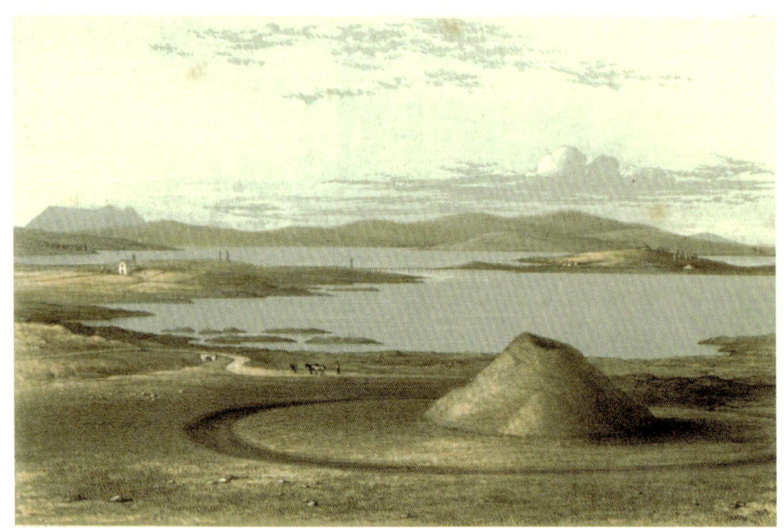

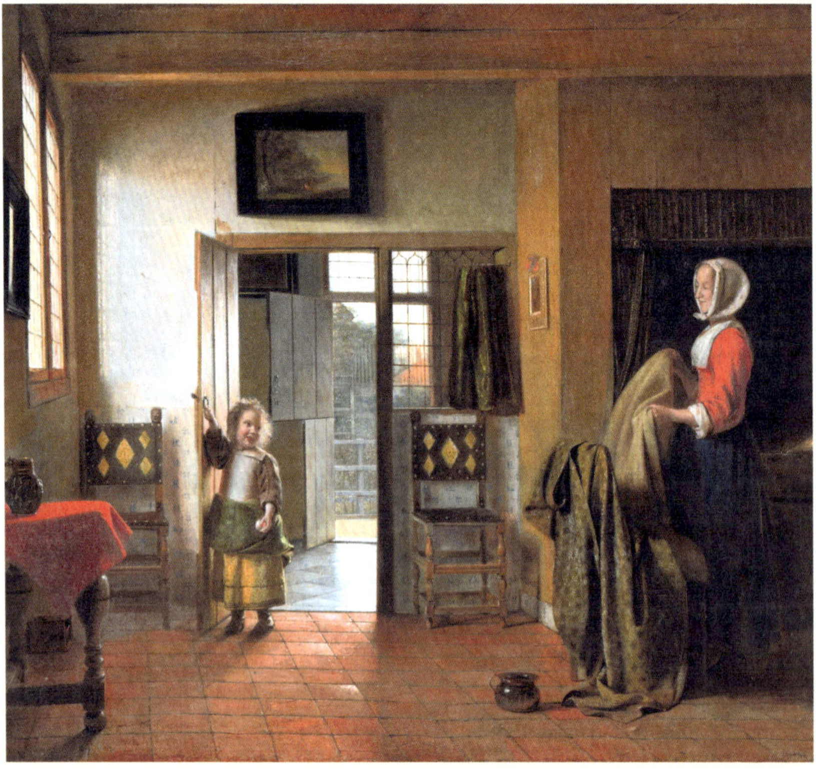

(*top*) James Farrer, *General View of Maeshowe*, 1862

(*bottom*) Pieter de Hooch, *The Bedroom*, c.1658/60

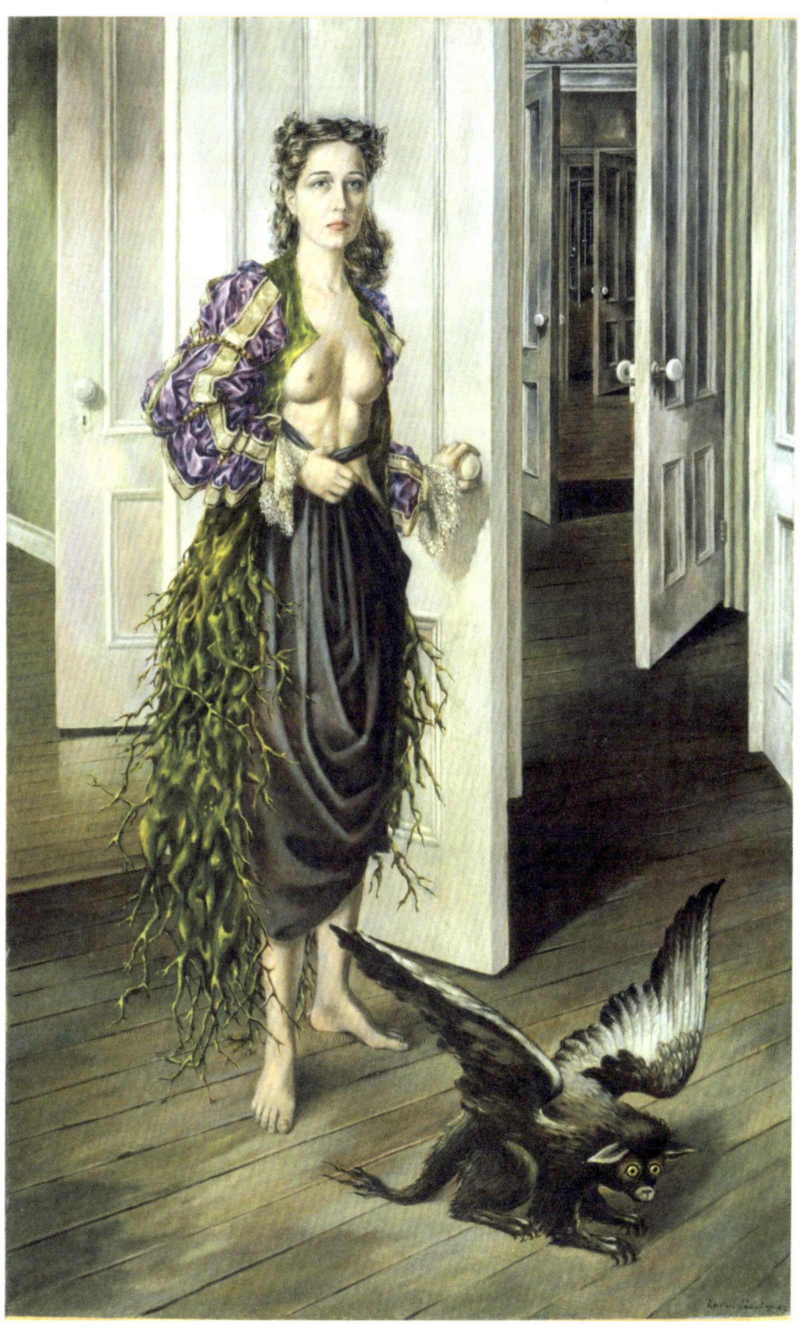

Dorothea Tanning, *Birthday*, 1942

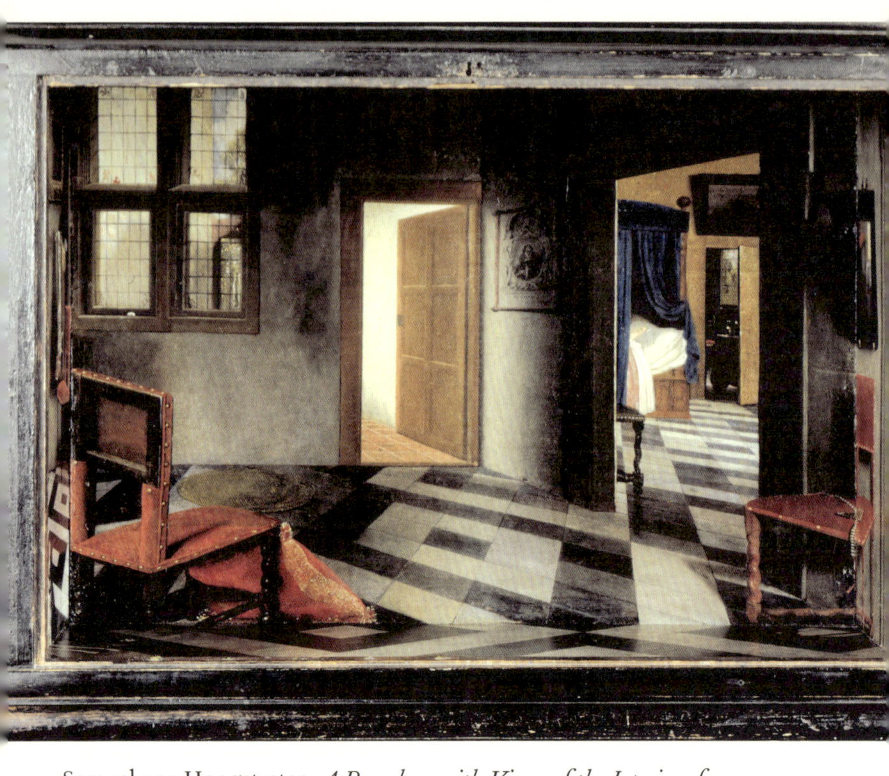

Samuel van Hoogstraten, *A Peepshow with Views of the Interior of a Dutch House*, c.1655–60

rarely feel I have to prepare or concentrate when going for a walk, so my looking is often casual and distracted. Sometimes, although I am looking, I take in nothing at all. If I stop, I don't know how I got to where I am or how to get home.

In setting out to observe a moment of planetary alignment, I looked differently. I was thinking about movement, cause and effect. That spring I went south to the Fal Estuary, where the equinox arrives with such extreme tides that seaweed is cast into the arms of the oaks that line the valley. This is a deep, high-sided place shaped by glaciers and one of the largest natural harbours in the world. I was taken around the river in a dinghy which suddenly felt very small when we turned a corner and came up against a ship. The river has been a haven for centuries, and ships lay up here for all kinds of reasons – they might be between charters, or caught up in political difficulty or a bankruptcy. A commercial ship is something you see in places of international business – a port, where its impact is softened by other ships, or in the distance at sea. This ship was moored among oak woods and mussel beds.

We approached the bow, passing between massive anchor chains, and came to halt right up against the hull, which was at least sixty feet high. The angle felt so steep, the hull narrowing to a blade, that I couldn't understand why it didn't tip over. Looking up made me dizzy so I looked down into the water, which was so still that it reflected the ship perfectly. I could look up or down and see the same thing. I became dizzier.

The loss of boundaries that extreme tides bring, the flooding of woodlands and the sudden deep water suggest a moment of access or openness that has been brought about by a breach. While we associate spring with soft, delicate emergences, it is a season full of violence and rupture. Water surges upstream, flooding marshes that drain just as quickly, revealing detritus and abandonments. Amidst this muddle and merging, everything seems to be calibrated towards a precise set of conditions. The extreme incursions are the momentum towards the rupture (the split in the seed, the crack in the egg) needed to bring about a return of possibility, opportunity, another chance to lay the ground for a good year.

I made these journeys at the turn of the century and felt reassured by the patterns that were revealed to me. I could go to each of these places now and little will appear to have changed. But I will see the landscape and light differently because now I stand in a less certain place, one that has been unsecured by freak weather of all kinds. Each part of the machine needs to function. Mis-timings and failures, such as late migration or the disappearance of a certain kind of larvae in a particular pond, lead to the wrong kind of rupture and surges that cannot recede.

3

Few people pay attention to the strange, sad moment of the summer solstice. They're too busy looking forward to summer, not realising that for the natural world it is already over. I find summer a difficult time and become low in July as others do in November, my mood compounded by the fact that I look and look, and nothing seems to move. The winter solstice has focus and transience as the sun emerges and then plummets. The light of summer can be too constant and generalised. There is a loss of momentum that pulls me into the ground, evoking childhood memories of tedium and loneliness. The sky is full of stuck grey clouds and there is far less song in the garden. Night is more of a change of colour than a loss of light. I find it hard to bear the sagging atmosphere of dull warm days, migraine-inducing build-ups of pressure, and the heat.

For the summer solstice, I went east to Blakeney Point, a shingle spit on the north Norfolk coast that stretches for five miles. On one side there are marshes and on the other, the North Sea. The spit isn't straight but more like a plant about to unfurl. Its shape is also perpetually shifting as it erodes to the east and grows to the west, towards land. Walking it, I felt suspended between land and water just as the day was at a point of hesitation between six months of lengthening and the six months in which it would contract back. The machinery of time – the stones, circles, dials, the counting and accumulating – felt less relevant than this dilation and contraction of light. The light of midwinter had crept towards the chamber at Maeshowe only to peter out. In the spring, on the flooded river, it felt as if light had filled the day to capacity and would force it to grow. Now the days were full and for me, in my summer mood, the light had nothing to do other than be there, to hang around for a day and then set off back towards winter.

I usually find a landscape such as Blakeney exhilarating and relish its shifting nature and all that space bouncing off flatness. But there are days that take on a veneer of dullness and this was one of them. The atmosphere plunges, my mood sags and the tremendous view becomes oppressive. I live in these flatlands and most of the time feel reassured by the ways in which nothing seems to change while nothing is fixed. Again, this is the reassurance of time when observed through the punctuations of light: we return to the same point but we are not stuck there.

Only sometimes we are, or feel we are, as I did that day. It was the northern year's most endless afternoon:* so much constancy that the time, the space, lacked punctuation.

Despite there being no clouds, I was sure that sooner or later it would start to rain. The sun had lost all character. Its light was remote. I felt fundamentally untouched by it and did not understand that it was I, and not the sea or the sun, who had been dulled. The place wasn't stuck even if I was. The creek filled quickly as the tide rose and the dramatic pull of planetary alignment had its effect here as elsewhere. Even flatness is relative to your point of view. I met up with the artist Greg Poole, keen to be shown what I wasn't managing to (feel or) see.[2] Greg's paintings are powerful abstractions of the colours and forms of plants and birds. He had been working out on Blakeney Point all day in the sun and wind, and seemed to thrive on it. He first described the place as looking 'very neutral' which might explain why I couldn't be bothered to engage with it. Neutral suggests that it was resisting making a statement or taking up a position. Greg was looking closely at what we were standing among, reading the ground through shading and colour. 'There's just a vegetable green spreading inland but you know that within that there's such diversity of form that it's only superficially flat.' It was as if he were looking through a microscope and I through a telescope. He had to point out the flowers, which I hadn't noticed beyond a vague sense of yellow. They were low clumps of biting stone crop (so acidic a shade that Greg described it as biting your eyes). To me they looked harsh and alien, like the yellow of the rape that arrived in the fields in

* Someone said that Dutch painting, with its still lifes and fields and kitchens, was 'one long Sunday'. I can see how one might feel overwhelmed by the lack of event.

the 1970s. For Greg, there was no harshness just 'the right things in their right place at the right time . . . this is their season and their habitat'. The predominant colour at midsummer is yellow but this will gradually turn to blues and mauves. He could see 'a catalogue of things that are saying it is midsummer . . . a whole series of things that add up'. I couldn't. He could pinpoint the date just by looking at the sea campions which were starting to fade and the stonecrop, which had only come out that week.

Greg was aware of those birds still defending their territory and nests. Others had already gone: 'It's the very beginning of movement. The birds come in like a tide and this is when they are starting to leave again.' I told him that it hurt me to look so far into the distance. He said, 'I've been looking at a computer screen for the last few days and it's such a relief to let the eyes see real space.' Maybe what hurt me was this space and how it would pull me out of myself if I let it. Depression has its own gravity and the mind is 'turned agonizingly inward'.[3] The desire to escape meets the impossibility of doing so as the self presses in. Looking out from within such a state is possible but the effort of doing so hurts. I was shivering in the wind on Blakeney Point but got badly sunburned.

4

At the time of the autumnal equinox, when my brother was buried and my father died, there's usually a pause that either precedes or follows a storm. This year, summer intensified week after week into drought and record-breaking temperatures. I lived in the corners of each searing day, getting outside before dawn, retreating as the sun rose and returning as it set. The storms that followed in the autumn were unsettling. The weather was too warm, the lightning foreign, and the rain intense and specific in ways I did not understand.

A good autumn fills up with colour and light that then slowly dwindle. It's like watching a fire burning itself out, a way of making ready for the time when there will be no light left. It is a period of consolidation, thanksgiving and harvest home. In the year of travelling the punctuations of solstice and equinox, I went to a wood in the West Country in the middle of the night to watch the river.

> When a boar comes, the stream does not swell by degrees, as at other times, but rolls in with a head . . . foaming and roaring as though it were enraged by the opposition which it encounter.
> Thomas Harral (1824)[4]

I stood on the edge of the River Severn at midnight, waiting for a twelve-foot-high wave to roar past in the wrong direction, a phenomenon called a tidal bore. The Severn Bore is one of the largest in the world. When the tide comes into the estuary, it's forced into an increasingly narrow channel. About twice a month, the tide is moving faster than the water further inland can flow and the pressure of this creates a large wave which travels miles at about 25 miles an hour before wearing itself out. The overflow of the spring tide felt like a benevolent flooding, a move towards conception, a breaking down of barriers. Even before I saw the bore, it felt like a purge.

I was cold in a way I hadn't been for months, and the woods around me were intensely dark. Before I saw the wave coming, I felt an unfamiliar kind of silence fall: a profound lapse in the atmosphere as the background rustle and murmur among the trees fell away. Then I heard a noise – like wind but more consistent. The noise grew until it sustained itself in a permanently breaking wave, which is what the bore is. My brain could not make sense of it and the hairs rose on the back of my neck. The sound came crashing through the trees, giving me time to imagine what I was about to see: an enormous force of water coming from a direction I could not locate. It sounds as if someone has unpinned the world and it's rolling itself up very fast towards you. For what seemed like a long time – but was probably less than a minute – all I could do was try to make sense of this noise. It started as grain rushing into a silo, then scree tumbling down a mountainside, then buildings falling and finally an abstract roar of monumental collapse.

Had I stood by the river in daylight and seen the wave coming, I doubt my reaction would have been as strong. There was a dislocation of my senses; an experience of sound rather than vision, and as sound I felt rather than heard. It was as if the wave had travelled not past but through me.

Staying put, locked doors, wallpaper

1

We grow familiar with where we live without trying, unaware of how intimately we know it until something is out of place. If you stay put, you become alert to the patterns and rhythms that underpin the world around you. If you stay still, you notice movement – how light crosses a window, how a street empties and fills. In a new place, you have to be present. You are trying to name what's around you or to take in the view. You won't know which button to press, how the taps work, where to buy milk or what that milk might taste like. Knowing a place is what makes us feel at home. You have the words you need to ask for what you want, and the everyday takes care of itself, leaving your mind to travel.

I haven't been to the places I dreamt of as a child – Zanzibar, Minsk, Madagascar and Samarkand. Instead I've spent thirty years living in the part of London in which I was born. My great-grandparents are buried in the churchyard at the top of the hill. If I walk down the street where my father's surgery used to be, I notice only what's gone: the cinema where the manager introduced each screening in evening dress, the leather-workers, the shrimp-seller, the lamp-lighter, the record shop. The surgery became a dentist's office and the last time I passed by, was a pop-up café. The pet shop where we used to admire a roomful of snakes was empty for a decade but kept its fancy wrought-iron signage long enough for that to become an asset. It, too, is now a café.

If I had lived elsewhere and then returned, I would have noticed more gradual and fundamental changes. Languages I used to hear are gone and now I hear new ones. Every street has a permanent hem of parked cars. The road I could confidently cross as a six-year-old is now a one-way red route coagulated night and day. Poverty is less visible but the tension surrounding its concealment is palpable. There is more superficial tolerance and less evidence of difference. The shops are those you'd find everywhere making this anywhere.

The Italian writer Cesare Pavese is supposed to have said: 'Travelling is a brutality. It forces you to trust strangers and to lose sight of all that familiar comfort of home and friends. You are constantly off balance.'[1] Is it such a bad thing to be forced to trust strangers? Or to lose sight of the familiar? And how else are we going to do such things than by leaving home? I am a bad traveller and easily thrown off balance. I approach any journey in a state of tension and regret. Yet I believe travel is good for me. Even when it has been exhausting or frightening or dull, I have come home feeling stronger, clearer and more experienced; relieved that it's over while glad it occurred. But for much of my life I have been free to travel and free to come home.

Staying put, you might not notice change. Your experience of a place could become as shallow as that of someone passing through, who is focused only on where they are going. Even those things that don't change can be renewed through observation. You can stop and look and keep looking until they unravel into something strange:

I have nothing in common with experimentalists, adventurers, with those who travel in strange regions. The surest, and the quickest, way for us to arouse the sense of wonder is to stare, unafraid, at a single object. Suddenly—miraculously—it will look like something we have never seen before.[2]

Cesare Pavese did not travel to 'strange' regions but his life was defined by historical events. The kind of undisturbed observation he describes above would not have been easy to achieve while living in a place and time caught up in political extremism and world war. He was nostalgic for an era he must have imagined more than remembered when 'there was time to study every stone in the gravel along the tracks, every tie, the down of a dry thistle, the fat stems of two cacti in the hollow below the road.'[3]

To some people the slowness of such time, the smallness of such drama, is unbearable. To others, it speaks of the constancy they crave. We stay put as a preventive act against loss but the world does not stay with us. Pavese refused to publish his work while it was subject to Fascist censorship. Instead he translated Ernest Hemingway and Gertrude Stein, among others, opening a window on the distant elsewhere. His best-known novel, *The Moon and the Bonfires* (1949), is the enactment of the life he might have had if he'd chosen to leave. A foundling emigrates from the Piedmont to America, where one day he meets a stranger in a bar who he knows, at first glance, must be from his village. This reminder of home prompts him to return and he finds that the hills of his childhood have become a battleground, his friends shot as partisans. He struggles to reconcile somewhere he thought he knew with what it has become.

Staying put is not staying still. It is an act of continuous return – to the front door at the end of the day, to the same bed at night. In doing this, you are applying yourself to the world you inhabit: 'Something has also happened to the one who never moved, a destiny—that idea of his that things must be understood, made better . . .'[4]

You are also returning to yourself and refusing, for better or worse, to be displaced or remade. After a disastrous love affair, Pavese took a fatal overdose at the age of forty-one, just as his work was receiving acclaim. His diary suggests that he had given up hope of making a true human connection. Perhaps to do so requires placing your trust in strangers, letting go of the familiar and allowing yourself to be thrown off balance. The desire for travel is a desire to be unanchored and disarmed. We let things slip and get lost, diverted and carried away. If Pavese could have travelled, perhaps he could have loved.

2

The eighteenth-century naturalist Gilbert White might be a good advertisement for not subjecting yourself to the brutal effects of travel.[*] He made his parish his subject and died in a house a few hundred yards from the vicarage in which he'd been born. White lived in an age of epic voyages of discovery but the furthest he travelled was 200 miles north to Derbyshire. This was the time of the American Revolution, the discovery of Uranus and the madness of King George. While another British clergyman, John Michell, was discovering black holes,

[*] See 'Seeing clearly, glimpsing, picturing', p. 86, for White's study of a field mouse and her nest.

White was noting that twelve inches more rain fell in Selborne in 1786 than in 1780.

His intentions were those of the scientist, with the result that he treated the fields outside his door as a foreign land. The combination of focus and detachment that good observation requires, whether by an artist or a scientist, is that of the good traveller – receptive and ready to make room to receive new impressions by jettisoning preconception. The world revealed to him is one of constant movement and change, with patterns as precise as they are mysterious.

> How strange it is that the swift, which seems to live exactly the same life with the swallow and house-martin, should leave us in the middle of August invariably! while the latter stay often till the middle of October . . .[5]

The Natural History of Selborne is now a landmark text in nature writing.[6] White's house is a museum, his garden has been restored and a gift shop sells beer and jam with his name on the label. The man who never left home is now part of the tourist itinerary. I visited on a hot and somnolent day and, wandering the meadows and woods beyond the village, found myself somewhere so lush and serene that I felt compelled to lie down and sleep. When I woke, I wasn't quite sure what century I was in. Now I think I must have dreamt the whole thing.

Staying put can be an evasion, an introversion, a way of never waking up but it is not a serene state. It requires the continuous deflection of influence and change. For White, this involved rejecting offers of better positions in the church. We do not know why he never married but not having a family would have added to his isolation as well as to his consistency. Perhaps, like Pavese, he had little faith in human contact.

White describes an old oak known as the Raven Tree. A swelling of its trunk made it impossible for the local youths to reach the nest however much they tried, so the ravens bred there each year, undisturbed. The day came when the wood was to be levelled and the oak chopped down. The raven was sitting on her eggs and remained there as the tree was hacked into and eventually toppled. As it fell, she was flung into the air only to be 'whipped down by the twigs, which brought her dead to the ground.'[7]

This could be a fable about what happens if we stay too long. We might not survive the act of leaving. But White is only interested in the fact that the raven was hard-wired to stay put and specifically during the nesting season. A few weeks later, she would have encouraged her young to go. We spend our lives building permanence, structure, routine, accumulating the familiar, just as we plan our escape – for an hour, a day, a week or forever.

3

In her essay on Gilbert White, Virginia Woolf described *The Natural History of Selborne* as 'one of those ambiguous books that seem to tell a plain story . . . and yet by some apparently unconscious device of the author's has a door left open, through which we hear distant sounds . . .'[8] She means that his seeing and picturing do not confine his subject to his table. His prose makes us wander outside to see the thing for ourselves.

There was a time when I was often away from home and would return to find my front door wide open. It was hidden from the road and might have sat open for days. Nothing ever happened and no one seemed to notice but however consciously I locked up, it would be open when I got home. I had seen myself close the door and turn the key. Or had I? Sometimes we leave a door open in a different way in that our brain fails to complete the picture. One afternoon I came home and went straight to the kitchen to make a cake. I was in a hurry and irritated by the cat, who was behaving oddly and kept getting in my way. Two hours later, as I took the cake from the oven, I noticed the cat stretching up towards some high shelves in a half-hearted way. I looked to see what he was interested in and there was a pigeon sitting on a teapot. It did not appear to be injured although I then saw what I hadn't seen before – a scattering of feathers on the side. The cat, elderly and half blind, must have somehow brought it in via the cat-flap but the bird was too large to have easily passed through it. I couldn't understand what I was looking at and thought for some time that I was making a mistake. My eyes must have passed over it several times but I only saw what was always there, the teapot. I managed to wrap the pigeon in a tea towel and took it outside where, after a while, it remembered itself and flew away.

Rooms that are this familiar become wallpaper* and we see them as we remember them. A wild bird in a kitchen is not part of the design. It should not have entered my image of the kitchen and it needed to get out. Walls become wallpaper in that they gradually absorb whatever is placed in front of them so that furniture, pictures and curtains flatten into backdrop. When moving house from anywhere lived in for a long time, we see how easy it is for that backdrop to be dismantled. Our eye travels towards a mirror or woodland scene and meets only wall.

* See also yellow wallpaper in 'Black and white and colour' (p. 113) and dissolving into the wallpaper in 'The body, open, itself' (p. 135).

180

The artist Dorothea Tanning grew up in Galesburg, Illinois, a place where she said 'nothing happens but the wallpaper'.[9] Nothing happening is itself a kind of wallpaper, a backdrop waiting to be filled. Tanning described her prevailing mood as one of 'longing for a displacement'. This suggests that she felt unable to act and needed something to happen to her, an event that would shake Galesburg loose and let her fall out of the scene. A willingness to be displaced is vital to an artist's vision. It is not enough to stay put with your studio and your subject. Everything must be tested – that is thrown into the air, including yourself. Tanning said that when she worked, 'Everything is in motion.'[10]

Her painting of her thirtieth birthday came from 'a dream of countless doors'. She has her hand on one of them but turns away from where that door leads (to more doors) and instead looks out of her dream and past us, her gaze underlined by that of a daemon, an awkward presence who looks like a thought she rather wished she had not had. Her costume seems incomplete and not just because it exposes her body. It's as if it hasn't integrated into something to be worn but has come into being as a series of aspects, part ceremonious, part shadow, part wild. It is intended, perhaps, for someone who has many selves and accommodates them without compromise.

> . . . behind the invisible door (doors), another door. You might say I lead a double life. Or a triple or multiple life. In fact, outside my studio, I am not who I pretend to be. There is no showing who one really is.[11]

In another self-portrait, she stands on a mountain edge, contemplating a fantastical lunar landscape that reminds me of the way the Dutch used to paint imagined mountains – part hangover, part fairytale. It is a chilly and daunting vista but there she stands with her back to us and all we can take in is her perfect hair and the fact that she is wearing a bathing suit; perhaps she is about to take a plunge. But Tanning preferred to remain behind a door: 'the decibels of nature can crush an artist's brain . . . So I lock the door and paint interiors . . . A white and dark picture would muffle the red outside.'[12] This landscape is similar to that of Sedona, Arizona, where she was to live with her husband Max Ernst from 1946, only the rich red rocks have been drained of colour. It's as if she needed to turn the world down – and in terms of realism, upside down – in order for it to become clear.

This susceptibility to the effects of the extreme elsewhere can be vital and fruitful. An artist has to identify and sustain the conditions that they need in order to work, and in order to feel themselves take or lose or change shape. For women, in particular, retaining artistic or intellectual freedom has meant being elsewhere and foregoing a more connected life. Georgia O'Keeffe went to New Mexico in pursuit of a wide-open and above all undeflecting elsewhere. She wrote to her husband Alfred Stieglitz in 1929:

There is much life in me — when it was always checked in moving toward you — I realized it would die if it could not move toward something . . . I chose coming away because here at least I feel good — and it makes me feel I am growing very tall and straight inside — and very still —[13]

There is a place you can point to whereas *elsewhere* is anywhere – everywhere – that is not *here*. The word is both sufficient and vague, and somehow deflects further enquiry. It's the indescribable and the unknown, a cloak of invisibility that we can apply to our feelings and thoughts as well as to our travels. Our hearts, minds and interests can all lie elsewhere. We can stay put in silence, in focus, in imaginative release. Or go elsewhere and find that all we needed was to place ourselves in tension with home. But if you stay at home, you might stop noticing. You might think you know. You won't veer in size or be struck dumb or find everything familiar but different. You won't know what there is to discover in yourself by setting out for somewhere else.

Journeys are defined by the visual – what we're leaving and what we're travelling towards. But sometimes we have to leave without being able to prepare for the journey, perhaps without a guaranteed destination. How does someone know when they have to leave? Is it always either too soon or too late or is there ever a point between? When is the exact moment you can tell that a threat is undeniable but escape still possible? Doesn't the one preclude the other? You might have to decide to send your children into the unknown, or to grab what you can and run out of the back door, and you may never know if you really had to. What does it mean to have to go into a future you cannot see?

As a child, if I saw an image of someone trapped by fire, flood, conflict or siege, I would wonder why they had not left before it was too late. Now I understand that you cannot imagine yourself having to leave; that visual rhythms of the familiar are a form of freedom that comes from the luxury of security. To feel secure, we have to be able to predict what we will see next. The image I remember most clearly is one when I was watching the news and saw someone high up in a building on fire, clinging to a window sill. They were deciding whether to let themselves fall only there was nowhere to fall to – no elsewhere that they, in the next moment, could reach.

Some choose to stay put and close their eyes or they do the last thing they can, which is to meet what is coming, to *look*.

4

I can sit in London and travel to Galesburg or Selborne or Turin. I will know more of each place than I did this morning but I can't say that I've been anywhere. I will form an idea, or adjust an idea I already had, but I will not have smelt the air, felt the heat, touched the walls or, crucially, gone through the process of leaving home to get there. There won't have been the time for my idea of a place to meet the place itself.

A journey should confound our expectations (especially those we do not know we have). If we only find what we already know, we have not travelled. A journey takes us along with it. If the imagination is allowed to get involved, then the experience can be just as powerful and affecting. But if we let the internet do our imagining for us then we are just absorbing information. We need to be present in our journeys, we are part of them.

In late August 1871, William Morris boarded a boat home from Iceland where he'd spent six weeks trekking around the country. Full of the bravado and satisfaction of completed travel, he was baffled by a fellow passenger. The man had arrived in Iceland that morning. He'd spent three weeks getting there only to walk round Reykjavik in the rain and take the next boat back to England. He went no further than the point at which actuality met his expectations. Perhaps he found Iceland too familiar or too strange; or he knew what he was looking for and had found it or realised he wasn't going to. Whatever his reasons, his journey was evidently about the journey itself: the leaving, the travelling towards, the arrival, the being there (even just for a walk in the rain), the turning round, the heading home.

Eye-catchers, furniture, peepshows

1

When I know I'm not going to be able to reach what I'm looking at, my vision relaxes. I feel pleasantly arrested, as if some responsibility has been lifted. It's a feeling I can trace back to childhood, standing by the Thousand Pound Pond on Hampstead Heath and staring at the sham bridge. The bridge is an eighteenth-century eye-catcher, a feature inserted into the landscape to draw the gaze and a more active proposition than something intended for the eye to rest on, such as a lake. An eye-catcher should stand out, even at a distance, but not announce itself. The experience should be that of glimpsing someone across a crowded room and setting off to meet them only to have them slip from sight.

The pond sits at the foot of the sloping lawn below Kenwood House, a stately home which always surprised me as I trudged out of the woods. I felt as if I had inadvertently entered someone's garden – which I had. The sham bridge is simple and mysterious, a series of three insignificant arches and a plain balustrade. It's a two-dimensional wooden struc-ture like a theatre prop. I accepted, and even enjoyed, the fact that I could not reach it and failed to realise that I walked past the back of it most days. It is referred to as sham, not a fake or a *trompe l'oeil*. A fake would try harder. It would be more elaborate in its finish and detail, and more effort would have gone into making it look real. A sham is not so determined to fool the eye.

There's a strong distinction at Kenwood between front of house and behind the scenes. The neoclassical villa is not original but a reinvention by one of the leading architects of the eighteenth century, Robert Adam. As Adam laid out the building and its gardens and ponds (did this one really cost a thousand pounds?), he added the bridge as a little joke. When in 1793 Humphry Repton, the first to call himself a landscape gardener, proposed a redesign of the grounds, he wanted to get rid of the bridge, which he felt to be 'below the dignity of Kenwood', and replace it with a real one. Why did such authenticity matter when his other ideas were further shams such as screening the encroaching city with more trees and opening up the grounds so as to suggest the ponds were a single lake? By catching the eye but not convincing it, the bridge reminds you that this is all surface. The house is no more real than the bridge or the view, and it is all a series of diversions and concealments.

Among the picture collection in Kenwood House, which includes a Rembrandt and a Vermeer, is Aelbert Cuyp's *View of Dordrecht*. Cuyp, who died in 1691, is not now well known but his paintings were hugely popular in eighteenth-century England and it is not surprising that at least one ended up at Kenwood. Sales of Cuyp's work were at their peak when Repton set about his renovations. *The Large Dort* is another view of Dordrecht but the foreground is dominated by monumental cows gilded by sunlight squeezing through distant clouds. It might be read simply as a vision of bountiful ease: the milkmaid looks as if her work is no more onerous than pouring tea while the labourers on the hillock are enjoying a companionable encounter. Or it might be read from a more connoisseurial perspective: four meticulously rendered cows dominate a landscape well-known to the artist and exactly given in its foliage, townscape, high sky and expertly evoked light. The figures are naturally posed, at ease in their environment and clearly at work. The ambiguity of Cuyp's art – simple celebration or artistic interrogation – must have ensured its broad appeal. It is poised on a cusp of the ideal and the actual, enabling it to satisfy different needs.

Cuyp was the son of a painter and was put to work early painting backgrounds. He was admired by fellow artists for his handling of light. He did not travel to Italy, like many of his contemporaries, but borrowed from those who did, gilding northern vistas with a southern glow and deploying a contre-jour perspective, in which light slants across the scene from the back of the frame, throwing the foreground into relief. This approach transforms his looming cows but also announces a painterly emphasis on volume, depth and scale. His pictures are large and usually intended to be looked up at rather than into. We are not invited in by a welcoming gaze or winding path. The scene is averted: one cow gives us a sidelong look while the dog appears to have been caught glancing our way. We are made to crouch, held back by the undergrowth that seems to jut from the frame.

The warm tone of Cuyp's magical light does not disguise the northern chill in the air. Constable* noted that 'Chiaroscuro is by no means confined to dark pictures: the works of Cuyp,

* See 'Unanchoring, sinking, at sea', p. 213, on Constable attempting to capture a storm.

thought generally light, are full of it. It may be defined as that power which creates space.'[1] This is what makes the cows so muscular and the folds in the milkmaid's blouse so heavy — form heightened by light. Some found this emphasis on atmosphere disappointing. Joshua Reynolds said that 'It is to the eye only that the works of this school are addressed.'[2] We can focus on lichen and dead leaves or look far into the distance at the hazy town and flying birds. This is not about drama so much as visual experience.

The eighteenth-century English viewer would be looking for a landscape painting that was recognisable but also aspirational: the image of a devout and tranquil way of life that was within reach. It should be, above all, harmonious but rich in gentle variation. If these pictures had to include people then they should be 'inferior beings' who signify 'a connection between all ranks and orders [that] mutually support each other's existence . . . the whole vast and magnificent fabric.'[3] There was no blurring of boundaries. Each part, each figure, had its place and kept to it. Careful delineation (or division) of form, tone and detail isolated each element beneath a harmonious surface. Cuyp's compositions contain a striking range of scale, perspective and tone beneath that pervasive, cohesive light.

Tastes were changing and those who collected paintings wanted to see the woodcutter and the milkmaid rather than the shepherd and shepherdess of classical Arcadia. Cuyp was painting the modern scene, in that it was local rather than classical, and made use of the vales and fields Horace Walpole rued English landscape painters 'neglected as homely and familiars'.[4] The labourers look attractive yet convincing and while a town signals modernity, it is not encroaching on rustic space. Most labourers in Holland were landowners rather than tenants, and they occupy this terrain more confidently and less symbolically. Land did not connote repressive power as it did (and still does) in England.

Labourers of that time were supposed to be depicted as modest but not vulnerable. There was to be no muck on their clothes. It was hard to make such characters convincing, as Stubbs' *Haymakers* of 1783 shows. Stubbs fiddled about with the light and altered the number of labourers, rearranging them as if they were chairs. These uncharacterised men and women are overdressed. The women pose with their rakes as if they're on stage rather than in a field. They are as synchronised and stiff as dancers on a vase. The brown, buff, pink and grey of their outfits embed them into the trees, the hay, the lane and the rosy glow of a setting sun, yet there's no real sense of immersion. Their white shirts and aprons are spotless. Such labourers' lives were increasingly precarious. Most were tenants and the Enclosures were cutting off their access to common land while industrialisation threatened the familiar 'fabrick' of their world.

Cuyp was able to balance old and new, the actual and the ideal with a coherence that made it a 'fabrick'. There was nothing fractured or jolting, just a pleasing place for the eye to land. If what is going on outside the window is troubling, how cheering to have a reminder of what the world should be like: fruitful, comfortable, ordered and in place.

2

When we travel, we seek out experience in order to build memories. We have invested in this time and want it to reward us with scenes to be remembered and shared. We cast around for something to catch our eye. The idea of looking at a view led to the construction of views and then to directions on where to look at them from and what to see. This drew attention to how we look. Plain sight and a description in a sketch book or journal gave way to the telescope, the camera obscura, the diorama, the photograph. We brought the view home in snapshots and models. With each of these developments, we moved further away from just looking. Visual disjuncture can bring about the renewed vision of surprise. We turned our backs, closed one eye and went indoors in order to look at the outdoors in a more concentrated way.

As the excitement of being able to see further wore off, looking was no longer enough. The feeling of contact became harder to achieve because we were less easily surprised, impressed or unsettled. We became used to vision's hypermobile, elastic, magical capacities, and needed to do more to feel contact with what we saw. We needed to enter the picture. We visited replica stage sets, and entire worlds built under domes in fields; we met characters and touched walls. How could we experience more? The walls started to move, the ground gave way and we were tossed up into the air.

I was in New York with my daughter when the rain came down, flooding the streets and stopping most things happening. We looked around for somewhere to shelter and saw a sign for a tourist attraction that promised not just a tour of the city but one in which we would fly over the streets and be submerged in the river. There was nowhere else to go, so in we went to a room arranged like a lecture theatre with raked wooden benches. There was the kind of screen you find in a small cinema and the place smelled like a cinema too – unaired, sweet and dusty.

When we sat down, we were asked to do up our safety belts. I peered into the dimness and realised that there were levers and wheels right there below me. It was like being strapped to a threshing machine or a factory loom and waiting to see what I would be processed into once it was switched on. The show began and we were, according to the screen, on a bus caught in traffic. The bench juddered a little. And then we were off, weaving through traffic, swerving to avoid trucks and pedestrians, the bench tipping us from side to side in such perfectly calibrated motion that it felt as if I'd consigned my motor responses to some outside agency. There was a continuous loud clunking as the machinery moved the benches but it didn't interfere at all with my belief that I was zooming around the city. The immersion was not visual, like that of the VR helmet, but kinetic as my body was firmly and specifically jolted around. The accompanying film wasn't particularly sophisticated but I inhabited its scenes without hesitation because I was already moving through them: 'I don't think the brain is interested in what's real. It's interested in what works.'[5]

There is something restful about disorder when it is orchestrated like this. It concentrates the mind on the body. Some of the art that has delighted me most has been bodily experience: rooms full of balloons in which the space around me filled up with tickling gentleness;[6] hurtling down spiralling tubular slides* that were a monumental version of the helter-skelter I loved as a child at the fair;[7] blundering around a series of rooms wearing a suit that made it almost impossible to see. This last was in Berlin in 2017 when I visited 'Limits of Knowing', an

* See Mendelssohn hurtling through a railway tunnel in 'Boredom, repetition, fixatives' (p. 63).

interdisciplinary exhibition aiming to draw its audience into 'states that are less popular in our knowledge-based society, like anticipation, premonition or bewilderment'.[8] The works were immersive and intended to transform 'concepts into "felt" sense'. I was familiar with immersive experiences of sound or light but Haptic Field was described as 'spatial'.[9] I had to zip myself into a body suit covered with sensors and put on a helmet that obscured my vision before being led into a series of rooms. I could hardly see but if I was near a person or a wall, the sensors vibrated or lit up. I was navigating by vibration or by the lights on other people's suits, reading small signals. Putting on the suit was an extension of strapping myself to that bench in New York. I was excited because I was about to be unsettled but if I had any premonition it was that I would be safe.

A decade after the New York experience I went to Cambridge to experience virtual reality for the first time.[10] This was at the invitation of Paul Fletcher, who was working on the uses of VR in the treatment of psychosis. There's a film of me in what looks like a stationery cupboard, sitting in front of a computer and wearing a headset. I am turning in my chair, looking up and down and around while murmuring 'oh' and 'ah' and 'uh-oh'. The first place I found myself in was a forest. It was a simple cartoon but forests are never simple places. I kept trying to find the edge of the picture but wherever I turned my gaze – up, down, behind me – the scene continued. We experience the world as if we can see in all directions at once and here it was, everywhere I looked. Next I was sitting in a chair and when I looked down and saw a pair of crudely drawn cartoon hands, my brain was convinced they were mine. The chair was on a plank protruding from the top of a skyscraper. The plank wobbled, tilted and

I fell. This I saw coming, so didn't mind. The most disturbing scene came next – an ordinary room, with a sofa, armchairs, plants and a rug. I waited. Nothing happened and then I realised that the room was getting smaller and that it had neither windows nor a door. At this point I had to keep telling myself that this was not real, which did nothing to lessen my physical dread. Perhaps because the room was so ordinary, my body did not agree. I was offered a chance to try a virtual funfair ride and was pleased to find myself in one of those gondola swings that thrilled me as a child but when it swung back, it did this so steeply that before it swung forward again, I felt sick and had to take the headset off.

Five years after that I was sitting in an armchair in a gallery, wearing another VR headset. This time I was on a tropical beach that looked extremely real.[11] I found out later that it was Christmas Island, and the detail of what I was floating among had been taken from a NASA spacecraft orbiting and mapping the moon. I also had a handset with which I could control where I went. After wandering around for a bit, I found myself far out in space from where I could land on the moon. Walking on the moon involved the same ponderous leaps that we see in footage of astronauts. I was sitting in a deep armchair and I knew there was someone nearby to guide or help. The sea, planets and stars looking both beautiful and real. If I wanted to look more closely at something, I could move myself towards it. I came out of the experience feeling refreshed but also as if it had all been frictionless. There was none of the difficulty or constraint that we usually encounter when wanting to see far and look deeply. My eye had not been caught and nor did I need to fix my gaze.

3

At eleven, I began to realise that I was visible and might be looked at and so became concerned with appearance.* I cared about the impression I made. I wasn't yet interested in furniture and accepted the bed, chair, chest of drawers and desk I had been allocated as a kind of domestic bedrock. It wouldn't have occurred to me that I had a choice and I didn't. I also knew I was lucky to have more privacy and space than many of my friends. Furniture accumulates history and associations which have nothing to do with its worth. It can affirm, consolidate, obstruct, clutter, distract, conceal, haunt or loom. Our house was a mixture of old and modern but rarely was anything new. The idea of getting rid of furniture or altering décor because your taste had changed did not arise. You used what you had, or what came your way, until it no longer functioned even after extensive repair. Our dining table was one of the few contemporary purchases my parents made as young people setting up home in the Sixties. It was slender, oval and out of place. The chairs around it were unstable and when my little brother's kept collapsing, my mother tied it together with string. When I was thirteen and wanted nothing more than to be like everyone else, I found this mortifyingly eccentric. Our chairs should at least match and not collapse. What would people think? I begged her to throw the chair out but she said he was fond of it and he explained that it was fine, and didn't give way if you eased yourself in from a particular angle. But we kept forgetting to warn

* For more on childhood, disappearing children and adolescent concealment and exposure see 'Invisible, unseen', p. 258.

visitors and several ended up on the floor.

I was eager for my room to reflect the person I would, any day, become but my idea of who that should be kept shifting. There would be a look I had noticed, admired and decided to emulate as it achieved critical mass and became The Look. As I cycled rapidly through North London bohemian, provincial teenybopper, disco girl, hippy, punk and new wave, my room was recast. I destroyed as much evidence as possible of the last person I'd been, ripping down posters that I was proud of only a week before. I started to daydream about boys, and one of my earliest fantasies was not of being kissed but of my crush entering my room and seeing me sitting on the floor by my record player (an old box gramophone) wearing just the right clothes and with just the right book in my hands. I was extending my attention from myself to my setting, and what I read and listened to were a part of this.

Books and music no longer have to be integrated into the furnishing of a room because they do not have to be visible. What you read or listen to is no longer automatically seen. Does this make books and records less potent signifiers of taste? Do we have to talk more about what we read or listen to because no one will notice?

At twenty-one, I joined a housing co-op that was given derelict buildings on yearly leases. These were my first unfurnished rooms and I filled them as my parents had with what came to hand while also starting to think about furniture as an extension of style. I was unconcerned about the bare floorboards and peeling plaster or the fact that the ceiling was held up by props, and spent hours painting the door to my room an unlikely glossy scarlet.

Once I stopped to consider the table, I started to notice when it wasn't clean and took up housework as I would later take up gardening. My teenage bedroom had been somewhere I could figure out who I was through what I liked and what I wanted to look like. Now my domain extended to a shared living space, kitchen and bathroom. Friends started to come over for meals. I noticed cutlery, glassware and plates, and my time in charity shops was spent more in the crockery section than among the clothes.

Pieter de Hooch, who died in 1684, is known for tranquil scenes of women and children secured within a framework of rooms, doorways, windows, corridors and courtyards. These pictures offer vistas that connect, in carefully determined steps, home and the world. This is a *door-sien* or 'through view', one that requires the negotiation of a number of hurdles. It does not look easy for the women in his pictures to leave home. When Peter Mundy travelled to Holland in 1640, he found Dutch households to be full of pleasure and contentment, and noted that even 'a house of indifferent quality' might have 'Ritche Cupboards . . . Imagery, porcelain. Costly Fine cages with birds, etts.' They would also be extremely clean 'within doors, as in their streetes.'[12]

For people to notice that a house is particularly clean, this needs to be brought to their attention. A bed will not simply be made but tidied, smoothed, plumped and tucked; the linen will be stiff and spotless. A table will be wiped and polished, and the cloth placed upon it starched and pressed. There will be crispness and shine, smoothness and glow as well as charming things to meet the eye and to suggest comfort (if not wealth): a cabinet of porcelain, a goldfinch in a cage or the 'imagery' of paintings. De Hooch knew his market and its appetite for domestic scenes.

He contrived this serene atmosphere out of components (which turn up in other works) rather than from life, and extensively rearranged scenes. Who these women and children are does not matter. They are part of a scene that is itself an emblem.

The tension in de Hooch's paintings is often liminal, in the sense of the actual threshold. The idea of private space was relatively new, and rooms had a less defined purpose. 'The Bedroom' (1658–60) might be a living space in which there happened to be a bed. The child's action here is assertive, opening a door and letting in light, while the woman's is that of concealing – making a bed, emptying a chamber pot. This child is one of de Hooch's most moving figures: her flyaway hair full of static, the reach of her arm, her confidence and sturdiness, the way in which she accepts the light, all contrast with the woman who fades into the interior,* bound by her headscarf and that heap of linen. They are exchanging a smile, which draws attention to the child's comparatively wild energy. She looks delighted to be seen and even commanding – Look at me! The woman's smile is weary. She's got so much to do and will not take up the idea that the child seems to suggest, that they go outside. The external world begins in the next room with its opulent marble floor, which bounces light unlike the absorbent terracotta of the tiles within. This is where you receive visitors – a place of shine where surfaces deflect scrutiny but reflect you. You appear in your furniture as well as in the pictures on your walls.

> As for the Art of Painting and the affection of the people to Pictures, I thincke none other goe beeyond them there . . .

* See Vuillard's sister folding into the wallpaper in 'The body, open, itself' (p. 135).

All in general striving to adorne their houses, especially
the outer or street roome, with costly peeces, Butchers
and bakers not much inferior in their shoppes, which are
Faurely sett Forth, yea, many times blacksmithes, Coblers,
etts., will have some picture or other by their Forge and in
their stalle . . .[13]

De Hooch's compositions are also making us aware of how we look into them. Artists in his milieu were experimenting with perspective and his work is most interesting for its visual push and pull. We see nothing happening and so look harder. This is an intimate space but the figures within it ignore or elude us. We can glimpse further but only through views which are restricted even as they proliferate. We have to negotiate a number of openings that could let us in or shut us out and either way make us conscious of our passage.

The women at the centre of these paintings hover between subject and object. They would be oppressed by decorum or the dangers or temptations that lie beyond these walls. Such women were confined to their homes, possessed by their absent husbands, and expected to maintain themselves at a point of strict moderation. They were invested in as the embodiment of virtue, yet viewed as inherently weak and in need of containment and protection.

De Hooch was under pressure to sustain a rate of production and to compete for clients. He was socially aware, adapting his style to fashion and demand as his clients became more sophisticated and would be flattered by a work's subtle and ambiguous effects. He struggled, never earning enough to pay taxes and working briefly as a servant. He is not mentioned in contemporary writing on art, and his figures are awkward and out of scale when compared with those of ter Borch or Vermeer. They make me feel as if I'm being told too emphatically to pay them attention but however crudely modelled, they have greater life and depth than many more refined such presences. When I turn from de Hooch's women to those of Vermeer, the latter seem more like an instrument on which to play with light.

Some women with time and money, who never made a bed or emptied a chamber pot, put their energies into constructing reproductions of their homes. In the Rijksmuseum in Amsterdam, there is a hall full of small Dutch houses. They aren't dollhouses but models. Like the actual houses of the rich, they are too large to be inviting and too expensively made to be touched. Petronella Oortman's model cost as much as an actual house in her very expensive street. The house is made from marble, walnut and pewter, its linen monogrammed and its dishes made of the same fine porcelain as those from which she ate.

Oortman would have been constrained by her luxurious existence even though it offered such resources. A model of home enabled her to place herself outside it.* She had contrived respite or escape, a place from which she could observe her world. Oortman's exactness might have been intellectual, aesthetic, competitive, whimsical or, most likely, all of these things.

There is an inescapable assumption that the more accurate a representation – the same materials, the same design – the more 'real' a copy will be. Was she trying to see her world more clearly? Or having completed her home, wanted the pleasure

* See also Elizabeth Bishop's image of her childhood village in 'Disorder, slippage, glare', p. 238.

200

of repeating the experience? What really brings this house to life is the painting of it undertaken by Jacob Appel in 1710.[14] We are used to paintings as evocations of reality and models as representation, and so our eyes read this differently.

Samuel van Hoogstraten was unusual among artists of his time in that he worked in all genres and was as much a writer as a painter. He was known as a dramatist and poet as well as for his treatise on painting. In the preface to that work, he presents himself as one who 'interchanges his brush with his pen'.[15] Like de Hooch, he was born in Dordrecht (in 1625) and trained under his father. At thirteen, when his father died, he was apprenticed to Rembrandt and at twenty-one set out on a career as an independent artist, travelling to Vienna, London and Rome. He appears to have been gifted and curious but restless, as his treatise shows. In writing about perspective, he pulled together the work of others before saying that he knew an easier way to achieve perspective, which he would write about later if he could be bothered. He never was, although he stressed the importance of knowing how vision works:

> There is nothing more easily tricked than sight. But I
> say that a painter, whose work it is to trick sight, should
> also have enough knowledge of the nature of things that
> he fundamentally understands by what means the eye
> is tricked.[16]

In order to demonstrate this, he built what he described as a *wonderlijk perspectyfkas* – a 'curious perspective box'.[17] These were then a popular form of entertainment, but this one is a serious demonstration of perspectival theory. It is not a model of a house but of a typical painting of a Dutch interior. It is furnished with the tropes of both subject and technique: the chequered floor, the glimpses into other rooms, the faithful dog, the letter on the chair. There are, unusually, two peepholes, and the three-dimensional effect when looking through either of these is so powerful that it is not remotely compromised by the fact that one side of the box is open and its construction revealed. If anything, this opportunity to figure out how the illusion works makes it all the more effective.

The experience of the real depends here on the illusion of space. Looking through a tiny aperture with just one eye, you will see a room at full size and you will feel it recede into other spaces. The anamorphic distortion used to achieve this, combined with the peepholes, forces you to take a particular position in order to see something clearly. You are rearranged. You are looking *into* rather than *at*, and will be aware at all times that the size and construction of this house make it impossible for you to follow your gaze inside. You will never find out who the shadow at the window belongs to, to whom the letter on the chair is addressed or why that person is in bed.

When you're thinking about how you're seeing, it's difficult to keep what you're looking at in sight. Studying art history, I learnt to look through and behind the painting at the artist, their techniques, materials, context and milieu. I set aside the question of whether or not I liked the work, and focused on what it revealed about making and reading the image. Reading history and theory, I was being placed in specific points of view. Some of them felt as I did when visiting van Hoogstraten's peepshow in London's National Gallery. I found a small dark box on a plinth in a side room: a cupboard inside a cupboard. The plinth was low, forcing me to double over in order to find the right position at the peephole. I had to contort myself in order to bring the inside of the box to my eye.

Unanchoring, sinking, at sea

1

The double passivity of being a passenger and being at sea can be unbearable. It's also what some people long for. They pay a lot of money to enjoy it on a boat built on such a scale that it makes the sea irrelevant. At sea, we discover how much the sea moves, and we move with it without moving ourselves. We have no control over a situation that is both perpetual and unpredictable. We might be looking at something still – a cabin wall or a calm horizon – but we are being swung, rocked or thrown about. The eyes argue with the ears (our sense of balance) about what is happening. The body is being moved in ways it's not used to and can't make sense of. It cannot anchor itself and sinks under a confusion of sensations and signals.

I'm prone to seasickness, which developed with age. As a child, I was on a ferry crossing the Irish Sea during what was later called 'the worst storm for fifty years'. I was too young to be afraid and felt not a hint of nausea. While adults gripped the table as their faces turned green, my siblings and I amused ourselves by trying to climb up and down the stairs while the boat lurched around. It was a free fairground ride, endless entertainment even as we dodged the puddles of vomit and the staggering men. Where were the women? All I remember is giant men, falling down and crawling about. Perhaps the women were under the tables.

It didn't occur to us that we might get hurt. We were at the age when we charged at the world and trusted it not to damage us. Most of the time it didn't. I wonder how a child's vision is shaped by that lack of fear; how open the world must seem before you are taught to creep through it, testing every unknown step. We learn to hesitate and so do our senses. No wonder the body starts to over-react.

In my thirties, I went on a whale-watching trip in New Zealand. The sea looked calm although we were warned that there was 'a bit of a swell'. The boat was cramped and we had to sit inside in tight rows whenever it was moving. After around half an hour of minor and repetitive lurches, I found myself trying not to be sick. The boat was pulling me forwards into this endless repetition and my mind was pulling backwards to the steadiness of the shore.* The nausea extended into dizziness, and I went hot and cold. My vision narrowed to the back of the seat in front of me. I was dimly aware of my teenage daughter to one side of me preparing to be mortified and the stranger on the other side readying herself not to notice what happened next. A gloved hand appeared and passed me one paper bag and then another. When the boat stopped, the hand beckoned me towards deck where I found I could barely stand up. My temperature was veering up and down, and I was shaking so much that I couldn't speak. The young crew member, whose hand had been guiding me, was kind. This was evidently something he saw most days but also perhaps that he couldn't imagine suffering from. He looked steady and resilient.

The guide announced that we were now above one of the

* See Mendelssohn, seasickness and repetition in 'Boredom, repetition, fixatives', p. 61.

deepest sea canyons in the world just as another boat arrived. Identical to our own, it sat there demonstrating horribly clearly the situation I was in. It looked absurdly frail teetering about between great heaves of water. Even the whales looked small as they occasionally almost surfaced.

It was not enough to see part of a fin or the curve of a back. We wanted to see a whole whale, to feel it close but at a safe distance; to stare and take pictures without any sense of having disturbed it. All I could think of was what I couldn't see – the canyon below. There were three more hours to go before I would be back on dry land. The young man advised me to sit somewhere with the coast in view and to keep watching it. Was this supposed to fool my eyes? Was it enough for my vision to meet solid ground while my body was still out at sea?

I don't remember how I felt for the rest of the whale-watching trip, just that the shaking eventually lessened as I stared at the coastline and willed the boat closer. At sea, it is difficult to make sense of how fast you're moving, how far you are from land or how long it will take to reach port. Your senses either flail or contract as you adapt to the lack of co-ordinates. The ship may be moving quickly but you slow down. Time passes in the sky, in the sun, moon and stars, and only if you can read them do you know that you are still moving and that, at some point, you will arrive.

2

Boats in medieval art often look far too small to contain everyone on board. The artist is prioritising the story and is not yet concerned with matters of scale. We need to be able to see who is present and how they relate, and so they loom as if crammed into a bath. Like their story, they are larger than life. Everyone is visible and no one can leave.

One ship, in a manuscript illustration by Évrard d'Espinques (1450–1500), is certainly too small to contain its story. Any ship would be. The woman is Isolde – being carried across the sea from Ireland to Cornwall to be delivered to King Mark, whom she is about to marry. In terms of life as well as this journey, she is not in control of how she's moving and unable to see where she's going. The narrative is repetitive and relentless but she's not seasick. Instead she tries to invoke a storm to unanchor herself from this situation. She would rather be dead. The man beside her (whose hand might be about to take hers, which she might be offering) is Tristan, Mark's nephew. He and Isolde have met before. She is renowned for her healing powers and years ago he was brought to her, badly injured, under a different name. She nursed this stranger even after she realised who he was: the person who'd killed the man to whom she was betrothed. She thought to kill him in vengeance but he met her eyes with such openness that she couldn't do it.

Time has passed and they meet again. She is now the object of his duty and must not be recognised as who she is. This voyage will be the passage between the time when she was not his and the time when she cannot be his. He has raised his telescope and is watching the green line above the blue horizon, knowing that it will become the point of their next separation. He stares out to sea because he must not see where he is and who he is with. Isolde is a mirror. If he looks at her, he will see his true self and his desire for her.

Isolde refuses to be contained by this ship, this situation. Less than passenger, she is goods to be delivered. Her only function is to arrive. She insists on the fact of her presence and will not retreat under the canopies put up to offer her shelter. She ought to remain out of sight. How can she stand there, so exposed? Tristan tries to conceal her from himself among company (such a small ship).

She sees him as the man she once healed. Without his armour, he did not know his own body, only that it was she who gave him back his wholeness. He doesn't want to see himself as he once was – wounded, brought to her as someone else, someone lost. He cannot stand that he let her save him and now he must give her away.

Land draws closer and Tristan goes to face her. They step into a dark corner where she offers him a deadly potion. They no longer want to see where they must go. But the poison has been exchanged for a love potion, and Tristan feels his heart bursting as he tries to find room for such feeling. The gaze of each pours into the other. From now on, they will see only their world.

In port, they compose themselves. Tristan must be seen to give Isolde to his uncle, and she must be seen to be taken. How quickly they have adapted – folding into one another so that being dead or alive or private or public are all the same thing. They can take up their roles because they are not here.

What next? Marriage and waiting. A night comes when the king is hunting in the forest and Isolde waits. How to wait when ready and alone? She's impatient to summon Tristan. She would be patient if she could see him or have some sense of him but the air is without charge. The summer dusk refuses to soften, spangling white and silver even when the day's rose and gold are long gone. The forest is too clear, its paths too open. She must wait for the king's men to go deeper among the trees. She asks the forest to lose them. She asks that dusk might blacken. And yet here can still be seen from there.

They've agreed on the signal of a torch, a small flame that could mean anything. It will be put out when it's safe for Tristan to come. Will he arrive too soon or wait too long? Or forget the signal? The little flame quibbles and jabs, its flicker reminding her that she is never truly safe or alone. It burns as a question, interruption, complication, hesitation. She gives the order for it to be put out. What she wants is the deepest dark, a night adrift without dimension or regulation.

The darkness in which they meet confirms that it's impossible to see anything beyond themselves. They sink happily into it. He asks if it is really her that his fingers are starting to describe. He had thought her made of emeralds and gold, brocade and silk, pearl-buttoned and petal-stitched. What he has in his hands – so live and changeable, barely graspable – is storm cloud. The length of her hair is spoken of as red and tightly braided. He did not know that that braid contained such feathers. This is what it means to meet out of sight, out of their own sight.

The sun is breaking down the door and the room fills with jangle and glitter. Tristan lies there, his eyes too wide like those of a young owl caught in the forest's net and made to face the day. He knows that he should be gone and that she ought to be left to wake in such a way that would not condemn her. But why hide the truth? They have fallen out of their days and have destroyed their names. Those who enter the room want only to cast shadows. They draw their swords but Tristan refuses to move. He wants to be seen beside her.

Isolde wakes to hear voices rise and fall. She watches people rage and weep but she is at sea. They cannot reach her. She says that if they cut him down they must cut her down too. Then no one will see.

Tristan, badly wounded, is taken home back across the water. All he knows is that he is not beside her. He lies among himself in a place he did not put himself. He wakes under a wall and does not know if it keeps him out or in, or if it is his own skin. Words pile up and drop. He has the thought to speak but finds that he is just a heap of stones that prop each other up. The world is a wall from which he is leaning. The night is uncontrollable. He keeps stumbling on a piece that is missing.

It is a song that saves him. It gives him something to imagine. It is sung outside his window and not for him but it conjures a childhood scene of spacious days under a simple sun. The song lets itself down inside his mind like a rope spooling into a well. He starts to climb its notes and the rope becomes a chain and then a place he can name. He has hauled himself back and is present once again but only in outline. He rests in the song and he waits.

She arrives at the height of day. She is free to be there and he is free to turn towards her: a man of wounds, who asks forgiveness for his injuries. He pours forth all that he has had to contain for so long and does not know that this is how he is leaving.

Isolde watches the moon rise. At first its light creeps over a ridge and then the moon slides out from behind the mountains. Nothing moves – not the moon, not the mountains. Yet, moment by moment, space opens up between them. In such a manner is he leaving. With each breath, a little more of him. A dissolution into light and air. He is still here but is becoming, with each breath, everywhere. She will follow him.

My love, you are now what you have always been:
as miraculous a presence
as dust drawn up from the earth
to float and spin in the sun
seen as one thing by one person
in a moment of passing.

And the clearest thing in my life has been
to see and be seen by this one person
in a moment of passing.

3

A storm is something we like to watch from a safe distance. Caught in a storm, we look only to find a way out of it. The scale and drama, the anticipation of thunder and lightning, can be enjoyed if the storm doesn't threaten your safety, livelihood or home. I was walking across a bare field at dusk with a friend when a huge storm broke. It was getting dark and we were in a place neither of us had been to before. The footpath we were following was a shallow track across ploughed earth and was instantly washed away. I turned round and then back and couldn't remember which side of the field we had come in through. Where was the gate? The rain was so intense, the thunder and lightning so near that we made for the edge to find shelter. Only we couldn't work out where the edge was. The storm had overwhelmed our vision. We couldn't see and just like that we couldn't remember. We decided to walk in as straight a line as possible. Even that was difficult because a straight line is defined by the consistency with which it relates to the things around it and anything we might have fixed on was dissolving into mud. Somehow we reached an edge only it was a steep bank of thin trees that provided no shelter. By this time I was laughing because I was scared. I didn't want to watch the lightning; I scuttled away from it. I have no idea how we found our way out.

I was in Florence for the first time and not taking notes. There were saints and angels and holy families, miracles and agonies, and they flattened in my mind into one long fresco. Someone put money in a slot and bare electric bulbs illuminated images intended to be seen by lamplight and candlelight. If the brightness revealed anything it was how frail and worn these paintings were. In a recess in a chapel that I immediately forgot the name of, I found a small fresco at floor level which was not a religious story. There was a lot of sky and weather, men and horses, a boat, and an arrival in a different land. A small sign down on the skirting board said that this was 'the earliest known representation of a storm in Western art'. The only bit of the story I remember is that an emissary had been sent to Scotland and his boat got caught in a terrible storm. I don't know if he survived as I was only interested in the weather. The fresco was not in good condition but even allowing for that, the storm was roughly handled. The artist would have seen storms but didn't know how to paint them because they had no artistic precedent. Art teaches the artist how to make something look real, not the thing itself. There was a long visual history for the artist to draw on of men kneeling and riding, horses cantering and standing, and boats at sea, but what of the weather? This artist appeared to have become absorbed in making sense of the storm as a meteorological phenomenon. Water is drawn up into the air, spun round in clouds and released. On that long hot day in Florence, it seemed to me the one thing I saw that sprang from (and to) life.

When we watch a storm, are we thinking about what it looks like or how it works? An image can address both questions at once. When Constable made his sketch *Rainstorm over the Sea* (*c.*1823–8), he was spending what time he could in Brighton, having moved his family there for the sake of his wife's health. He sat on the beach with a tin of paints on his knees, the picture propped in its lid. He was teaching himself to work faster, to grasp more of what was passing, and in doing so had to decide what mattered in terms of remembering. He is not thinking about appearances or the conventions of representation. His wife is dying, the sky is moving, he is up against time. For once, he looks straight out to sea and doesn't bother with human presence. There are interruptions on the horizon but they don't amount to detail. This small late work seems so powerful now because it conveys how we experience and remember rather than what the storm looked like, which is truer to how we see. In its almost abstraction, the sketch becomes diagrammatic. Like the painter of the storm in the fresco, Constable has become (however inadvertently) interested in how this weather works. He is trying to make visual sense while also letting himself paint like someone who is sitting hunched on the beach watching turbulent skies that will soon reach him.

When it was shown in London in 2021, this sketch was lauded as evidence of Constable's overlooked wild side. People weren't used to thinking of him in this way but the same force, the desire to reach past the act of painting, can be seen in his more finished and conventional works.

From the southern edge of East Anglia, you can look across the mouth of the Thames estuary to the coast of Kent. This view is somewhere between looking across a river and looking out to sea. You don't have to go far to be able to see further, but can climb a small rise to the negligible ruin of Hadleigh Castle, which Constable once sketched as a 'hasty memorandum'.

> At Hadleigh there is a ruin of a castle . . . it commands a
> view of the Kent hills, the Nore and North Foreland &
> looking many miles to sea . . .[1]

Constable was almost forty and earning his living as a portrait painter: dowagers in lace, gilded youths, a banker's eight starched children. He'd been wooing Maria Bicknell for five years. They married and had seven children, and Constable was eventually able to turn to painting his 'places': the barns, gardens, fields and mills. In November 1828, Maria died of consumption. He wrote 'I shall never feel again as I have felt – the face of the world is totally changed to me.'[2] He dressed in mourning for the rest of his life and returned to the view from the castle although he did not visit it again.

He worked next on a small oil sketch (1828–29), finding his way towards something darker, an atmosphere, the opposite of a view; something that he had not noted when there but somehow remembered. Around the time that Maria died, he returned to the subject in ink, placing the castle at more of a distance, raising himself to a gull's-eye view, glancing off the

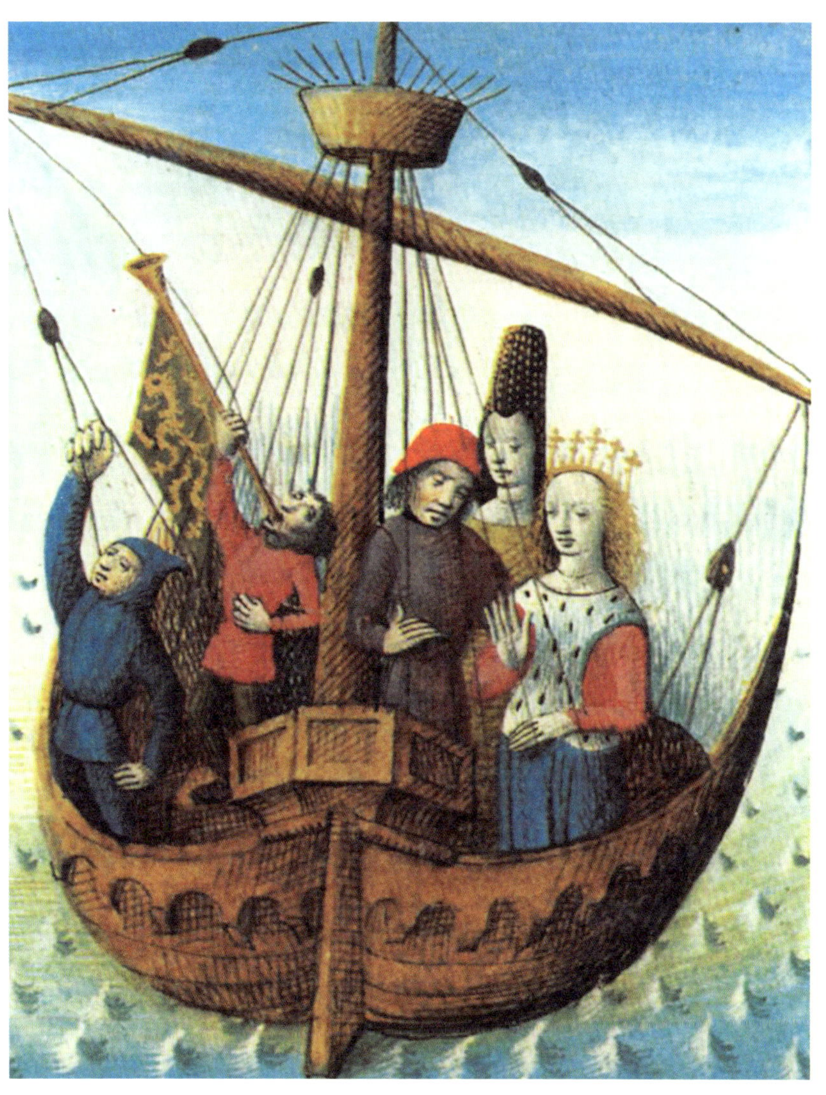

Évrard d'Espinques, *Tristan and Isolde Travelling to Cornwall by Boat*, c.1450–1500

(top) Jacques de Gheyn II, *Study sheet: lobster and two depictions of witches*, c.1602

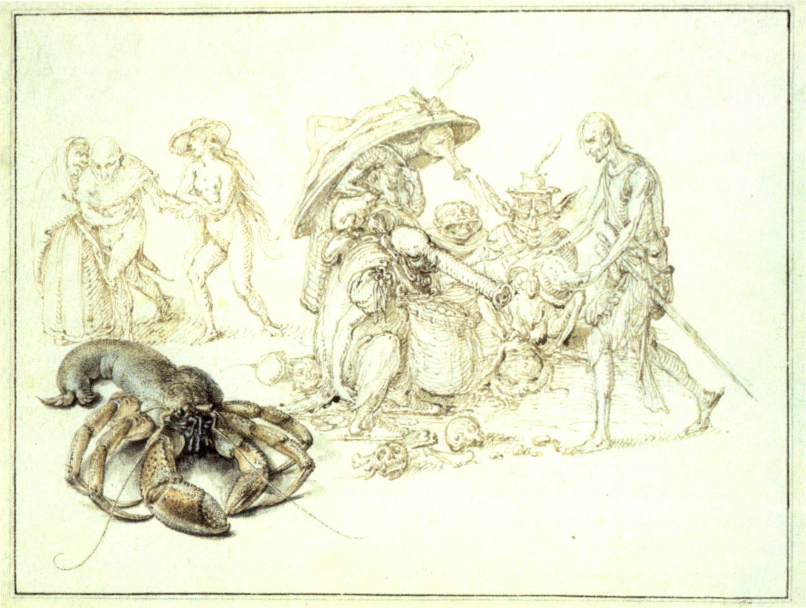

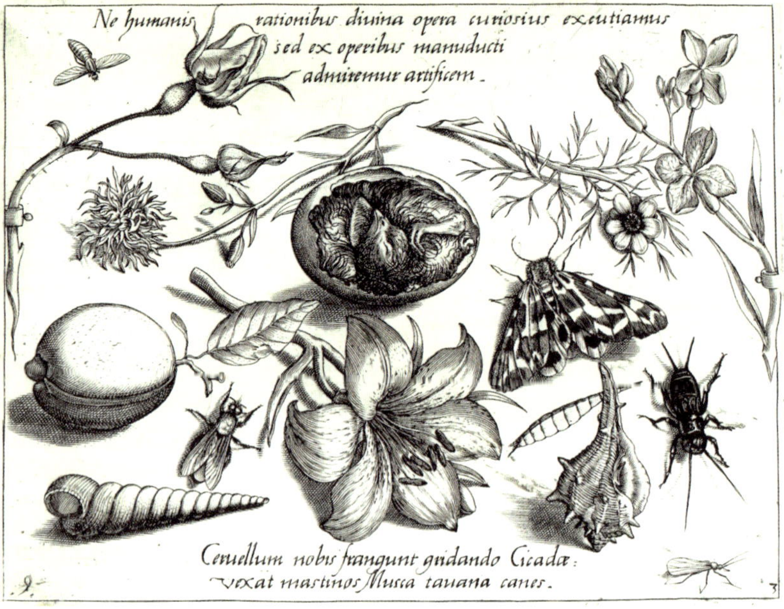

(bottom) Jacob Hoefnagel and Joris Hoefnagel, *Insects, Plants and Shells around a Chick in an Egg*, 1592

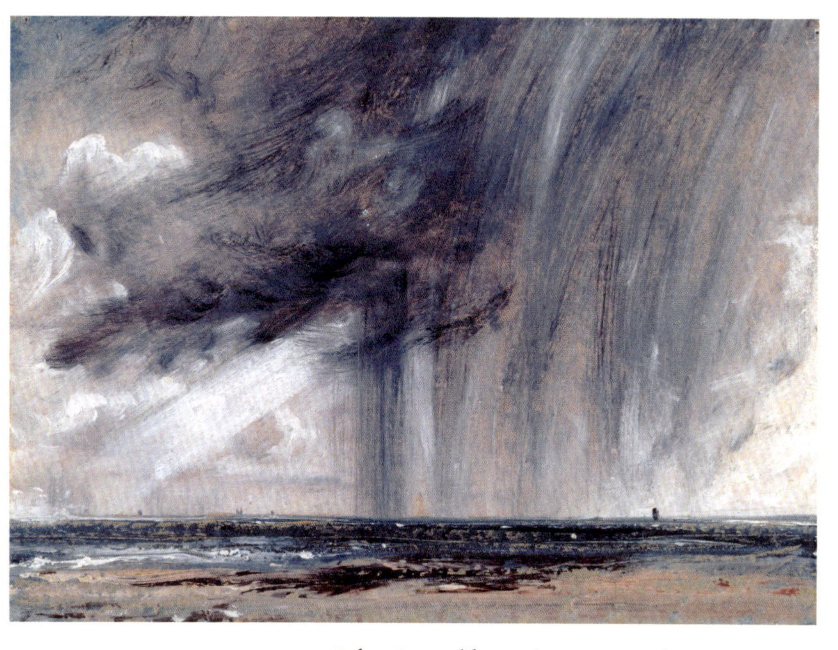

John Constable, *Rainstorm over the Sea*, c.1824–8

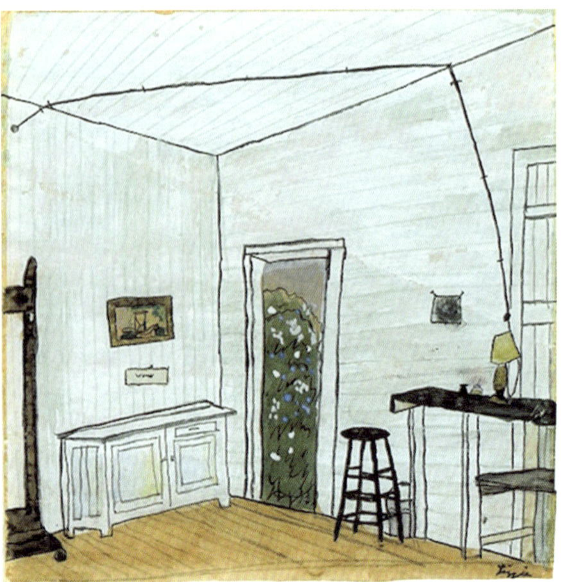

Elizabeth Bishop, *Interior with Extension Cord*, 1996

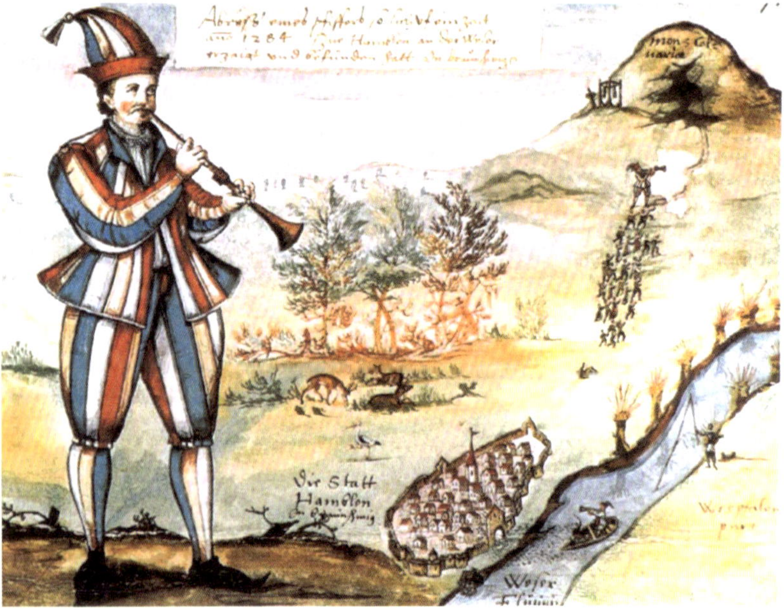

Augustin von Mörsperg, Pied Piper painting from *The Tale of Mörsperg*, 1592

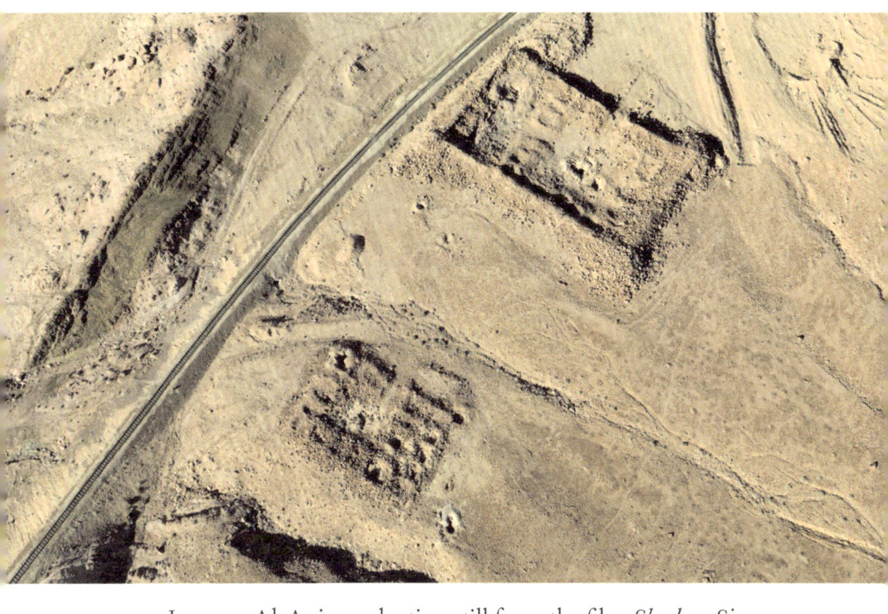

Jananne Al-Ani, production still from the film *Shadow Sites 1*, 2010

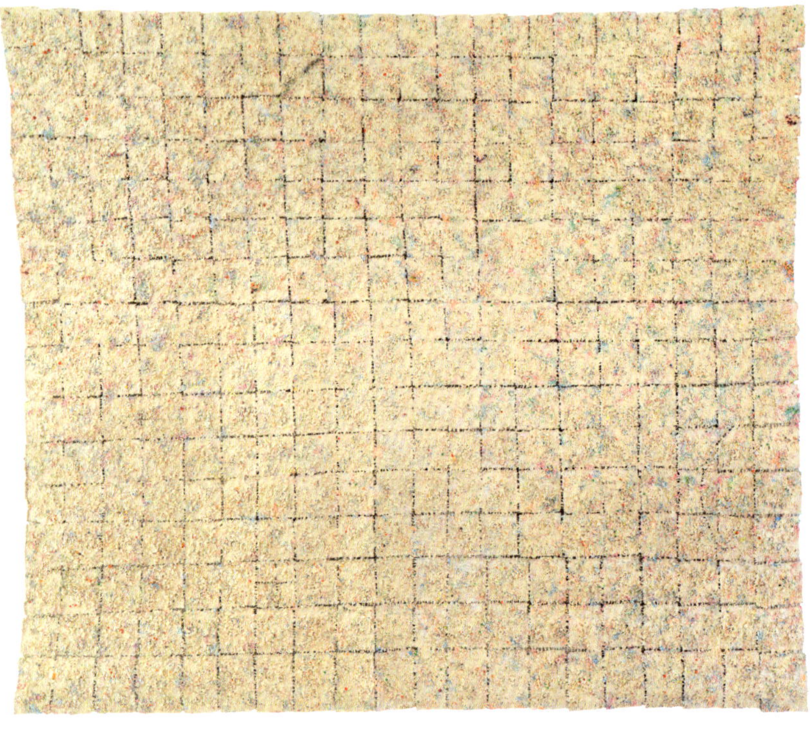

Howardena Pindell, *Untitled #24*, 1978–9, mixed media on canvas, dimensions 219.7 x 261.6 cm, 86½ x 103 in. © Howardena Pindell. Courtesy the artist, Garth Greenan Gallery, and Victoria Miro

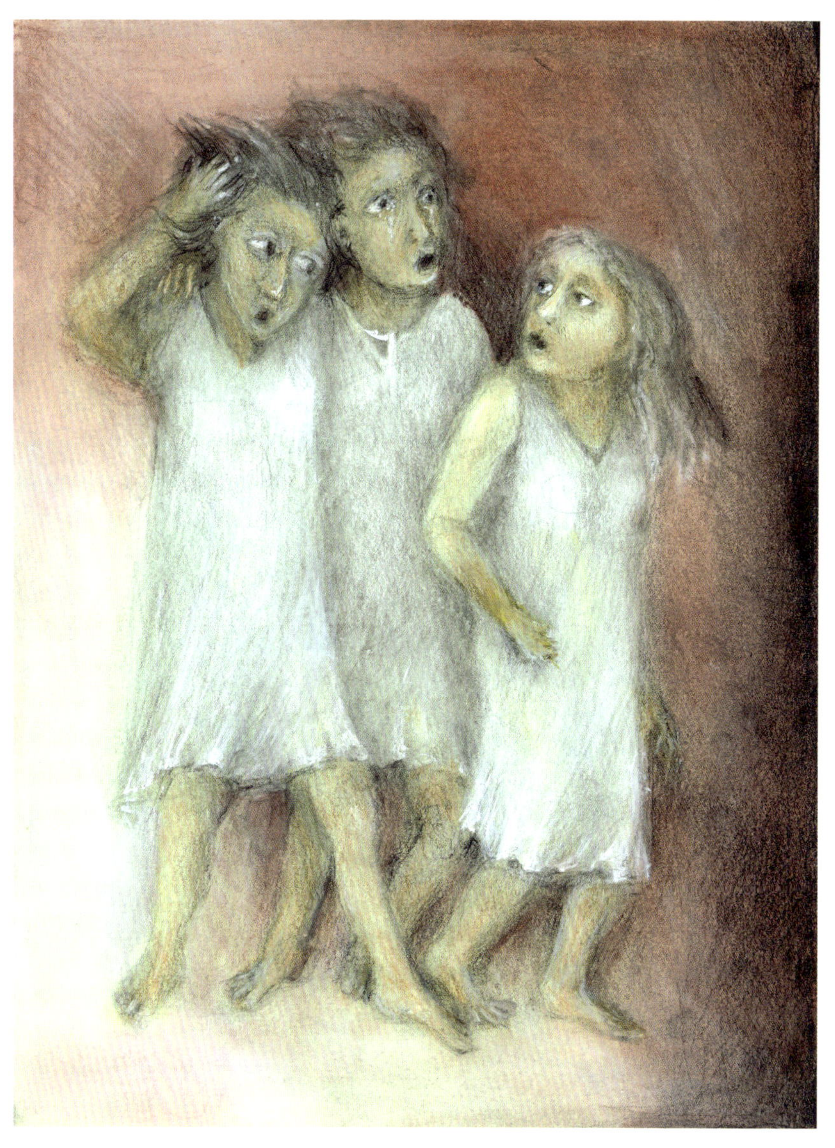

Ana Maria Pacheco, study for sculpture *(Remember)* 4, 2018

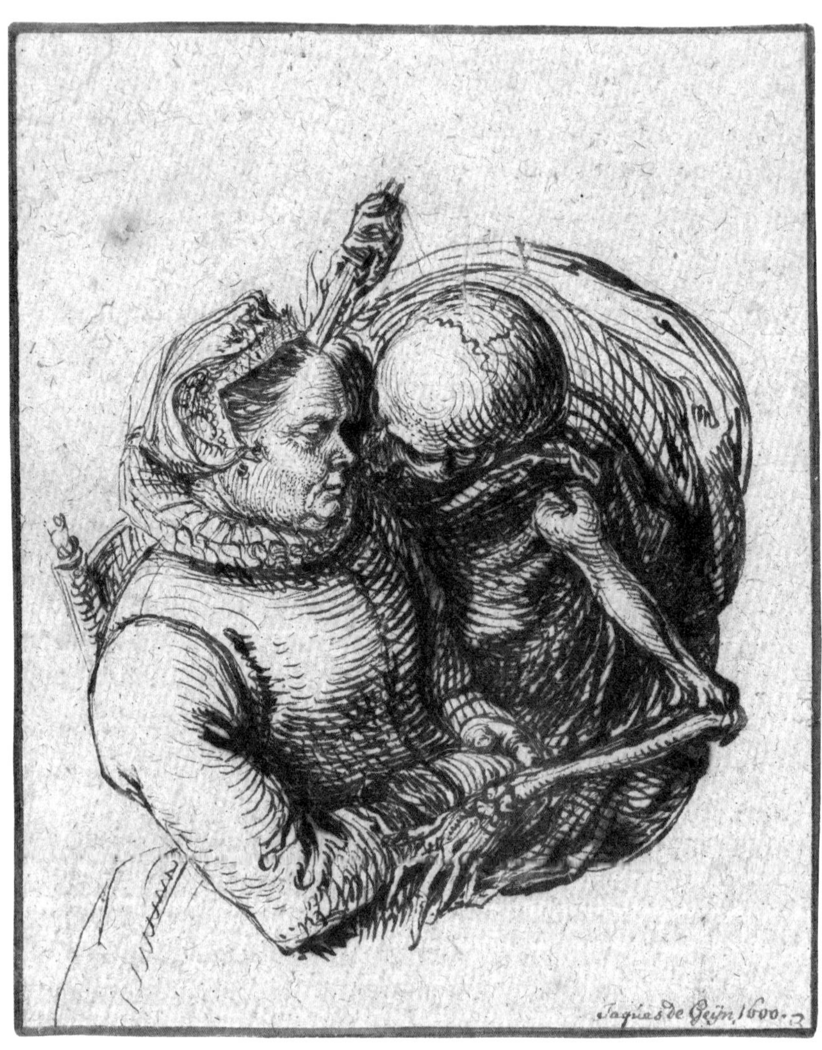

Jacques de Gheyn II, *Woman and Death*, 1600

ruins, expanding the sky and opening up the sea. He added a shepherd and dog, who neither stand out nor tell a story nor take up space. The more he added, the more space.

The next study is a large oil sketch. Gulls are now circling the towers but they crumble into the air as if the castle itself is crumbling and being blown away (it was). This broad spill of land is a turmoil of hedgerow and hawthorn, mud and stone. The sky is a vertical force, heaping and tipping white while the sea is flattened to nothing. The castle is hard left and low. It looks like a couple of broken drains. This is the edge and offers neither foothold nor a way back.

The eventual work *Hadleigh Castle, The Mouth of the Thames: Morning after a Stormy Night* is dated 1829.[3] He is focused on the idea of 'after'. A storm has unpainted the view and exposed the sharp tips of things. Brightness catches like wool on barbed wire. The air has been scoured and Constable's highlights are so cold, so crystalline that they were referred to as 'Constable's snow'. They hurt. Turner dismissed them as 'splashes of white-wash that might have dripped from a newly painted ceiling' (I think of Constable's mind, unfurnished by losing Maria, as an empty ceiling).

At the Royal Academy, when the painting was hung and Constable was putting the final touches to it on Varnishing Day, the eminent sculptor and committee member Sir Francis Leggatt Chantrey pronounced the foreground too cold and taking Constable's palette from his hands, muted the scene. Constable, watching, said only, 'There goes all my dew.'[4] He did not object but once the great man had gone, removed all trace of his interference. Constable was deferential and gener-ous, accepting the long wait before he was admitted to the RA and trusting Chantrey's dubious expressions of support. Yet he knew better than any great man how his paintings quickened under the touch of his 'dew'. He also knew the difference between pursuing the true nature of an image and extending this pursuit for the sake of it: 'the great vice of the present day is *bravura*, an attempt to do something beyond the truth'.[5]

4

The empty sea has become a subject like the empty church or the empty room. It has no visual anchors or at least none that automatically capture the eye. Vija Celmins' family left Latvia for America when she was a child, ahead of the Soviet occupation in 1944. In the 1970s, she started to work with satellite imagery of the ocean and the surface of the moon. Her ocean is a surface that we experience without the anchorage of presence, location or scale. It is a drawing that looks like a photograph – a different way of resisting bravura and coming to rest at a point of truth. I have the same response to this precision that I do to the roughness of Constable's storm. I'm being invited to think about how something works – the movement of water – and in doing so see it more deeply. Celmins says that she sees 'drawing as thinking, evidence of getting from one place to another'.[6] 'Evidence' suggests that what emerges is autonomous and uncontrived, formed in process rather than preconceived.

Celmins talks of working in 'very small increments' and of investigating the limits of her medium, graphite: 'It's almost as if I was exploring the blackness of the pencil along with the image that went with it.' This might seem like a dry and constraining thought when we're looking at the uninterrupted ocean but working in this painstaking way, in tension with her instrument, might have been what anchored her.

The fast-changing, unanchored world of seventeenth-century northern Europe depended on drawing to record and disperse new knowledge. Drawing was aligned with documentation, planning and scientific enquiry. It was the medium best suited to the empirical approach that the North was embracing: knowledge through observation. Johannes Kepler used the word *pencilli* for that which 'paints' the 'picture' on the retina and Samuel van Hoogstraten followed his lead: 'The shapes of things with their colors are received thus directly by the eye. We shall call these shapes forms and images or refer to them by our usual technical term as the "drawing" of a thing.'[7] Van Hoogstraten sees the world as if from another planet 'thanks to the art of drawing'.* The pencil is the most direct medium emphasising the directness of 'from life'.† The description of phenomena is different to the illustration of theory – as different as a study of mice is from a history painting. The former has no narrative context. It is not a framed moment in time but a thing out of time, like Celmins' sea.

5

We live with unknown depths both inside and outside ourselves. Our well-lit world suggests that it will be possible for us

---

* See 'Peering and noticing, flits and swerves', p. 145, for the full quote.
† Two hundred years after Kepler, the pioneering photographer William Henry Fox Talbot (see 'Boredom, repetition, fixatives', p. 68) spoke of the 'pencil of nature' in order to stress the absence of the human hand in the making of a photograph. (Buckland, *Fox Talbot and the Invention of Photography*.)

to illuminate every corner. We want to see everything but at the same time we know that to light the dark is to change it. There are obvious reasons for our fascination with the seabed. It's the unknown and unreachable on a vast scale, filled by our imaginations with monsters, drowned cities, wreckage and treasure. Looking down into the depths is like looking into ourselves: a bumbling exploration involving effort and risk that casts a weak light on a few details. The light doesn't seem to accumulate. We just move our tiny range of focus from one thing to the next.

We may no longer believe in the creatures of the night – witches, devils, ghosts – but those of marine darkness (and of our inner darkness) have not only proved to be real but have remained beyond us. From time to time, new technology sends the explorers back to make a better map, to go further. We reach the ocean depths by means of a submersible, a bubble in which we bring our own atmosphere and pressure, tools and lenses, laws and logic and system of measurement, imagery and language. A stratified pile of rock brings to mind a Doric column and we can't help but wonder again about drowned cities.

As we get used to the dark, we begin to make out a kind of landscape and start to draw a map. The earth's surface is an articulation of disturbance, which continues here on the seabed. There are cliffs, ravines, valleys, channels, peaks and bridges – a drama of eruption, depression and suspense. Then we come to something for which not even the explorers have a word. It resists any idea of form but there it is, and they are reduced to calling it a 'structure'. There are some creatures that can't even be called that. Look, the explorers urge each other, look at that *thing*. It is barely anything – more like a thickening of the water, a large slow ripple that we can only discern by its lacy opacities. There is a part that looks a little more solid and might be a head or heart but it is not to be made sense of. We cannot turn it over in our hands or bring it back to the surface. What comes next is horribly familiar: a huge fish with a crushed face, blobby and encrusted, and swimming with a pair of fused hands. We cannot bear what we recognise of ourselves in its enormous tragic eyes.

There is too much that doesn't make sense. We find creatures we know but here they behave differently. Shrimps swim happily in the near-boiling black water spurting from hydrothermal vents on the ocean floor, and are equally happy in the freezing water nearby. Just as we don't believe in life without light, we can't believe what life is capable of.

To be squashed into a tiny submersible and dangled among all this, to have to peer through a porthole, is like being inside our own heads, our perception limited by the range of our vision. We try to enlarge our experience by filming in 3D but while this is stunning, memory seems to flatten it out again into pictures. If only something down here would look back. We might then feel that we had properly seen it. But most of this deep-sea life is barely formed heaps of stuff that look like matted black wool or cotton wool, tangled threads and tubes.

The depths have become conscious of our presence. A ghostly octopus with ribboning tentacles blanks out the camera and those seething prawns attach themselves to its carapace as they do to a crab covered in krill. Some of them will come back to the surface along with all the other samples to be analysed and named. Raised into light, these parts of the dark are raised into noise: at first the clatter of pulleys and chains and alarms,

the machinery that brought them up, and then voices desperately trying to describe.

James Elkins, writing in 1992 about 'visual desperation',
referred to the fossils found in the Burgess Shale in the 1970s,
specifically the Hallucigenia, which was so difficult to make
sense of that for some time, the palaeontologists simply could
not see it.[8] When it was eventually recorded, it still made no
sense and belonged to no genus. Some years after Elkins' essay,
it became clear that they had been looking at it upside down and
back to front. It has been re-envisioned over the last forty years
as a trace on a rock, a magnification, an illustration, a model
and an animation. It is now known to belong to the same class
as velvet worms and water bears, which does not help most of
us to see it any more clearly.

Curiosity, wonder, rupture

1

Few scientists are ever seen in science museums, of which the function is, in any case, to memorialize or recruit, not to inculcate craftmanship or enlighten public taste. Unlike art, science destroys its past.

Thomas Kuhn (1969)[1]

Science does not destroy its past so much as render it obsolete. Over time, science becomes history and instruments become artefacts. A scientist would not choose a three-hundred-year-old telescope over a modern version but the experience of trying to use one might make them more aware of their visual habits and conditioning. Seeing differently could sharpen their awareness of the framework in which they operate, and open new aspects and angles of approach. This also applies to artists although unsettlement can be convention, ornamentation or habit as well. Scientists still learn from, and even draw on, their past. Wanting to see further and move faster sometimes involves looking back at what might have been missed.

More than half a century from the time when Thomas Kuhn was writing, we invest more – not less – in the scientific past and in the past altogether. A world that can only be contacted through traces, fragments and murmurs is enticing. As science evaporates into electrical impulses, we dust off what we have of it in solid form in the attic: brass, paper and glass. How tactile and demonstrative! Scientists don't need all those redundant objects but they may need to be reminded of how solutions can arise: a lot of data, endless repeated experiments and then, sometimes, a notion that comes from the mind connecting differently.

In the summer of 1997, I had a correspondence with the Czech immunologist and poet Miroslav Holub – an exchange about science, museums and science museums. We wrote to each other by fax, a now obsolete but pleasing technology that retained some of the character of written correspondence. Holub, who died the year after our exchanges, is the only person I've met who was as much a scientist as he was a poet. He was internationally renowned in both fields. Too many scientists announce that they are 'also a poet' simply because they write the stuff in their spare time. I might say that I'm also a physicist because I struggle with quantum mechanics now and then. I have such respect for scientists that I assume they are intellectually superior and also that they share a poet's wide-ranging curiosity. Some are and do but some have a romantic idea about the 'poetic' which I don't expect. Poets seem naturally interested in how things work. My notebooks are full of details of how fossils, black holes or crystals are formed; of lazy language, rain dances, suspension bridges and binary star systems.

When I invited Holub to give a talk in London, my immunologist sister came along with some of her colleagues. They kept laughing at things no one else understood and I realised that his poems are full of immunological in-jokes. They are also welcoming, exacting and scrupulous. Holub had a broad vision, strong ideas and a true capacity for wonder, which he wrote about in his first letter:

Dear Lavinia,

Recently I had to answer, for Czech TV, the intriguing question, what are your seven wonders of the world? . . . I noticed in the answers of all participating scientists that we tend nowadays to find more wonders in nature itself, not in technology, not in the human artefacts which used to be the wonders two thousand years ago. This says something important about the human mind. We are less surprising to ourselves, our culture and our civilisation are less surprising. They are simply our identity. The real wonders are in the wide and cool world of stars, photons, genomes and neurons as we replace soft words with hard facts. Not only the so-called Known is expanding but the Unknown is expanding even more. And that's the real thrill . . . Is it possible to show not only the achievements of science but also the drama of science? We should show science as it is, which is a purposeful process of doubt and uncertainty.

Dear Miroslav,

When I was working in the Science Museum, I realised how much easier it was to marvel at Watt's Steam Engine than a fibre optic. The first calculator, Babbage's beautiful intricate Difference Engine was far more exciting to me than the black-box computer technology that has succeeded it. Is this not because earlier inventions were more tangible, their processes more easily demonstrated? For the non-scientist, it is far more interesting to trace a series of levers, wheels, pulleys or ropes, than to attempt to understand an electronic circuitboard or to guess what's going on inside a disk drive. This may be partly why we have ceased to wonder at our technological advances. We are less surprising to ourselves, as you say, because while what we are offered performs miracles, it does not fire the imagination.

The 'wide and cool world' of stars, photons, genomes and neurons you describe is for most of us no easier to understand than the black box. The difference is, I think, that it does fire the imagination with its uncontrollable human reverberations. Scientists are rightly infuriated by the way in which maths and physics are misappropriated and laden with human significance . . . But the universe is what we measure ourselves against and what we steer by; light, however analysed, defines our atmosphere; genetics and neurology confront assumptions we may not have known we had about the relationship between body and soul.

Dear Lavinia,

Speaking of body and soul, everybody has in their chest, behind the sternum, an organ called the thymus. Once upon a time, it was 'just a gland'. Once upon a time, it was the site of the human soul. Fifty years ago it was just tissue producing the white blood cells, the lymphocytes. Today it is the key organ of our immune system, a cellular university where lymphocytes learn the basic cellular logic and knowledge, what is the Self and what is the Non-self. The structure and the functioning of the thymus can be best understood as some sort of an organic computer within your own body. People spend their active scientific lives studying and modelling just one of the immense number of communications, interactions, movements and refinements which go on in the thymus.

My life was enriched by my fragmentary knowledge of the thymus. It is another universe I live with. Without this knowledge, I would just believe in a couple of soft words, like self, memory and wisdom. Science is the way to eliminate soft words and to create new universes and find new internal computers. Or, in Medawar's words, 'in science we have at least something important to be smart about.'

Dear Miroslav,

I agree that not enough is shown of the drama of science. Just as people assume that being a poet is all drama, they believe science to be a world of unflustered logic. The poet must be logical within the world of each poem and the scientist must take imaginative risks. Perhaps if the process of discovery and invention were more visible, scientific endeavour would be better understood. But there is also the hard and tedious work you describe which I think was more obvious when all the nuts and bolts were on display. With Watt or Babbage, you can sense the sheer laboriousness, the effort and sweat and repetition required. How can the same be shown for more recent discoveries and inventions? How can the scientist be humanised without their work being romanticised?

Dear Lavinia,

Sure, some sciences advance into the invisible and the unimaginable, and the popular mind trails behind. In fields such as mathematics, cosmology, genetics, biochemistry,

and of course in all kinds of modern technologies, the gap
is widening and the popular mind can't grasp both the
Unknown and the Known, so that the drama of science is
lost.

But, on the other hand, there is something very positive
about the gap: we are taught that there is an increasing
number of domains where we must just accept the opin-
ion of the experts. That nobody is supposed to have their
Theory of Everything and to elaborate on it in public.
That's one of the great lessons of civilisation, and it is a
moral lesson.

Dear Miroslav,

When scientists talk about probabilities instead of cer-
tainties, and about the unknown (not only that we may
discover but that which will always lie beyond us), I have
more faith in them than when they are sure. This is not
because I like my facts to be softened round the edges, but
because I like to think how active and changing and endless the process of discovery can be. Alterations in how
we look at the world, from Copernicus to Heisenberg, are
surely good for us: they lead to the humility required to
acknowledge the unknown. Perhaps the desire for a Theory
of Everything is the desire for a portable, adaptable answer
to all life's questions. Something that can sit in a pocket and
be used in all sorts of situations.

This palliative use of science is as bad as the ignorance
and superstition it has replaced, if not more so because
science can sound reasonable even when it has been turned
into such hocus pocus.

Dear Lavinia,

I like your 'palliative use of science'. It ranges from scientific mimicry used by modern shamans to newspaper statements on another cure for tumours. Sometimes it sounds like the football news: that from now on Newcastle is going to beat Manchester United fifteen times in a row.

For the general public, it is rather exceptional to hear the real scientific discussions and communications. And it is hard to blame the scientists. In Prague we now have a Learned Society, sort of a Royal Society without the kingdom. There, molecular biologists listen to physicists and astronomers to historians. They listen more attentively than poets listen to poets; poets get tired too soon. The only learned man who never listens, because he never comes, is a postmodernist philosopher . . .

Dear Miroslav,

My family are all doctors and scientists and coming across them at work has taught me something of the two extremes of the scientific experiences we have discussed.

My sister is an immunologist and one Sunday morning, I gave her a lift to her lab as she had to feed some cells. I was excited, imagining smoking test tubes, colourful jars of pharmaceuticals, Bunsen burners, and those hungry cells bubbling away somewhere. I thought her lab would be full of the drama of her work. It wasn't. It was a room full of inscrutable electronic equipment and cupboards of discreetly labelled jars. She pulled on a pair of rubber washing-up gloves, took what looked like an ice-cube tray out of a kitchen fridge and dosed each square with a drop from a pipette. I suddenly realised how much of her day was spent in an endless sequence of small repetitions and variations in the hope of getting a useful result.

My brother did a PhD in astrophysics, a study of spectra around a cluster of stars. I asked him once how it was going. 'I've had a good month,' he replied, 'I got a result.' 'What was that?' I asked, excitedly. 'Twenty million light years plus or minus twenty million light years.' He was struggling with an extremely abstract state of affairs but like my sister, needed to be methodical, just as my sister needed, however routine her work became, to remain imaginative.

Dear Lavinia,

That's exactly what I feel. I never go to the lab with the hope that today I will discover. I go to the lab hoping that we will be able to repeat the measurements we did six times before, that the labelling of the cells which failed three times may work at last and that the tissue samples were not displaced in the freezer. I go to the lab with the feeling I remember from high school: I have learned something but it's not enough. We must try again and again, and that's the moral of it, try again. And if we get, after a month, some suggestion . . . it will be like opening the gate of the unknown again . . . My problem with philosophy and human visions of our past, present and future is that I regard the mechanism of catching cold as intriguing as the problem of the natural world or the human soul, or even more.

Reading this exchange now, I want to take issue with myself. The ease with which someone understands the steam engine will depend on more than its parts being visible. If you have grown up in a world of cars and trains, you will understand it more easily than someone who has never come across an engine of any kind. And is something always more comprehensible if it is visible? I grew up before technology became invisible but for those born later, the invisible might be instinctively easy to understand.

Miroslav Holub was far more open to uncertainty than I, for all my talk of contingencies. I am also as susceptible to the romance of science as anyone else, casually exaggerating for effect. I remembered my brother's conclusion as 'Twenty million light years plus or minus twenty million light years.' It was a story I liked to tell and no one questioned it. When I mentioned it to him one day, he said, 'I was working on Omega Centauri which is (rounded up) 20,000 light years give or take . . . er . . . 20,000 light years. 20M light years would be extra-galactic and I wasn't doing that stuff.' His gentle correction, his intimate and understated relationship with his subject reminded me of Holub, the good scientist quietly pursuing their own small wonders.

2

Let us not too curiously examine divine works with human reasoning, but having been led along let us admire their artificer.[2]

This epigraph was added to Joris Hoefnagel's *Insects, Plants and Shells around a Chick in an Egg* (1592) by his son Jacob

(1573–1632). He – Joris – was renowned for adding images to text in a radical act of interpolation.* While his animals and plants invaded the page in ways that dazzled and disarmed, his son's intervention did the opposite, in this case advising the viewer to step back. Jacob made many engravings of his father's work and must have judged the market for these prints to be one which preferred to be told what to think. Or, in this case, not to think: you can be curious but just curious enough. If your interest strengthens into examination or you try to make sense of what you are looking at in terms of reason, you will lose sight of the image's purpose. It is a reminder of the infinite variety and mystery of a divine plan.

Seventeenth-century wonder was an experience of submission to something beyond 'human reasoning', with the consolation that you knew what lay in that beyond. Your mind could shelter in a sense of its own smallness and limits, and feel taken care of. The shell of the egg has been carefully broken. You want to see inside the shell but not be the one to break it. You don't want to disturb the chick and feel queasy about the ambiguity of it being neither dead nor alive. Without the title, you might not realise it is a chick at all. Its arrangement seems to be what interests the artist, not its status. The world is there to be looked at, to be visually explored and documented. No thought is given to the impact of this. We are only looking.

Curiosity is flattering and reassuring. It is about saying, 'I know something new,' rather than, 'This is new.' It gives us

* See his additions to the Bocskay Manuscript, the flora and fauna breaking out of the margins to take over the centre of the page, in 'Seeing clearly, glimpsing, picturing', p. 76.

230

more to talk about and less to think about, whereas wonder renders us speechless. Curiosity carries little risk of wonder's destabilising effect, which Aristotle and Plato agreed was the impetus for all philosophical questioning.*[3] If wonder depends on being prepared not to know then so does the gaining of knowledge. Hoefnagel's near contemporary Jacques de Gheyn II† seemed to be fascinated by the difference between curiosity and wonder. While we can only be curious about what is imagined, we are filled with wonder by what is actual but unexpectedly strange. The juxtaposition of *Study of Hermit Crab and Witchcraft* (c.1602) insists on the crab as more fascinating than the fantastical scenes behind. This is perhaps why de Gheyn's studies of witchcraft seem so ineffective in generating wonder. They have the air of being another branch of knowledge (such as folklore) and their cartoon-like shadows might be pointing to the preposterous importance attached to such practices. How much more magical is a crab who moves house!

While wonder is disorientation at seeing beyond what is known, curiosity can be an assertion of how much you are able to know. You acquire knowledge to show that you can. But curiosity can also be a healthy impulse. The travel writer Freya Stark, who was curious on an epic scale, deplored the fact that 'indifference should be so generally considered a sign of superiority the world over . . .' and talked about the difficulty she observed in others of concealing 'the strain which a total

* Socrates: I fancy, at any rate, that such [logical] puzzles are not altogether strange to you.
Theaetetus: No, indeed it is extraordinary how they set me wondering whatever they can mean. Sometimes I get quite dizzy thinking about them.
† See more on their relationship in 'Seeing clearly, glimpsing, picturing', p. 75.

absence of curiosity entails.'[4] Stark suggests that we are naturally curious and that the suppression of a spontaneous and active interest in the world around us takes considerable effort (or is the symptom of an inner malaise). We may be able to stop ourselves reacting but we cannot help but look.

3

The book that Joris Hoefnagel filled with animals and plants belonged to Emperor Rudolf II, who had a *wunderkammer* (a curiosity cabinet) full of marvels. These not only celebrated the infinite variety and mystery of the world but asserted the emperor's power and reach. He could not have a rhinoceros, but he could have its parts: a tooth, some skin, the horn. A painting of them was sent to Rudolf by his ambassador in Spain. He bought the lot.

In 1515, Albrecht Dürer produced his woodcut of a rhinoceros, an animal he had never seen.[5] The print became immediately well-known and has remained so. In his note above the image, Dürer makes clear that this specific rhinoceros is one that was sent from India to the Portuguese court and then on to the Pope, only the ship sank and it drowned. He based his depiction on descriptions and images, and while it is recognisable as a rhinoceros, it has the visual feel of something made up of parts. If you haven't seen something, and have to rely on other people's versions of it (which may contradict or confuse each other) then maybe you can never achieve a coherent image.

The seventeenth-century investigative artist or scientist was finding that the more they looked, the more there was to see.

Whether through a microscope or telescope, or with the naked eye, this would lead them beyond the bounds of vocabulary and knowledge into a wordless state of receptivity. We now equate the secular, objective (empty) eye with 'true' knowledge. An artist such as de Gheyn,* though, would have been influenced by Bacon and Galileo, not Heidegger, who lived some three centuries later. Both of the former signalled a disapproval of surrendering to irrational experience, associating it with the kind of knowledge they were looking to refute and replace. Curiosity may be 'useless', but wonder was 'broken' knowledge, pointing to a deficiency, an arrest in comprehension, an investigative collapse:

> . . . for if any man shall think by view and inquiry into these sensible and material things to attain that light, whereby he may reveal unto himself the nature or will of God, then, indeed, is he spoiled by vain philosophy; for the contemplation of God's creatures and works produceth (having regard to the works and creatures themselves) knowledge, but having regard to God no perfect knowledge, but wonder, which is broken knowledge.
> Francis Bacon (1605)[6]

It is at these broken moments that something leaps out at us – like one of de Gheyn's freed and projected images. The philosopher Mark Kingwell uses Heidegger's model of 'something going wrong with the equipment of the world', so that a quite ordinary object 'stands out'. If you hit your finger with a hammer, suddenly you consider the hammer. When something goes

* See 'Seeing clearly, glimpsing, picturing', p. 75, and 'Black and white and colour', p. 103.

wrong with *our* equipment, that is the tools with which we build a perception, we experience the same thing. An image jumps out at us – it makes an *impression*. The Platonic metaphor is of a block of wax on which we impress our sensations and conceptions 'as we might stamp the impression of a seal ring.'[7]

For de Gheyn, little had stayed in place so much would have stood out. His heightened forms appeal to the eye but resist penetration leading to a paradoxical state in which the observer is visually captivated and intellectually baffled. He was working in ways, and with subject matter, that had yet to be theorised. For that moment he, and his images, were speechless.

4

De Gheyn was contemporary to Galileo, whose mathematical model of the world was to replace the old system of correspondences. Galileo was tortured by the Inquisition for insisting that the earth moved around the sun. He discovered planets, established the law of falling objects, and when he heard of the telescope from the Netherlands, taught himself to grind lenses and make better ones. His drawings of the phases of the moon revealed its craters and mountains. No wonder he wrote with disdain of the *ometto curioso*, the idly curious little man or in this translation, 'funny little fellow'. This is in a critique of the poetry of Tasso, which he compares to a cabinet of curiosities:

> Here I feel as if I am entering the studio of some funny little fellow, someone who took pleasure in decorating it with things that, either because of their antiquity or their rarity or some other feature, have an out of the way air

about them, but which are in fact just trifles, perhaps a petrified crab, or a dried chameleon, a fly and spider frozen in a piece of amber, some of those little clay figurines that they say are found in the ancient tombs of Egypt . . .[8]

On 'entering' the poetry of Ariosto, however,

I see opening before me a treasury, a tribunal, a royal gallery, adorned with one hundred ancient statues of the most celebrated sculptors, with an infinite number of complete stories, and the very best of the most famous painters, with a great number of vases; crystal, agate, lapis lazuli and other gems, and filled, finally, with rare, precious, marvelous, and the most exquisite things.[9]

We are not to take this fellow with his funny little treasures seriously. He has no taste. He collects anything old or 'out of the way': withered and dusty items of uncertain provenance. His collection sounds unconvincing and somewhat depressing. Not that I would expect to enjoy Ariosto's room either with its committees and categories, those hundred canonical works, and the endless stories whose endings are already known. There is so much of everything in his room, and it is all gorgeous and perfect. In both cases, style is manifested as an act of vision, as a kind of collecting and arranging. It is about what has been noticed and how the author will be seen.

The pandemic reminded us that seeing is often not enough. We want to be in the room or under the sky, to hold each other and to stand in front of things. The visual contact that we experience through physical presence is quite different to that we receive from virtual images. When Europe's borders re-opened, I went to do some work in Vienna and spent what spare time I had in galleries and museums. In the Kunsthistorisches Museum, I found a number of objects from Emperor Rudolf's collection. They were in a series of small, dimly lit rooms, which felt like being inside his curiosity cabinet. Rudolf's collection moves freely between the natural and the artificial or artful, often combining these in displays of virtuosity. Intricate scenes depicted on a nut or shell place him on high, able to take in a vast panorama, to hold it in his hands. As I wandered back and forth, I noticed that there was one case that attracted every man who passed through. They lingered beside it, looking wistful. It contained one of the emperor's automata: a golden ship which moves itself across the table as pipes and drums are played and cannons boom. The ship is laboriously mechanical and utterly unlifelike – but it is golden and it moves!

This collection is five hundred years old but doesn't look it. So many of the emperor's objects are gilded or polished into agelessness – their beautiful colours, brilliant gleams and smooth surfaces evoking timelessness to the point of sterility. These days we like things that look old but only in a certain way. They should appear to have had a lot of respectful human contact reflected in their worn forms and surfaces. They have substance and strength, and have endured. They should express time as a slow passing. I don't imagine that the emperor was interested in time.

That day in the Vienna museum, my curiosity was most strongly held by two books which I could barely see as they were contained within a black box to protect them from light. The room was so dim that I felt the light of my gaze, the force of my curiosity, might erode them. I pressed a button and the table top slid back revealing a single page that I couldn't touch or turn. There were virtual facsimiles available which seemingly took me through the surface of the image, but they had none of the thrill of touch, the artist's touch with pencil, brush or crayon.[*] Touch disturbs the surface of the page, and so the artist's presence is a form of disruption that is recorded in the work and can be seen but not felt in a reproduction.

Wonder is the purest form of belief. We accept the existence of something for which we have no words even if we have encountered it as something written or said. Heidegger distinguished wonder from curiosity by its quality of unknowing: we come up against the limits of comprehension and articulation, and have to feel our way into something and then find a way to describe it. It is the point at which knowledge runs out and we are asked to believe in what we have never seen.

I like to be taken to the edge of my understanding and language and ideas, and to have my mind slowed so that I can experience what I would describe as wonder. Something has such an impact that I detect a moment of emptiness before the brain rushes in to build an explanation. A moment of wonder is a tremendous relief. There are no words. I can rest now.

* See 'Seeing clearly, glimpsing, picturing', p. 79, on high-resolution images of manuscripts.

Disorder, slippage, glare

1

When Elizabeth Bishop was five years old, her mother had a breakdown. One day, while being fitted for a dress, she started to scream. She was committed to an institution and while she lived another sixteen years, Elizabeth never saw her again. The shock to the child was perpetual: 'A scream, the echo of a scream hangs over that Nova Scotian village. No one hears it; it hangs there forever . . .' Bishop was born in Massachusetts in 1911 and while she is celebrated as an American poet, it was not America that formed her. Her father died shortly after her birth and her mother returned home to Nova Scotia when Elizabeth was three. It was an agonisingly uncertain time as this auto-biographical story, 'In the Village', shows:[1]

> First she had come home with her child. Then she had gone away again, alone, and left the child. Then she had come home. Then she had gone away again, with her sister; and now she was home again.
>
> . . .
>
> The dress was all wrong. She screamed.
> The child vanishes.

The mother has the power of presence or absence while her child can only wait. She has been wearing mourning for two years, since the death of her husband, and this new dress is to be purple. She panics, perhaps she should still be wearing black, and her scream is itself an obliterating blackness. The child survives by absenting herself (something she may have learned from her mother). The scream is in the past but the child's own vanishing is in the present – perhaps she will never stop vanishing. Where can she go? She vanishes into herself.

The narrator places this event at a distance. The child becomes 'I' halfway through while the mother remains 'she'. But we are confined within the child's point of view and are forced to look at everything except what happens. The child cannot face the scene and so she concentrates on what might be generalised as the furniture: the pinned purple dress and the wallpaper's 'wide white and dim-gold stripes'. She looks first at how 'the wallpaper glinted' and then stares out the window: 'the elm trees outside hung heavy and green', focusing desperately on the blacksmith's shop just beyond the garden, her gaze straining towards the moss on its roof just visible above the lilacs. She conjures the blacksmith – friendly, reassuring and utterly present – and the heat and noise (the life) of his forge. As soon as she can, the child goes to him and when she comes back, she is not allowed upstairs but joins her aunts who are unpacking her mother's things.

'Things' is a large loose net of a word and it dredges up a motley but specific collection of stuff. The child becomes 'I' when she starts to 'examine' these things as if the writer emerges with a notebook in her hand. There are black clothes and white clothes, collars and trims, hats and parasols, a case for calling cards and a small silver-mesh bag. Her mother is described through this fussy apparel as uneasy, elaborate, black and white, and offering little in the way of comfort. The child plays with a spilt bundle of crumbling postcards, listing the colours of their ink, the stamps, the handwriting. Focusing on what things look like, catching your own eye, can help you not see what is happening. And if you're busy looking at something, you are not expected to meet anyone's eye. The child is sent to postpone the dress fitting for a second time and, unable to face the dressmaker, records every detail of the dressmaker's house with its heaped offcuts, lettered pattern-pieces, lace and buttons. She even scrutinises the beard of the king on the five-cent piece she is given.

When her mother reappears, the child notes only the dress she is wearing before going out to take the cow to pasture. On that walk, she passes new store-window displays of summer hats and shoes, which she saves up to examine on her return. For now, she makes do with the minister's hat as he passes on his bicycle, the design of iron railings and the colour of the cow's fresh dung: 'fine dark-green and lacy and watery at the edges'.[2] Before long, her mother is returned to hospital but the child limits her observation of this to itemised lists of the cake, chocolate and books – Longfellow, Tennyson, the New Testament – sent weekly to 'the sanatorium' by her grandmother. The colour of the dress reverberates in the purple tassle on a bottle of scent and the indelible purple pencil with which the packages are addressed. It is the child's job to take these to the post office, and she carries them so that no one can read the label. Her mother's scream persists:

No one hears it; it hangs there forever, a slight stain in
    those pure blue skies . . . too dark, too blue . . . the colour of

the cloud of bloom on the elm trees, the violet on the fields
of oats; something darkening over the woods and waters
as well as the sky . . . The scream hangs like that, unheard,
in memory – in the past, in the present, in the years
between . . . Its pitch would be the pitch of my village. Flick
the lightning rod on the top of the church steeple with your
fingernail and you will hear it.[3]

Trapped feeling is displaced into sound trapped in the air.
The child can see her mother's scream as a 'small stain'. It is
no more perceptible than a sheen, a dusting, something others
might not notice but that she will always see. Unlike the summer hats or the blacksmith's clang, the scream will not become
part of the furniture. There is no weaving into fabric or settling
into memory. Instead there is an overloaded sky that looms
above the village, which shrinks away from both the story and
the reader. All we can do is flick the lightning rod on the tiny
steeple as if it were an emotional tuning fork.*

In 2007, I spent a week in this house. It is as neat and white
as its neighbours, which sit close by. Bishop must have seen and
heard a great deal, and she would have been seen and heard
herself, indoors as well as out. The floors creak and the walls
are thin. Her bedroom, where I slept, is compact but (as is characteristic of Bishop) its space is used well. A cupboard, wardrobe and set of drawers have been built flush into one wall as
in a ship's cabin. She probably enjoyed the suggestion of being
at sea. She later wrote about her 'proto-dream house' being

* Looking at the world through a screen also shrinks it and places us outside
it, neutralising and muting any experience we might think we have had. See
'Staying put, locked doors, wallpaper', p. 174.

a remote shack on a cliff that she used to see in the distance, an improvised structure, a crooked box that was never quite secured. When I traced the lines of her room they wobbled and when I tried to close the door it jammed on the ancient linoleum. Those cupboards and drawers reminded me of her belief in 'closets, closets and more closets'.[4] She was reticent and private, and found herself with much to contain just as she resisted settlement, neatness, permanence – the kind of life where lines are clear and always meet.

An unpredictable, unsecured childhood changes your approach to mapping the world around you. If things are harder to fix, you grasp them more tightly and contrive order where you cannot find it. The world needs to be predictable to the extent that its impact can be managed and so you invest things with meaning, find a way to connect and explain. The acuity that results from this can be productive – there is richness in attentive vision, and you can read the smallest signals and detect every resonance. But it can also disturb. You lose control because you want so much of it, which can lead to a state in which significance, connection, cause and effect are amplified by an overriding internal narrative. You might feel you are seeing more deeply but you will be more easily persuaded that you are mistaken. The unsettlement that amplifies your powers of perception also undermines them. If you know that your experience of the world is unreliable, why would you trust your senses?

While childhood trauma is formative, it is not what makes a good poet. Bishop was as precise as she was receptive, and always in control of her work. She knew that while poetry is driven by the self, it enlarges out of that into something more broadly human, an imaginative act that depends upon discipline and technique in order to succeed.

Nova Scotia is where Bishop established a visual preoccupation with pattern, process and form. Even then she was weighing up aesthetics and arrangements: 'The summer before school began was the summer of numbers, chiefly number eight . . . Four and five were hard enough but I think I was in love with eight.'[5] When she got stuck on 'g' she decided with characteristic independence of judgement that 'My alphabet made a satisfying short song, and I didn't want to spoil it.'

The intimacy of Bishop's poetry is not that of sharing the self. What she shares, to a remarkable degree, is how she sees. The thrill is in the live-action replay of her adventure with her subject: the initial surprise, the feeling out, the determination to describe. Her best poems are landscapes into which the human experience has been dissolved or panoramic accounts of an animal knitted into the fabric of its place such as the armadillo or the moose. She directs and revises our gaze, charting surfaces before following through to any narrative or investment (which she does not deny as part of how we see).

This is not the poetry of the corner of the eye. Bishop adjusts her gaze but keeps looking, unwavering, alive to revision, and always outwards. She is interested in what things do to each other rather than to her. The young Elizabeth stayed on with her grandmother for just three years but retained her connection with Great Village all her life, returning every summer. Wherever she lived, Bishop sought out 'the intimacies and improvisations of village life'.[6] She relished the everyday and wasn't afraid in her poems to wade in, to grab and prod, to get her hands dirty with 'the muck and mire of life'. In this, she was not romantic: 'I want to avoid the picturesque.'[7]

Nova Scotia is the setting of many of her best poems, and its geography of vast skies and wild coastline offers the sense that Bishop is on the edge of something deep and dangerous into which she might disappear and into which she might want to – an ambivalence that is one of the most striking aspects of her work. She admits rather than conceals uncertainty, and transforms volatility into the dynamism of poetic vision, concealing great swoops of focus and scale beneath her measured surfaces: 'As we lie down to sleep the world turns half away/through ninety dark degrees;/the bureau lies on the wall . . .'[8] She was a traveller, intent on new sights and experience. She found contemporary British poetry cautious and reserved: 'I like fanatics, people who go all out.'[9]

The hard brightness of the light in Nova Scotia concentrates its colours. The iridescent firs, blazing red barns and luminous bare fields explain why Bishop writes so often of this landscape as if it were painted: 'You know about the Bay of Fundy and its tides, I imagine, that go out for a hundred miles or so and then come in with a rise of 80 feet. The soil is all dark terra-cotta color, and the bay, when it's in, on a bright day, is a real pink; then the fields are very pale lime greens and yellows and in back of them the fir trees start, dark blue-green. It is the richest, saddest, simplest landscape in the world . . .'[10]

The scale of the Bay of Fundy is hard to convey. You look out over miles of mud and water while the bay cuts so far inland that you forget that this is the sea. The tide roars in and retreats, and things come to rest only to be washed away again. I might be describing a Bishop poem or her life, any poem or any life:

'The world is a mist. And then the world is/minute and vast and clear.'[11] This movement between the contingent and the absolute is something she understood and was able to articulate. Nova Scotia is the place that described it for her.

2

There is a place in Lapland called Arctic Circle. You can step across a painted line and receive a certificate for doing so although the actual circle changes position all the time. It wavers over the north pole like one of the lassos the Saami use to catch reindeer, and slips according to the tilt of the earth on its axis. When the reindeer are rounded up, they run in a circle, always anticlockwise, the opposite direction to magnetic flow.

When you come to the Arctic, even just this edge of it, the feeling of slippage is immediate. In midwinter, the nights are twenty hours long and the world is snow. While my mind let go of time, my body clung to any sign of it. Late each morning, a small sun inched into view and rolled along the horizon. The sky lightened to grey for three or four hours and there might be a faint wash of yellow and blue, like the glimpse of a real day happening somewhere else. Then the sun tipped away again in a spill of earthy red. As I watched it go down, my eyes uncontrollably closed. I turned to apologise to the person sitting next to me only to find that he had fallen asleep.

Arctic darkness is anything but consistent. The only constant is the magnetic north, over the pole, a black haze like iron filings in a physics experiment. When the Northern Lights appear, their wild streaks and sheets and pillars reminds us of how volatile darkness can be. The aurora borealis are a form of elemental disturbance (electron showers stirring up hydrogen and nitrogen) and the rawness of their colours, like that of the small sunset, suggests a time when light was first occurring. The Finns call the Northern Lights *revontulet* or foxfire, after a mythical fox who swept snow into the air with its tail, igniting it. If you talk to the Northern Lights, they will come down and grab you. If you don't wear a hat, they will clutch at your hair.

There is a time of day when this world becomes very clear, a winter twilight called *sininen hetki* or the 'blue moment'. Blue light rises out of the snow and, because everything is covered in snow, the whole world turns blue. My mind was trying to make sense of this and wanted to trace the blue back to its source but I couldn't find it. The dark sky seemed to have nothing to do with this as if it had switched itself off. The blue appeared as if it rose out of the world. It even rose out of me. It was a blue without texture and offered no association other than that of atmospheric perspective – how things turn blue in the distance.* How peaceful it was to stand out there in the dark and snow and blue light, watching the world fill up with its own space.

The Arctic Highway runs north along a river which was buried under fields of snow. The road was buried too, and the few cars that came this way followed its compressed grey trace past signs that could not be read because they had been wiped out. This was fairytale snow, hanging in glittering swags from trees that doubled over under its weight. It emphasised telegraph wires and heaped up cosily against windows.

Snow scatters light and flattens perspective. It is visual absence and physical substance. There was nothing to read in

* See 'Black and white and colour', p. 103, on blue and distance.

it, just a fundamental continuity. I couldn't feel lost because I didn't expect to know where I was. I had no compass and anyway from the North Pole, whichever direction you head is south. It was impossible to travel fast, or on foot, and impossible to make much noise as the snow imposed a muffled acoustic. I let myself fall backwards as I would into a feather bed.

The bedrock of Finland is so old that it contains no fossils (and so no fossil fuels). Ice sat on Finland for ten thousand years, causing it to sink, and when it melted and the glaciers shifted, they snapped the tops off mountains and lacerated the ground which filled up with water. The land is still rising, more quickly in the north, a tilt that is causing lakes to tip themselves out. Medieval ports are now fields while new islands are emerging. And now the snow is disappearing, the ice is melting, and more of the world will start rising and sinking.

Some days it was minus ten which is the temperature at which ink freezes in a pen and water thrown from a cup will become ice before it hits the ground. Your lungs might bleed. Even now when buildings are heated and sealed, and streets can be as brightly lit as a film set, there is a genetic inheritance of cold and dark. I met a Finnish psychiatrist who was an expert in Arctic Personality Disorder. He said that darkness is less of a problem than the cold, which makes the body hoard blood around the heart, depriving the brain. He explained that the Arctic personality is characterised by *sisu* – adaptability and perseverance. Such people had a tendency to be greedy, stingy and ruthless. They hoarded information, were suspicious of strangers and 'sexually specialised'. His other interest was suicide, and he remarked that women had started to kill themselves in the same way as men. They used to take an overdose or drown themselves, 'so as not to leave a mess', but now they were just as likely to use a gun.

At Arctic Circle, you can visit Santaland. Local teenagers work there as elves but the atmosphere is more like that of a craft shop than a theme park. I asked Santa what he thought of the idea that the long winters caused depression. He laughed: 'We've lived in darkness for a thousand years, why should it trouble us now?'

3

Summer evenings can feel like a perpetual late afternoon, a time of winding down as the northern light graduates through dusk to darkness so slowly that we barely notice it happening. It takes time to get dark, which gives us a chance to adjust as the body reacts, adapts and moves towards sleep. If the light didn't fade, time would stop. This happened when I returned to the Arctic Circle at midsummer. The sky dimmed a little in the small hours but no more than that, and my stay flattened into a single very long day. It was like living in a sun-filled present tense with no hint of yesterday or tomorrow. The white nights had another kind of profound physical effect. They filled me with joy, but it was joy without purpose or limit. I lay on my bed at three or four in the morning, craving sleep as the sun filled the room and continued to pump me full of euphoria. Being endlessly happy is exhausting.

My first night was spent in the port of Bodø in northern Norway, where every building from the fishery to the church was compact, functional and low. The town looked as if it had been constructed from a kit and could be packed up and driven off in a single day. The hotel room was more of a cabin and there was no blackout at the window, just curtains made of thin strips of flameproof material. Only the sea and the great stone harbour walls looked as if they had any permanence. My mind had set out to meet the dark but here it retreated. I found it difficult to concentrate or to engage.

Even softened by cloud, the midsummer light was insidious. It could be as jarring as the striplights under which we queue or wait for a transaction, a decision, news. I was waiting for something to happen, for the sky to break, but nothing would happen and all night people circled the harbour square or rode back and forth in cars and on motorbikes, trying to make time pass. I lay down for three hours and once or twice dipped beneath the surface of sleep.

The next day the ferry left at what would have been dawn if the sun had gone down and sailed for five hours towards a dark line that eventually broke up into islands. The light was strong and the sea blue-black with a far more terrifying depth than when in midwinter darkness. There were hundreds of islands. Their cliffs were so tall and sheer that each sat in black shadow, giving the impression that it was hovering on the sea. Everything was unanchored. There were too many islands, too much water and too much light. One passenger stayed inside, videoing a map of the islands on the cabin wall.

Unqualified happiness is unnerving, too. Like a cloudless sky or an empty page, it is boundless, blank, unreadable. The French writer Henry de Montherlant said that 'happiness writes white', meaning you can't see it – it is shadowless white on white. It isn't interesting. A well-lit white room is without atmosphere and brings to mind the clinical and sterile: think of the operating theatre. It is an unnatural space and the objects within such a place can also appear unreadable. Whiteness is undisturbed light. It has no form, no detail and can be so bright that we cannot meet it with our eyes. It is through cloud that we can look at the sun, through pollution that we can trace the progression of a sunset as the ultraviolet end of the spectrum breaks up in the filthy air, leaving us a glorious residue of rose and gold. In our stories, we need a beginning, a middle and an ending, and that is how we map our days. We need change, to feel ourselves moving and a sense of what we are moving through.

Vaerøy is one of the Lofoten Islands, where the sun does not rise for a month in winter or set for two months in midsummer. The beach is little more than a ledge of blanched sand and the sea is so thickened by cold and light, so vitreous, that it is somehow more than clear. During my visit, the sea was calm but whatever washed up had been pounded and scoured. There were heaps of stones worn down into huge, beautiful eggs shot through with quartz; a sheep's vertebrae, eye socket and jaw as smooth as paper; the translucent shells of crabs, sea urchins and limpets; fraying husks of seaweed.

This was bird land. There were no trees so they had to make do with the ground cover of rock and gorse, and their eggs lay hidden beneath my feet among the egg-shaped stones. Oystercatchers hurtled past screaming, warning or distracting. Redshanks blurted from fence posts, their nests scattered among whatever grass they could find. Masses of gulls and terns exploded out of the cliffs where auks, which come into land just to breed, built nests on tiny ledges. Their eggs are tear-shaped so that they won't roll. Crows mobbed the oystercatchers, after their fledglings. Cormorants wheeled and dived.

People kept their own hours and the guesthouse served up slabs of halibut or cake whenever anyone wanted a meal. There were children outside playing football at three a.m. I read all the books I'd brought with me in the first thirty-six hours and started pulling Norwegian volumes off the shelf in hope of pictures. I found photographs of a man catching an eagle by hand. There used to be a lot more sheep-farming on the island and eagles were considered such a threat that the government paid for each one caught. Just as their children earned pennies scraping out cod cheeks in the fishery in winter, the islanders supplemented their income by catching birds. Three men climbed a mountain but only two would come down. It was said that crows could only count up to two and so would not realise that someone had stayed behind. The third man was entombed in a stone cairn with a small gap, next to which he laid some bait attached to a string. The crows settled to eat, which reassured the eagle who moved in on the feast. The man had to inch the bait back towards him, make a grab for the eagle's claws and pull the bird into a small space where it couldn't spread its wings. These days the eagles are protected, the sheep are more or less gone, and new ways of making money have to be found. As my landlady said: 'We can't all be cutting one another's hair.'

Midsummer is the feast of John the Baptist, and also when the trolls come out to make mischief and the witches go to meet the devil on the mountain top. In the late afternoon, people started to appear along the coast building fires. They shared the traditional midsummer feast of dark beer, salami and semolina but this was not a festive affair. The light was so bright that the flames were invisible. There were no leaping shadows, no glow. They stayed long enough to make sure that their unwanted furniture and tyres had properly caught alight, and went home long before midnight.

I waited on the beach as the sun made its way to the centre of the view. At midnight exactly, it started to sink down onto the sea so smoothly that it looked like a ball about to bounce. And then it did bounce – immediately rising again. I felt thrown into reverse. For all my years in the city and my nights diluted by tungsten, neon, sodium and halogen, I was more attuned than I knew to the setting of the sun. It was my body, and not my mind, that insisted that this bouncing sun was all wrong. It was wrong to be able to see so far that the earth curved, wrong to have a fifty-foot shadow, wrong to be sleepless and wrong to be so happy. It did not feel like happiness after a while. Happiness is a burst of connection, coherence, harmony or equilibrium. It is not constant. The loss of darkness had me trapped; light met every thought and glance. I had no imagination there.

4

An eclipse is a planetary peepshow – the picture forming beyond our control and only briefly becoming clear. It's as difficult to hold onto the experience of watching one as it is to remember that it's an optical illusion. The sun is four hundred times the size of the moon, which only appears to cover it because of angle and distance (the sun is also four hundred times further from the earth).

For scientists, the dimming of the sun is a chance to study it more closely. I just wanted to know what it felt like to see it disappear. In March 2015, there was a total solar eclipse that could only be viewed onland from two places: Svalbard in northern Norway and the Faroe Islands, which lie halfway between Scotland and Iceland. I decided to travel to the Faroes, even though there was a good chance that clouds would block the view. My flight was full of 'eclipse chasers' who wanted to experience totality, the moment the moon blocks the light of the sun and the sun's corona becomes spectacularly visible. Laden with meteorological and camera equipment, they exchanged nervous remarks about the weather forecast. The mood was a mixture of deep yearning and business-like intent. They knew they could do nothing to ensure a clear view, or any view, of the eclipse but they would cross the world for the possibility. Almost all of them were men.

The Faroes consist of eighteen volcanic islands scattered roughly in the shape of an arrowhead. They erupt out of the sea on some of the tallest basalt cliffs in the world. Waterfalls spill down tiers of rock behind villages of maybe a dozen houses. It rains often, and fog and cloud descend. As ten thousand visitors arrived in the days leading up to the eclipse, the sun barely appeared. When it did, it was blinding. The Faroes are muted and low-lit. The soft greens, reds, yellows and greys of the landscape are echoed in the colours of the houses. There is gentle street lighting and very few signs. If you are used to the level of brightness found in most city centres, you might think all the shops were closed. The cruise ships anchored nearby for the occasion blazed away in comparison.

Everyone was asking everyone else from where they were planning to watch the eclipse. Which island? Which side of which island? On top of a hill or down by the sea? The weather forecast kept changing but the eventual advice was to climb a hill but not to go too high as you might find yourself surrounded by cloud, which could settle on roofs and roads. There would be thirteen planes circling above the islands but the rest of us had to accept that whether we headed north-east as advised on Wednesday or north-west as advised on Thursday, the odds remained at two to one against clear skies.

A total solar eclipse happens in the same place on average every 375 years. The next one to be seen from the Faroes will be in 2245 but the last was relatively recent. This was the second eclipse that Finnur Johansen had been able to experience by going no further than his own backyard. He lived just along the road from the house where, in 1954, he watched his mother-in-law's chickens rush into the henhouse as the sky grew dark, tuck their heads under their wings and go to sleep. Minutes later when light returned, the cock crowed and the chickens re-emerged. It was midsummer and he could also remember the flowers closing and opening, and how after that brief dark moment he was struck afresh by their colours. The islands were not troubled by global media and cruise ships then. State Geologist Jóannes Rasmussen wrote in his diary: 'Rain and foggy, impossible to work, the solar eclipse was from 11.06 to 1.32.' Sverri Dahl, the Keeper of National Antiquities, noted simply, 'The solar eclipse. The cathedral and colours. The birds are flying, but silence this very moment.'[12]

Eclipse day dawned and I was woken by people outside my window excitedly photographing a patch of blue sky. After three days of cloud, its brilliance was shocking. I went halfway up the hill above the town from where there was a grand view of the bay over which the sun would ostensibly be shining at

254

8.38 when 'first contact', the moment the moon starts to consume the sun, was due to occur. The speed and direction of distant planets are easier for us to predict than the weather over our heads. People stared at the sky as clouds appeared and disappeared as if by sleight of hand. No one seemed able to make sense of it. All around me men were nursing their cameras, putting on filters and hoods and taking them off.

In 1878, the American astronomer Maria Mitchell took some of her students to observe a solar eclipse in Wyoming. This party of women travelled unescorted and you can infer from Mitchell's tone in issuing directives to her students that she was not going to be impeded by convention:

> You will see Nature as you never saw it before – it will
> neither be day nor night – open your senses to all the
> revelations. Let your eyes take note of the colors of Earth
> and Sky. Observe the tint of the Sun. Look for a gleam
> of light in the horizon. Notice the color of the foliage.
> Use another sense – notice if flowers give forth the odors
> of evening. Listen if the animals show signs of fear – if
> the dog barks – if the owl shrieks – if the birds cease to
> sing . . .[13]

I prepared myself to see it all as clearly as I could: to open my senses, focus, observe, notice, listen. Ten minutes before first contact, the sun was fully visible. People cheered even as the clouds slid back into place. Now and then the sun slunk past behind a lacy veil of cloud, the bite in its side growing larger. This was the moment to put on the eclipse glasses. Their effect is the opposite of 3D, the view becoming a diagram of a tiny yellow disc being swallowed by darkness. The process was smooth to the point of indiscernable, rather like trying to watch a flower open.

It was hard to look away but important to do so because, as Mitchell says, an eclipse is not just about what is going on in the sky. As totality approached, heavy clouds rolled in and we lost sight of the sun completely but the air started to thicken and dull, the bay gradually blackening like an unfixed photograph. The bar of light on the horizon melted and we disappeared into the moon's hundred-mile-wide shadow. The Faroese weather is so local that people half a mile away were able to see what I had missed: the sun inked out, a moment's absolute blackness and then the corona flaring from its edges as light finds its way through the moon's uneven surface. After two minutes and forty-five seconds of totality, there was a smooth fade back up into light. What hit my eye after this brief darkness was colour.

In June 1927, Virginia Woolf travelled to the north of England to watch an eclipse which, like this one, was obscured by cloud. She travelled with a group to Yorkshire by train and records the same anticipatory tension, 'we kept looking at the sky' which was 'fleecy' and 'mottled'. Woolf was disappointed by the pale fields and grey farms, the families dressed in Sunday best black, as if already impatient for a rich visual experience. When they reached their vantage point high on the moors, the sun rose as a 'gold spot' and then moved in and out of the clouds as they pursued it with their 'smoked glasses', feeling anxious and already cheated until 'the colour was going out' and the valley darkened into a 'delicately tinted' red and black. 'Nothing could be seen through the cloud. The 24 seconds were passing' and then 'rapidly, very very quickly, all the colours faded . . .

the light sank and sank; we kept saying this is the shadow; and we thought now it is over – this is one shadow; when suddenly the light went out . . .' When it returned, Woolf too saw colours 'as if washed over and repainted.'

Phenomena such as an eclipse may not frighten us now that we can explain them but they confound us just the same. Counting those twenty-four seconds might have anchored Woolf however much she wanted to give herself up to the experience: 'How can I express the darkness? It was a sudden plunge, when one did not expect it; being at the mercy of the sky.' You cannot help but seek out the machinery. You find yourself trying to keep up with what you're watching and then, once it's over, speculating on when it might be seen again. Woolf ended her diary entry with 'Then – it was all over till 1999,'[14] which was when a total solar eclipse would next be visible in Britain.

As we wander away from such experiences, confused and amazed, the cosmos can seem like a perfect machine but there is slippage within it as well. The moon is slipping away from us and the sun expanding. There will come a time when they do not ever align and there will be no more eclipses.

1

Stories can arise from the need to explain something: why the sun disappears at night, why it's not a good idea to go into the woods after dark or why a hundred and thirty children disappeared from a small town in northern Germany in the late thirteenth century. The story of the Pied Piper hovers between history and myth, and is full of the kind of detail that settles into fact. There is a specific date, an actual street through which they passed, and the number of children is always given as a hundred and thirty.

> In the year 1284, on the day of John and Paul on the 26th day of June, 130 children, born in Hameln, were led out of the town by a piper, dressed in many colours . . .[1]

A watercolour of the Pied Piper in Augustin von Mörsperg's *Reisechronik* (1592) is said to be a copy of a window destroyed in the seventeenth century, which had been painted in a church in Hameln in 1300 to commemorate the event. The piper looms over the story while the town and the children are lowly and exposed. The way into the mountain is usually portrayed as a discreet opening that leaves its surroundings unperturbed, a manifestation or an apparition that you probably imagined and will never see again. We do not see where it leads. It is often left out of the picture, perhaps because it is the hardest part to believe. The hole in the mountain is a tear in the page. Here, it is a massive rupture that confronts us with the nothingness it holds.

Details add substance, especially in the form of statistics. An exact place and time make this a document rather than a story. It was not some children or many children who disappeared but 130: five classrooms or thirty families. The disappearance may be invisible but it has been witnessed, described, heard, recorded and read.

> All this is written in the town-book at Hammel, where
> many high folk have read and heard the same.[2]

The horror of the children being piped away is enlarged by how easily this moment flows from the ordinary. The town is plagued with rats. A man arrives who promises to get rid of them. The town tries to cheat him. Then the story takes an unexpected turn. When the Piper doesn't receive his promised reward, he repeats the act but this time takes the children, leading them into the mountain. His power is the music of his pipe, an invisible charm and one to which anyone could succumb.

The story extends from what is seen to what might be seen, the unseen and what cannot be unseen. No wonder it has lingered for centuries. To be lost inside a mountain is not to be invisible but to be unseen. The page, the painting, the window, the mountain, are all the surface of the visible and teach us about visual boundaries. We can replicate them on screen where we can magnify the detail, the brushstroke, the grain.* We can see

* See the high-resolution mouse in 'Seeing clearly, glimpsing, picturing', p. 79.

more but we cannot get any further. The surface remains. Did anyone actually see the mountain open? There are witnesses.

> A boy that being lame and somewhat lagging behind the rest, seeing this that hapned, returned presently backe and told what he had seene . . .[3]

He was too slow in following the Piper and too late to enter the mountain, and so he saw the other children disappear. Having been an outcast, he is now a witness although he cannot show anyone what he has seen. And he's not sure what he did see because it is impossible that a mountain could open and close like that. Perhaps he's haunted by other things he does not want to have seen. We might make a disturbing event invisible by replacing it with a version we feel able to look at.

> this a childrens' maid saw, who with a child was drawn after from afar, and turned about, and brought the report into the town. Büntingus writes that two of the children returned, and that the Kopfelberg had opened itself, and that the Piper had gone in with the children, of whom there were altogether 130.[4]

Büntingus adds that the mountain was where criminals were hanged. He also says that of the two children that returned, one was dumb and could only point and one was blind and could only tell. If you did not see it, you must take the word of someone who did, and their memory has to be ratified as testimony 'all compared with the original documents and the testimonie of the witnesses thereof, which let him that doubteth be condemned'.

If we swear we saw something, does that make us sure we did?

The children are often described as lost rather than taken or killed, as if it were an accident and they could still be recovered. They are the object and the Piper the subject: he 'led them out of the city gate into a mountain, where he lost them with himself . . .'[5] It is his story not theirs, and we cannot bear for them to become more visible – to see their faces or hear their names – because we know that they are going to disappear.

Whatever the legend's starting point, it has a palpable sense of being prompted by some actual event. There were reports of 'dancing mania' related to the consumption of bread made with rye infected by a fungus called ergot, which has the same hallucinogenic effects as LSD. These might have been an escalation of the dances traditionally held on St John's Day. The children might have joined the Children's Crusade of 1211 or an eastwards migration or, most darkly, might have been eaten during a time of famine. In Hamelin itself, the disappearance was treated as historical fact.

> . . . such a history is painted on a window in the parish
> church . . . The pitiful wonder is also inscribed in the town
> book, and the folk of Hameln are accustomed in their
> writing to date their letters from the loss of the children.
> Some set down this wonder in the year 1282 . . .[6]

The children are not only enchanted by the music of the pipe but by the piper's dress. He makes himself visible, drawing the eye so as to distract attention from what he is doing. He also makes himself motley (as if he could be anybody) and unreadable. He escapes convention, performs magic, appears from nowhere and disappears back. He is an arrival of colour and noise, excitement and strangeness, in this small, quiet world. Artists paint the children as caught up in the visual magnetism of the piper. They take on his shapes and rhythms, his gestures, the colours of his coat. They break down into the landscape as they are gently led off the sunlit slope of the mountain along a path that is sliding into a pocket of darkness. They could tell themselves that what lies ahead is only shadow. The piper draws them on, keeping himself in sight but also pulling away as if to say *Keep up or I will disappear*. They do not, or cannot, let him out of their sight.

The purpose of the story might have been to warn the young about the dangers of what lies beyond the mountain: do not let yourself be seduced by brightness, by music, by the different and new. Do not wander away because you will get so lost that you will be locked into darkness. You will never come back.

> and comming to a little hill, there opened in the side thereof
> a wid hole, into which himselfe and all the children, being
> in number one hundred and thirtie, did enter; and being
> entered, the hill closed up again and became as before . . .[7]

What we see depends on how it is described to us. A mountain is a towering vertical, a solid form of absence, one that is too large to be easily seen.[*] Maybe it wasn't a mountain at all but a 'little hill' that grew in the telling in order to match the incredible nature of the event.

The children's absence is held in place by silence in 'the street

* See mountains in 'Black and white and colour', p. 103.

in which no music is played', Bungelose-strasse, the street without drums, from where they are said to have left the town.

> . . . they could not but haue kept memorie of so strange a thing, if indeed any such thing had there hapned the folk of Hameln are apt to date their letters from the loss of the children.[8]

They could not but have kept memory of so strange a thing. They do not want to remember but they have to. The feeling of not believing what you've seen is aligned with that of not being believed. Both require a considerable level of visual confidence to be overcome. The story of the Pied Piper continues to haunt us. Children still disappear into mountains. Someone must have seen.

2

Before we were old enough to walk out into the night, my big brother and I went through a phase of slipping out of the house at dusk. We weren't going anywhere. Instead, we turned back to spy through the windows. We watched our mother tidying up the kitchen, our sister playing a game, our father doing paperwork, our little brother chattering to himself. We were out there in the not-quite-dark looking in on the ordinariness of early evening. No one realised we were gone, let alone came looking for us, but we could conjure drama from thin air. We pressed ourselves flat against the wall, inching closer to a window and straining to escape notice.

The aim was not to see but to become unseen. We were eight

and ten years old, and testing the idea of stepping outside family and home. It felt like discovering a new power. We had what now seems like a remarkable amount of freedom, spending all day out with our friends, but less sense of volition than a child might these days. We felt able to wander and so didn't need to gather the will to do so. I've been told I often slipped away, even as a small child. That, for me, is the point of invisibility – not being able to discover people's secrets but still moving among them and not being seen, not needing to respond. I didn't really want to be apart from my family. Had I looked in the windows and seen no one, had the lights gone off, I would have been terrified. I wanted to be able to step outside my life but only if I could easily step back. There is no point in being invisible unless someone is expecting to see you.

In their twenties, with both parents dead, Virginia Woolf and her siblings rented a house in Cornwall two miles from Talland House, where they had spent their childhood summers. They arrived at night and immediately walked up the hill to Talland, which they hadn't seen for ten years.

> There was the house, with its two lighted windows . . . all,
> so far as we could see, as though we'd left it that morning.
> But yet, as we knew well, we could go no further; if we
> advanced the spell was broken. The lights were not our
> lights; the voices were the voices of strangers. We hung
> there like ghosts in the shade of the hedge, & at the sound
> of footsteps we turned away.[9]

Those lights that invite us in only do so if they are 'our lights'. Otherwise we must remain in the dark, at an unintrusive distance, accepting that as far as these lights are concerned, we do not exist. This is what it's like to watch someone disappear into dementia. My father kept trying to go home and gave his address as a combination of four places he had lived in. He was coming home in the dark fifty years late. Who is that at the window? Where is the key? He managed himself as if stuck outside: sitting indoors in his coat and going to sleep on top of the bed while still in his clothes.

When I was eleven we moved to the country, where I found a darkness I could disappear into. As I approached the house at night, a distance of a hundred yards could fall endlessly open. I hesitated before wading in. Night swallowed my hand in front of my face. I was starting to learn that parts of myself could slip out of sight, could refuse me, and I welcomed the feeling that I might dissolve into this blackness. I had yet to be fixed by anyone's gaze. There was freedom in this but it also meant that I could not fix anyone, could not keep them.

The village had a scattering of lamp-posts but after dark, you needed a torch to walk down the main road. There were regular power cuts that first winter. The newspapers were full of pictures of families gathered around a vague source of radiance, looking plucky and happy and playing a board game or cards, as if spending more time together had to be restorative. We no longer gather round a hearth. We have learnt how to carry off heat and light, and build our homes accordingly with corridors and staircases, in a series of small rooms. So when heat and light failed us, we did what we could to preserve our habits and arrangements. We were allocated a candle, lantern or oil lamp, and each took their own small source of light away into their own private dark.

Virginia Woolf describes the core self as this, a private dark, and the 'being and doing' of life as a gaseous whirl around a black hole: 'To be silent; to be alone. All the being and the doing, expansive, glittering, vocal, evaporated; and one shrunk, with a sense of solemnity, to being oneself, a wedge-shaped core of darkness, something invisible to others . . .'[10] Evaporating and shrinking are ways of moving beyond notice rather than disappearing altogether, and essential to the freedom of being unseen.

When I turned on my bedroom light, I couldn't see anything out there and so assumed myself unseen. But we had moved from a city street shaded by large trees to the middle of a village where my room looked out onto the road, and I was clearly visible. One day my father said that someone had mentioned seeing me lying in bed reading when they passed on the bus. He thought it was funny but I was mortified. I found thicker curtains in the attic, devised elaborate ways to test their opacity, and drew them even during the day. The spell of invisibility, of slipping outside, of seeing nothing in reflection, had been broken. From then on, I could not help but see myself and could not imagine myself unseen.

The self-consciousness of adolescence was a wrenching into light. I stared into the mirror at flaws made monstrous by the scale of my attention. All my energy went into vigilance against exposure. I turned myself up, invested in surfaces – hair, make-up, clothes – and learnt not only to meet the gaze of my enemies but to stare so fiercely that I could turn them back on themselves.

To be seen too clearly is to be reduced. Much of you gives way, becoming transparent and so invisible. Only the basic

lines remain – anything from a sketch to a diagram depending on the level of attention and the determination of that
gaze, what it accepts and refuses. I dyed my hair and clothes
black, and stopped making noise to the point of speechless-
ness. I shut down at school and found myself unable to learn
or remember. Dispensing with 'all the being and the doing', I
simplified into silence and darkness. If I was lucky, this might
become a starting point.

3

The pilot Amelia Earhart suggested that you can observe the
world more completely from the sky: 'You haven't seen a tree
until you've seen its shadow from the sky.'[11] An aerial view
offers a shadow world in which vertical forms are laid horizontal and become clear. It is true that you cannot really see a
tree when looking up and towards it. When a tree lands on the
ground, its height and scope are always surprising. The reve-
latory nature of shadows seen from the sky is used by archeol-
ogists who make aerial surveys at either end of the day, when
the shadows are longest, in order to locate 'shadow sites', those
which are only perceptible when their shadow can be seen. The
artist Jananne Al-Ani made two films of such places across the
desert landscapes of the Middle East, not just the imprints of
archeological sites but of industrial, military, agricultural and
mining activities.* Al-Ani was specifically interested in the
conception of the desert as empty space, and in the representation of military conflict, atrocity and occupation: 'I began to

* *Shadow Sites I* (2010) and *Shadow Sites II* (2011)

investigate events for which there was no visual record, no photographic or filmed evidence: just verbal or written accounts.'[12]

In Seamus Heaney's last collection, *Human Chain*, there is an untitled poem that begins, 'The door was open and the house was dark'.[13] This elegy for a friend contains an undocumented emptiness. There is less than no one there, a negative presence. His dead friend's house has fallen open, as have the poet and the poem. The house, simply entered, has become its own emptiness – as we all will. He calls out his friend's name and the response is a silence that 'grew/Backwards', reversing him out of the place and reabsorbing his utterance.

Even though he does not belong here he meets 'no danger,/ Only withdrawal, a not unwelcoming/Emptiness . . .' By resisting the impulse to describe the unknown, he allows it to remain just that. More than that. He sets it beside another emptiness: 'as in a midnight hangar//On an overgrown airfield in late summer.' The hinge of simile keeps the house and the hangar apart. One cannot become the other any more than the poet can inhabit the death of his friend. In both places, the human presence has arrived at the wrong time of day, of the year, of the epoch, of life.

The door is left open by that final floating line but more so by the surprising conjunction with which the poem begins. The door being open *and* the house being dark is not things as they should be but things as they are. In a process of disinvestment, this poem, an elegy, rejects conclusiveness even when it comes to connection except in the form of conjunction. This is the falling short of the act of connection *by definition* or as Elizabeth Bishop puts it, 'Everything only connected by "and" and "and".'[14]

What we are left with is this 'not unwelcoming emptiness'. The poem does not come to meet us any more than the meaning of death or absence come to meet the poet. Instead it lets us in through an act of withdrawal, making way for our own specificities while providing us with conjunction rather than anything as contrived as consolation.

The accumulations and erosions that constitute ground.

What the drought reveals: gardens, airfields, ruins.

How others render us invisible.

How rarely we are unseen.

The power of the image that is unseen.

On not talking about what we have seen.

Of trying to unsee what we have seen.

How we close our eyes in order to feel more.

The imagined image

1

The work has neither name nor subject and yet it is a substantial presence, a painstaking and robust accumulation towards expression. Its density is assertive but poised. I am trying to say that it is measured rather than tentative, and that it achieves reticence, even silence, in the matter of meeting our expectations.[*] If we need more, we are left to imagine it.

The most rewarding step in the process of making art might be the moment of conception, which comes before knowing what the work will look like or express. It is a sensation, a visceral excitement and while the work is impossible to describe, it will never again be as perfect or as clear. You can see, inhabit, feel and understand it with a completeness, a coherence, that we generally only find in dreams. Leonardo da Vinci wondered why we see something so much more clearly in dreams than when we imagine it.[1] Imagining is the first conscious act of envisaging. We are applying ourselves to seeing this thing. We do not see clearly because our eyes are no longer empty.

When Howardena Pindell speaks of her work, you recognise an artist who is clear in her intentions: 'So then I decided to draw the grid. I numbered each square and then I put calibration marks

* See also Eva Hesse's studio works in 'Becoming, resistance, dissolve', p. 93, or Jacques de Gheyn's mouse studies in 'Seeing clearly, glimpsing, picturing', p. 81.

and either I used letters or numbers. And I would cut it in sections so that I could do a section at a time, sewing it . . .'[2] She knows that she will construct the work by hand because she does not want it to 'have any sense of being free of a mark'. Her abstractions hold us at the moment of an image about to be imagined and slow us down further through the deliberate, overt, methods by which they are constructed. They are a record of their own making. Her surfaces are cut, stitched and perforated; she punches holes in paper and uses the resulting little discs, sometimes numbering them but always at random. Paint is forced through layers and gaps, and occasionally sprinkled with glitter. These rich and complex textures entice us to stay where we are: on the surface having not yet reached an image. We are satisfied by their tactile intricacies. We remain even longer because of a commanding sense of intention. This practice is not about resistance or reaction. It is an intellectually autonomous act of investigation that allows its framework and instruments to emerge when already underway. A large canvas is rendered manageable by being broken down. It is cut up but its arrangement is held in place. There's a system for which numbers or letters are used as symbols. The parts fit and the engine moves.

2

In 1821, Charles Babbage designed Difference Engine No. 1, a calculating machine and a step towards the first computer. A portion of it was assembled by Joseph Clement, his engineer, in 1832. It had two thousand parts and represented less than 20 per cent of the design. The Difference Engine could not be easily grasped like an abacus or slide rule. Who could comprehend two thousand parts let alone twelve thousand? The Engine opened up possibilities that Babbage tried hard to envision: 'The whole of arithmetic now appeared within the grasp of mechanism.'

He had imagined one machine and once it had been built and he could see it, he was able to imagine another: 'A vague glimpse even of an Analytical Engine at length opened out, and I pursued with enthusiasm the shadowy vision.' In order to work out how to build the second machine, he needed to model it and then design each part. As what we imagine becomes clearer, it starts to reveal its mechanisms and then the components required for these to work. Babbage needed others to bring this vision into reach: 'Draftsmen of the highest order were necessary to economize the labour of my own head.' He was also hiring men to build the 'experimental machinery' with which he tested and adapted his design.[3]

Babbage gave up his role at Cambridge University and moved to 'a very quiet locality' where he had outbuildings and land. The coach-house became a forge and foundry, the stables a workshop. He built more workshops as well as a fireproofed building 'for my drawings and draftsmen'.[4] His primary assistant was almost tempted away to work on the construction of the new railways (which Babbage complained were stealing all the good draftsmen) but he gave the man a raise and swore to persist with his work, even though the cost meant that he lived on bread and cheese.

Babbage met his collaborator, Ada Lovelace, when he was forty-one and she was eighteen. He tried to amuse her with a mechanical toy but he was addressing someone who at twelve had researched the anatomy and principles of flight, written up a theory of 'flyology' and designed a flying horse powered by steam. Babbage invited her to see his Difference Engine and soon realised her genius as a mathematician. Her father was Lord Byron, whom she never met, and her mother Annabella Milbanke, a great intellect who was nicknamed by Byron the 'Princess of Parallelograms'. She had her daughter well-schooled, and Lovelace brought the confidence of privilege and the asset of an early mathematical education to her work. Her dexterity of vision made her indispensable to Babbage.

Ada Lovelace described her approach as 'poetical science'. Her ability to think about concepts and abstract processes, metaphysical questions, the 'poetic', directly informed her ability to draw out the potential of Babbage's designs: 'What is Imagination? . . . the combining faculty seizes points in common, between subjects having no apparent connection . . . Imagination is the Discovering Faculty, pre-eminently. It is that which penetrates into the unseen worlds around us, the worlds of Science.'[5] Through her understanding of the role of the imagination, Lovelace found a means of flight but she had no desire to escape. Rather, she wanted to see the unseen.

In 1842, an Italian military man called Luigi Federico Menabrea wrote an account of the as yet unbuilt Analytical Engine following a meeting with Babbage: 'The illustrious inventor having been kind enough to communicate to me some of his views on this subject during a visit he made at Turin, I have, with his approbation, thrown together the impressions they have left on my mind.' Despite this casual tone, Menabrea wrote eight thousand words which as Lovelace observed, took it for granted 'that the mechanism is able to perform certain processes, but without attempting to explain *how* . . .' Menabrea is dazzled by possibilities, as we are by new technologies, without being curious about their workings: 'To give an idea of this rapidity, we need only mention that Mr Babbage believes he can, by his engine, form the product of two numbers, each containing twenty figures, in *three minutes.*'

Ada Lovelace translated Menabrea's text, prompting Babbage to ask why she had not written upon the Analytical Engine herself, being so 'intimately acquainted' with the subject. She responded that it hadn't occurred to her (not that she could not or would not write but that it was inconceivable that she might). Babbage suggested that she add some notes to her translation, which she agreed to do. He credits her for taking care of the algebra, confessing that the one part he undertook himself, 'to save Lady Lovelace the trouble', she returned to him with corrections having found a serious error. Her eventual notes ran to twenty thousand words, three times as long as Menabrea's own text.

Babbage understood 'that the whole of the developments and operations of analysis are now capable of being executed by machinery'. The Difference Engine was a calculator but the Analytical Engine was a computer. It was Lovelace who could see that the language of symbols offered new forms of expression:

> This science constitutes the language through which alone we can adequately express the great facts of the natural world, and those unceasing changes of mutual relationship which, visibly or invisibly, consciously or unconsciously to our immediate physical perceptions, are interminably going on in the agencies of the creation we live amidst.[6]

Lovelace's notes give a thorough explanation of how the Analytical Engine would work, using the analogies of weaving and mills. Both processes require material and she is as clear about the limitations of the machine as she is of its possibilities: 'The Analytical Engine has no pretensions whatever to originate anything . . . it has no power of anticipating any analytical relations or truths. Its province is to assist us in making available what we are already acquainted with.'[7]

In 1852, Ada Lovelace died of cancer. She was thirty-six. Babbage died in 1871 never having built the Analytical Engine. Seven years later, a committee was formed to investigate the feasibility of constructing it from Babbage's papers. He had only produced models of certain parts and the committee's proceedings do not suggest much confidence: 'A large number of drawings of the machinery are also in existence. It is supposed that these are complete.'[8] They felt that Babbage had an 'utter disregard of any questions of complexity' (which is where Lovelace would have stepped in). The papers stipulated a thousand columns of fifty wheels each of which depended on 'a vast machinery of cams, clutches, and cranks for their control and connection'. This would cost at least ten thousand pounds and perhaps three or four times as much. They decided not to go ahead even as they understood the machine's potential:

we think the existence of such an instrument would place within reach much which, if not actually impossible, has been too close to the limits of human skill and endurance to be practically available.[9]

Ada Lovelace was the translator not only of a text about this invention but of Babbage himself. She could articulate his ideas as well as their implications: 'The science of operations, as derived from mathematics more especially, is a science of itself, and has its own abstract truth and value.'[10] The imagined image is given a place to remain unrealised in a language of symbols just as it is held in Howardena Pindell's surfaces.

3

Ana Maria Pacheco works towards her sculptures by drawing studies or making models 'as guides. If I was to recreate something small on a large scale I'd just be repeating myself, and that is not interesting to me.'[11] Making an idea visible is not just about a series of repetitions and enlargements. The work remains a process of meeting the unseen, the unknown. The three figures in her *Study for Sculpture (Remember) 4* (2018) might be the before, during and after of someone seeing a terrible thing. One is about to look but does not want to: her face is lowered while her gaze is pulling ahead. The next is caught up in the act of seeing and her eyes are fixed, while the third has already seen and is turning back in order to see something else.

We observe ourselves observing and think we see. For all that we want to see further, there is much that we do not want to see. This fear is bound up with what we expect to see, which is what we imagine. The most vivid images might be of things we never actually see just as our lives are shaped as much by what we do not do or have not encountered. The desire to see further can also be the result of the need to rush past. We can remain in a comfortable and anticipatory state of being about to look without the risk of contact or impact. To see means we have to respond, to act.

'Things that are not at all are never lost' says Leander to Hero in Christopher Marlowe's version of the myth.[12] We're tantalised by possibility but the fundamental potency of the imagined image lies in how it is designed by us to meet our needs. When Leander swims the Hellespont each night, he can see nothing except the lamp that Hero has set in the window of her tower. He has to imagine her, which might be why he is so determined. In his mind, she will be what he wants her to be. This lovely line has a sinister context: it is his argument against her sworn chastity.

> This idol which you term virginity
> Is neither essence subject to the eye
> No, nor to any one exterior sense,
> Nor hath it any place of residence,
> Nor is't of earth or mould celestial,
> Or capable of any form at all.
> Of that which hath no being do not boast;
> Things that are not at all are never lost.[13]

He is locking out her 'idol' by denying its perception. It cannot be seen, heard, tasted, smelt or touched, nor can it be found either in this world or that of the gods. It is not capable of form so cannot even be imagined. If something is unimaginable, its implications become meaningless. Leander's argument is spurious but it is an illustration of how we can persuade ourselves that something does not exist by dismantling the ways in which we might confirm its existence.

4

Death is also inconceivable on Leander's terms but we give it many forms. Jacques de Gheyn's drawing of a woman on her deathbed (1596) pulls equally towards presence and absence. Her hands and face are thoughtfully delineated but most of what we can see is that which conceals her. There's a surprising sense of radiance emanating from her peaceful almost smiling expression and the energy of those lines. Another study of de Gheyn's, *Woman and Death* (1600), has an invigorating formal freedom. It suggests that the woman is about to be re-absorbed into the black hole of non-existence, where there is no shape to take and no place to be. She is unperturbed by and even unaware of death, whose visage is concealed so that we are confused by the tenderness of his embrace as he lifts her into himself.

On one of the four days of my father's dying, my brother remembered a story he used to tell. One night during his National Service, he found himself flying alone in heavy cloud. All he had to go on was his instruments. He held his nerve, trusted the readings and flew blind until all of a sudden the plane rose above the cloud and he was flooded by the light of a full moon. I'm as interested in the instruments as I am in the cloud and the moon, and I try to be patient when I cannot see, to hold my nerve in hope of what might be revealed to me.

Sometime in the late 1980s, I asked my brother (who was then in his early twenties) how the elements were formed. He sent me a nine-page handwritten letter complete with diagrams, formulae and an explanation of fusion versus fission. It is the clearest description of the vast extent that I have ever read.

Dear Lavinia,

Everything in the universe is made up from molecules and atoms, and the molecules are in fact groups of atoms bonded together, so everything in the universe is made up of atoms.

An atom is made up of a positively charged nucleus containing neutrons and protons (and a few other particles) around which orbits a cloud of negatively charged electrons . . .

Electrons aren't made up of smaller particles but neutrons and protons are. In the beginning of the universe, just after the big bang, the energy was so intense that these elementary particles were flying around too quickly to form protons and neutrons. As the universe expanded, the matter in it cooled and protons were formed. As these have a positive charge, they would attract the negative electrons to them and so once the universe had cooled sufficiently, you would expect it to be made up mostly of proton–electron pairs orbiting each other. In fact this is just what you find and to this day the universe is composed of a vast majority of hydrogen . . .

Nowadays there is about 75 per cent hydrogen and 23 per cent helium and 1 or 2 per cent everything else. (These figures are extremely rough.) So how have the extra helium and the elements heavier than the helium (i.e. the atoms with bigger nuclei) been formed? The answer is in the stars.

Stars are huge furnaces fuelled by nuclear explosions, and hydrogen atoms are fused together to form helium, and then helium is fused to form heavier elements. The stars are heavy element factories . . .

It's after the big bang. The universe contains clouds of cooling gas; 80 per cent hydrogen. A cloud is out in space, hardly affected by anything else and so, in the vacuum, feels its own gravity pulling it inwards. So the cloud begins to collapse in upon itself. Now the whole of a star's lifetime is a struggle against this collapse: a struggle it finally, inevitably, loses.

As the cloud collapses into a ball which then continues to contract, the centre heats up. Its temperature continues to rise unchecked until it reaches several million degrees (centigrade or kelvin). At this point, the temperature is so high, hydrogen fusion reactions can finally take place. This generates energy and (i) the energy streaming out from the centre holds off the collapsing outer layers; (ii) the gas ball begins to 'shine', it becomes a star . . . The surface is only a few thousand °C so hydrogen fusion only takes place in the centre. (The trade's name for hydrogen fusion is 'hydrogen burning' but in fact it's completely different to actual *burning*.) . . .

Most of matter is in fact empty space, void. The thing

that stops you walking through walls isn't matter bumping into matter but electric charges repelling each other.

Hydrogen 'burns' to produce helium in this way for several thousand million years. The fusion produces starlight and stops the star collapsing under its own gravity. Eventually the hydrogen in the core is all turned into helium and the fusion reactions begin to die. The star begins to collapse some more and the core temperature goes even higher . . . the region outside the core then reaches a few million degrees and the hydrogen there starts to fuse. So you get a shell of fusing hydrogen which slowly moves outwards . . . but the shell cannot stop gravitational collapse alone. As the core temperature reaches several tens of millions of degrees, the helium that has been produced by hydrogen fusion (plus the 20 per cent that was there originally) begins to fuse too.

This gives off the energy to hold off gravitational collapse and keep the star shining for a few million years. Even before the helium is used up, the next reactions start happening . . . So these reactions keep the star stable and shining. Eventually, of course, they use up the helium in the core. Then these reactions falter, the star collapses some more and heats up, and they continue to take place in a shell, slowly moving outwards just behind the shell of fusing hydrogen.

The star then continues to collapse until the core reaches 50–100 million °C when the carbon and oxygen fuse in various ways producing various products . . . These reactions burn in the centre and, with the help of the shells of fusing material around them, keep the star going for a few

million years more. The core runs out, the star collapses a
bit, heats up and the reactions move out in a shell.

Now the core contains nuclei with 14 or more
protons . . . and they repel each other too strongly to
combine. The core collapses till the temperature reaches
2,000 million °C at which point the heat is so great, nuclei
start to break up a bit. Then the silicon nuclei (or whatever
kind it is) can fuse with the fragments of other nuclei . . .

Remember the fusing shells? They're all still there. The
star starts to look like an onion. The core contains nuclei
with about 56 neutrons and protons in them . . . nickel and
iron (Fe) for example . . . the star can keep fusion going
until it starts to produce iron, nickel and so on and then it's
the end of the road.

Where do the uranium, silver, gold, tin, iodine,
barium, platinum, bismuth and at least 50 other elements
come from?? There's a problem with the elements from
hydrogen to iron (weights 1–56) too: now they've been
produced in the star, how is it that they're here on earth?
How do they get out of the star?

(At this point I went to bed)

Hello Lavinia,
Sunday morning
. . . Yesterday I left the star hanging there, suddenly
run out of all possible sources of nuclear energy in its
core. The core collapses rapidly and as before, it heats up
enormously. At about 4,000 million °C, the iron it has so
painstakingly produced . . . is broken up into helium . . .
at 6,000 million °C the helium is turned into neutrons.

These neutrons stream out from the collapsing core and bombard the nuclei in the outer layers. At the same time the outer layers (where nuclear fusion possibilities have not been exhausted) are brought very rapidly to extremely high temperatures by the collapsing core. Explosive nuclear fusion and intense neutron bombardment simultaneously blast all but the core of the star into space *and* produce significant numbers of heavy elements by r-process [rapid process] neutron capturing. So, many heavy elements are produced *as* the star explodes, not before.

After the explosion, the material (still mostly hydrogen, even after all this!) is thrown into space and ends up in the gas clouds. This may stay as it is, or form more stars or even, heaven forbid, end up as a planet.

Some things should be said.

The core of the supernova collapses to a neutron star or black hole. There are two types of supernova. The other is caused by a star expanding and dumping its outer layer on a close binary star. At the height of a supernova explosion, the star can throw out more light than the rest of the galaxy (quite a death throe) but in fact most of the energy given off is *not* in visible light.

A lot of what I have said only applies to heavy, massive stars. Light stars don't go supernova.

The Chinese in 1054 AD observed a supernova which is now a shell of gas still spreading outwards from an intensely bright central spot. I think when this supernova went off, earth didn't have a night for several days it was so bright (as all these lovely heavy elements, silver and tin, were being produced).

Did you know 'helium' = 'helios' (sun) + 'ium'
(element? stuff?) because it was discovered in the spectral
lines in sunlight before it was known on earth?

The stellar spectra I've got on my desk left the stars of
the cluster Omega Centauri in 13,000 BC. Now they're on
my desk (in some form) . . .

love,

Reynold

One thing beside another (a foreword)
1 Elizabeth Bishop (1911–79), 'The Fish', in *The Complete Poems 1927–1979* (Farrar, Straus & Giroux, 1979)

Caves, sleep, absence of light
1 Frank O'Hara (1926–66), 'An Image of Leda', in *The Selected Poems of Frank O'Hara*, ed. Donald Allen (Vintage, 1974)
2 *Cave of Forgotten Dreams*, dir. Werner Herzog (2010)
3 O'Hara, 'An Image of Leda'
4 'Und dieses einen Weges kamen sie.' Rainer Maria Rilke (1875–1926), 'Orpheus. Eurydike. Hermes', in *Neue Gedichte* (Insel Verlag, 1907)
5 Edmund Burke (1729–97), *A Philosophical Enquiry into the Sublime and Beautiful: And Other Pro-Revolutionary Writings*, ed. David Womersley (Penguin, 1998)
6 This section draws on a conversation with the neuroscientist Professor Colin Blakemore (1944–2022), Institute of Philosophy, University College London, 14 August 2014
7 John Hull (1935–2015), *Touching the Rock: An Experience of Blindness* (SPCK, 1990), republished as *Notes on Blindness: A Journey Through the Dark* (Wellcome, 2015)
8 John Locke (1632–1704), *An Essay Concerning Human Understanding*, 1689, ed. Roger Woolhouse (Penguin, 1997)
9 Locke, 'Epistle to the Reader', in *An Essay Concerning Human Understanding*

Solidity, appearance, dullness
1 John Locke, *An Essay Concerning Human Understanding*, 1689, ed. Roger Woolhouse (Penguin, 1997)
2 J. M. Barrie (1860–1937), *Margaret Ogilvy*, 1896, cited in the introduction to J. M. Barrie, *Peter Pan in Kensington Gardens and Peter*

and Wendy, ed. Peter Hollindale (Oxford University Press, 1991)

3 J. M. Barrie, notebook, 1922, cited in the introduction to *Peter Pan*, ed. Hollindale

4 Vladimir Mayakovsky (1893–1930), 'A Cloud in Trousers', trans. Kathy Lewis and Bob Perelman, in *Russian Poetry: The Modern Period*, ed. John Glad and Daniel Weissbort (University of Iowa Press, 1978)

5 R. S. Thomas (1913–2000), 'Perspectives: Mediaeval', in *Collected Poems: 1945–1990* (Phoenix, 2000)

6 Pliny the Elder (23/24–79), *Natural History*, trans. H. Rackman (Loeb Classical Library, 1952)

7 John Lydgate (1370–1449), 'The Complaint of the Black Knight', *c.*1403 (HardPress Publishing, 2013)

8 George Crabbe (1754–1832), *The Borough* in *Life and Poems of the Rev. G. C. Crabbe*, 1834 (2nd edn, John Murray, 1847)

9 Crabbe, *The Borough*

10 Rembrandt van Rijn (1606–69), *The Sampling Officials of the Amsterdam Drapers' Guild*, known as *The Syndics* (1662), Rijksmuseum, Amsterdam

11 Virginia Woolf (1882–1941), cited in Peter Sager, *East Anglia: Essex, Suffolk and Norfolk*, trans. David Henry Wilson (Pallas Guides, 1998)

12 Samuel van Hoogstraten (1627–78), *Academy of Painting; or, The Visible World* (*Inleyding tot de Hooge Schoole de Schilderkonst*), 1678, ed. Celeste Brusati, trans. Jaap Jacobs (Getty Research Institute, 2021)

13 Autobiographical letter from Luke Howard (1772–1864) to Goethe, in *Luke Howard: His Correspondence with Goethe and His Continental Journey of 1816*, ed. with a commentary by D. F. S. Scott (William Sessions, 1976)

14 Autobiographical letter from Howard to Goethe

Distance, deception, glow of fire

1 Willa Cather (1873–1947), *My Mortal Enemy* (Alfred A. Knopf, 1926)

2 Cited in Cynthia Haveson Veloric, 'Golden Girl by Augustus Saint-Gaudens: The Regilding of Saint-Gaudens' Diana', *Incollect* (1 August 2014)

3 *New Yorker* (27 February 1965)

4 Ovid (43 BC–AD 17/18), *Metamorphoses*, trans. A. S. Klein (Border, 2014)

5 Ovid, *Metamorphoses*

6 Ovid, *Metamorphoses*

7 Stephen Crane (1871–1900), *Maggie: A Street Girl* (D. Appleton, 1893)

8 Crane, *Maggie*

9 Crane, *Maggie*

10 Crane, *Maggie*

11 O. Henry (1862–1910), 'The Lady Higher Up', in *The O. Henry Short Story Collection*, 1 (Merchant, 2019)

12 Henry James (1843–1916), 'The Real Thing', 1892, in *Complete Stories*, 4: *1892–1898* (Library of America, 1996)

13 *Evening News*, October 1911, Philadelphia Museum of Art Archive

14 Letter from Riccardo Bertelli to Henri Marceau, 17 March 1932, Philadelphia Museum of Art Archive

15 Letter from Harold Voorhis of New York University to Fiske Kimball, Director of the Pennsylvania Museum of Art, 7 March 1932, Philadelphia Museum of Art Archive

16 Letter from D. F. Kingsley of the New York Insurance Company to Dr Brown, Chancellor, New York University, 16 December 1931, Philadelphia Museum of Art Archive

17 Cather, *My Mortal Enemy*

18 Henry James, *The Awkward Age*, 1899 (Penguin, 2006)

19 Charles Norris, chief medical examiner of New York, cited in Harrison Martland, 'The Occurrence of Malignancy in Radioactive Persons,' *American Journal of Cancer*, 15 (1931)

20 Lavinia Greenlaw, 'The Innocence of Radium', in *Night Photograph* (Faber and Faber, 1993)

21 Florence L. Pflazgray, 'Radium Victim Battles Death with

Courage', *N.J. Daily Courier* (30 April 1928)

22 Cecil Drinker cited in Richard B. Gunderman and Angela S.
Gonda, 'Radium Girls', *Radiology* (February 2015)

23 Harrison Martland, 'The Occurrence of Malignancy in
Radioactive Persons'

24 Clarence Lee, president of US Radium, 1928, cited in R. E.
Rowland, *Radium in Humans: A Review of US Studies* (Argonne
National Laboratory, 1994)

25 'Radium Poison Hopeless', *New York Journal* (26 May 1926)

26 *Finger-ring*, c.300 BC, British Museum, excavated in a cemetery in
Naukratis, Nile Delta

27 Lucius Apuleius (*c.*124–70), *The Golden Ass*, trans. Robert
Graves, ed. and rev. Michael Grant (rev. edn, Penguin, 1990)

28 Apuleius, *The Golden Ass*

29 J. G. Ballard (1930–2009), *Miracles of Life: Shanghai to
Shepperton, an Autobiography* (Fourth Estate, 2008)

30 Apuleius, *The Golden Ass*

31 Ivor Gurney (1890–1937), 'After-glow', in *Collected Poems*, ed.
P. J. Kavanagh (Fyfield, 2004)

32 Crane, *Maggie*

Boredom, repetition, fixatives

1 John Ruskin (1819–1900), *Praeterita I*, 1885–9, in *John Ruskin:
Selected Writings*, ed. Kenneth Clark (Penguin, 1964)

2 Ruskin, *Selected Writings*

3 Karl Klingemann, letter, 10 August 1829, in Sebastian Hensel,
The Mendelssohn Family (1729–1847) from Letters and Journals
(Harper, 1881)

4 Felix Mendelssohn (1809–47), letter to his family, 14 July 1831,
in *Selected Letters of Mendelssohn*, ed. W. F. Alexander (Swan
Sonnenschein/Macmillan, 1894)

5 Felix Mendelssohn, cited in David Jenkins and Mark Visocchi,
Mendelssohn in Scotland (Chappell, 1978)

6 James Scott Walker, *An Accurate Description of the Liverpool and*

Manchester Railway (J. F. Cannell, 1832)

7 Felix Mendelssohn, letter to his father, Abraham Mendelssohn-Bartholdy, 25 August 1829, in *Felix Mendelssohn, A Life in Letters*, ed. Rudolf Evers, trans. Craig Tomlinson (Cassell, 1986)

8 Letter to Abraham Mendelssohn-Bartholdy, 11 August 1829, in *A Life in Letters*

9 Martin Butler and Evelyn Joll, *The Paintings of Turner* (Yale University Press, 1984)

10 *Reisebriefe von Felix Mendelssohn Bartholdy aus den Jahren 1830–1832*, ed. Paul Mendelssohn Bartholdy (Drei Brucke Verlag, 1862)

11 Felix Mendelssohn, letter to family, April 1829, in Jenkins and Visocchi, *Mendelssohn in Scotland*

12 Félix Nadar, *Exposé de motifs pour la revendication de la propriété exclusive du pseudonym Nadar, et Supplément au mémoire* (Dondey-Dupré, 1857)

13 Susan Sontag (1933–2004), *On Photography*, 1977 (Penguin, 1979)

14 Félix Nadar, *When I was a Photographer* (*Quand j'étais photographe*, E. Flammarion, 1900), trans. Eduardo Cadava and Liana Theodoratou (MIT Press, 2015)

15 William Henry Fox Talbot (1800–77), 'Brief Historical Sketch of the Invention of the Art', in *The Pencil of Nature* (Longman, Brown, Green and Longmans, 1844)

16 Fox Talbot, *The Pencil of Nature*

17 Charles Baudelaire (1821–67), 'The Salon of 1859: The Modern Public and Photography' in *Modern Art and Modernism: A Critical Anthology*, ed. Francis Frascina and Charles Harrison (Routledge, 1982)

18 Paul Fletcher, Bernard Wolfe Professor of Health Neuroscience, University of Cambridge, conversations in 2014

19 Mark Wallinger, *Ever Since* (video, 2012), Hauser and Wirth

20 Virginia Woolf, diary entry, 18 March 1925, in *The Diaries of Virginia Woolf, 3: 1925–30*, ed. Anne Bell (Penguin, 1982)

Seeing clearly, glimpsing, picturing

1 Georg Bocskay (1510–75), *Mira Calligraphiae Monumenta: A Sixteenth-Century Calligraphic Manuscript Inscribed by Georg Bocskay and Illuminated by Joris Hoefnagel*, ed. Lee Hendrix and Thea Vignau-Wilberg (Getty, 2020)

2 Karel van Mander (1548–1606), *Dutch and Flemish Painters* (*Het Schilder-Boeck*), trans. Constant van de Wall (Mcfarlane, Warde, Mcfarlane, 1936)

3 Denis Diderot (1713–84), 'Voyage en Hollande', 1772, cited in Svetlana Alpers, *The Art of Describing: Dutch Art in the Seventeenth Century* (University of Chicago Press, 1984)

4 Bocskay, *Mira Calligraphiae Monumenta*

5 Van Mander, *Dutch and Flemish Painters*

6 Van Mander, *Dutch and Flemish Painters*

7 'Four studies of a diseased mouse', in Rijksmuseum catalogue, rijksmuseum.nl/en/collection/RP-T-1880-A-98

8 Sir Francis Bacon (1561–1626), cited in Alpers, *The Art of Describing*

9 Karel van Mander, *The Lives of the Illustrious Netherlandish and German Painters . . .* (*Het Schilder-Boeck*), ed. H. Miedema, 6 vols (Davaco, 1994–9)

10 *Four Studies of a Woman*, 1602–3, Musées Royaux des Beaux-Arts, Brussels

11 Gilbert White (1720–93), Letter XII: 4 November 1767, in *The Natural History of Selborne*, ed. Richard Mabey (Penguin, 1977)

12 White, *The Natural History of Selborne*

13 White, *The Natural History of Selborne*

14 Beatrix Potter (1866–1943), letter cited in Linda Lear, *Beatrix Potter: A Life in Nature* (Penguin, 2008)

15 Extracts from a conversation with Zoe Kourtzi, Professor of Experimental Psychology, University of Cambridge, 2014

Becoming, resistance, dissolve

1 Eva Hesse (1936–70), *Eva Hesse: Studiowork*, Fruitmarket Gallery, 2014

2 Briony Fer, *Eva Hesse: Studiowork* (Fruitmarket Gallery/Yale University Press, 2009)

3 Sol LeWitt, cited in Lucy Lippard, *Eva Hesse* (New York University Press, 1976)

4 Eva Hesse, *Statement* (1968) in *Eva Hesse* (Fischbach Gallery, 1968) cited in Lippard, *Eva Hesse*

5 Eva Hesse, interview with Cindy Nemser, 20 January 1970, Cindy Nemser papers, 2013.M.21, Getty Institute

6 This version of the story of Lucretia is from Livy (59 BC–AD 17), *History of Rome* (*Ab Urbe Condita*) trans. Rev. Canon Roberts (Dutton, 1912–24)

7 Livy, *Ab Urbe Condita*

8 From the testimony of Artemisia Gentileschi (1593–c.1656), March 1612; see 'Artemisia's rape trial', National Gallery website, 29 September 2020, nationalgallery.org.uk/exhibitions/past/artemisia/artemisias-rape-trial

9 Testimony of Artemisia Gentileschi

Black and white and colour

1 Karel van Mander, *Dutch and Flemish Painters* (*Het Schilder-Boeck*), trans. Constant van de Wall (Mcfarlane, Warde, Mcfarlane, 1936)

2 C. S. Lewis (1898–1963), *The Lion, the Witch and the Wardrobe*, illustrated by Pauline Baynes (Geoffrey Bles, 1950)

3 Ruskin, *Modern Painters*, in *John Ruskin: Selected Writings*, ed. Kenneth Clark (Penguin, 1964)

4 D. H. Lawrence (1885–1930), 'Bavarian Gentians', in *D. H. Lawrence: Poems Selected by Tom Paulin* (Faber, 2007)

5 Francis Bacon, cited in Svetlana Alpers, *The Art of Describing: Dutch Art in the Seventeenth Century* (University of Chicago Press, 1983)

6 Antoni van Leeuwenhoek (1632–1723), *Alle de Brieven van Antoni van Leeuwenhoek* (Swets and Zeitlinger, 1939–79) cited in Alpers, *The Art of Describing*

7 F. Scott Fitzgerald (1896–1940), *Tender Is the Night* (Charles Scribner's & Sons, 1934)

8 Charlotte Perkins Gilman (1860–1935), 'The Yellow Wallpaper' (1892), *The Yellow Wallpaper and Selected Writings* (Virago, 2009)

9 Perkins Gilman, 'The Yellow Wallpaper'

10 Garry Fabian Miller quotations from a conversation with Lavinia Greenlaw, October 2001. See also Garry Fabian Miller and Lavinia Greenlaw, *Thoughts of a Night Sea* (Merrell, 2003)

11 Italo Calvino (1923–85), 'Quickness', in *Six Memos for the Next Millennium* (Penguin, 2016)

12 Garry Fabian Miller, 'Lecture 1: The Light Gatherers', Bodleian Libraries Honorary Fellowship Lectures, March 2022

The body, open, itself

1 Kester Rattenbury, *Building Design* (29 October 1993)

2 H. S. Souttar, 'John Hunter the Observer', *British Medical Journal*, 1/4600 (5 March 1949)

3 John Hunter's advice to Edward Jenner in Lloyd Allan Wells, '"Why Not Try the Experiment?" The Scientific Education of Edward Jenner', *Proceedings of the American Philosophical Society*, 118/2 (19 April 1974)

4 'John Hunter's Remains', *British Medical Journal*, 2/3955 (24 October 1936)

5 Sir Reginald Watson Jones, Hunterian Oration, 1959

6 John Berryman (1914–72), 'Dream Song 207', in *The Dream Songs* (Farrar, Straus & Giroux, 1969)

7 Heidegger's phrase as used by Mark Kingwell in 'Husserl's Sense of Wonder', *Philosophical Forum*, 31/1 (Spring 2000)

8 Zbigniew Herbert (1924–98), 'The Hygiene of the Soul', in *Selected Poems*, trans. Czesław Miłosz and Peter Dale Scott (Penguin, 1968)

9 Emily Dickinson (1830–86), 'My first well Day— since many ill—' (574), in *The Complete Poems*, ed. Thomas H. Johnson (Faber, 1970)

10 John Berger (1926–2017), *A Fortunate Man: The Story of a Country Doctor*, 1967 (Canongate, 2016)

11 Alfred North Whitehead (1861–1947), *Modes of Thought* (Macmillan, 1938)

12 Alfred North Whitehead, Lecture Six, 'Civilized Universe', in *Modes of Thought*

13 Max von Laue (1879–1960), cited in E. A. Burtt, *The Metaphysical Foundations of Modern Physical Science* (rev. edn, Routledge and Kegan Paul, 1949)

14 Francesca Woodman (1958–1981), note written on back of print, MacDowell Colony, 1980

15 Philips Angel (1616–83), *Praise of Painting (Lof de Schilder-konst)*, 1642, trans. Michael Hoyle, *Quarterly for the History of Art*, 24/2–3 (1996)

16 Ovid, *Metamorphoses*

Peering and noticing, flits and swerves

  1 Eugène Fromentin (1820–76), *The Masters of Past Time (Les Maîtres d'Autrefois)*, 1876, trans. Andrew Boyle, ed. Horst Gerson (Phaidon, 1948)

  2 Johann Heinrich Lambert (1728–77), *The System of the World*, trans. James Jacque (Vernor and Hood, and J. Cuthell, 1800)

  3 John Locke, *An Essay Concerning Human Understanding*, 1689, ed. Roger Woolhouse (Penguin, 1997)

  4 Robert Hooke (1635–1703), *Micrographia*, 1665 (Folio Society, 2022)

  5 Hooke, *Micrographia*

  6 Samuel van Hoogstraten, *Academy of Painting; or, The Visible World (Inleyding tot de Hooge Schoole de Schilderkonst)*, 1678, ed. Celeste Brusati, trans. Jaap Jacobs (Getty Research Institute, 2021)

  7 Hooke, *Micrographia*

  8 Antoni van Leeuwenhoek, letter 1694, in *The Collected Letters of Antoni van Leeuwenhoek* (Routledge, 1939)

  9 Van Leeuwenhoek, *Collected Letters*

10 'Do you reside now as formerly at Slough? If so the railway will prove an amazing convenience to you. I went by it the other day;

we reach Maidenhead in 50′ (ex. stopstages) I don't want to go
faster than that.' William Henry Fox Talbot to Sir John Herschel,
1838, cited in Gail Buckland, *Fox Talbot and the Invention of
Photography* (Scolar Press, 1980)
11 Constance Fox Talbot (1811–80), source unknown
12 Richard L. Gregory (1923–2010), *Eye and Brain: The Psychology
of Seeing* (5th edn, Princeton University Press, 2015)
13 George Eliot (1819–80), *Middlemarch*, 1871, ed. Rosemary
Ashton (Penguin, 2003)
14 Georgia O'Keeffe (1887–1986), cited in Calvin Tomkins,
'Georgia O'Keeffe's Vision', *New Yorker* (4 March 1974)

Pattern, machinery, punctuation
1 Louise Bourgeois (1911–2010), in Eleanor Munro, *Originals:
American Women Artists* (Touchstone/Simon & Schuster, 1982)
2 This conversation with Greg Poole (1960–2018) is from *The
Year's Four Corners*, BBC Radio 4 (2002)
3 William Styron (1925–2006), *Darkness Visible: A Memoir of
Madness* (Vintage, 1992)
4 Thomas Harral (1774–1853), *Picturesque Views of the Severn with
Historical and Topographical Illustrations* (G. and W. B. Whittaker,
1824)

Staying put, locked doors, wallpaper
1 Attributed to Cesare Pavese (1908–50) in the epigraph to Ian
McEwan's *The Comfort of Strangers* (Jonathan Cape, 1981)
2 Cesare Pavese, *Dialogues with Leuco* (*Dialoghi con Leuco*), 1947,
trans. William Arrowsmith (Marsilio, 1989)
3 Cesare Pavese, *The Moon and the Bonfires* (*La Luna e i Falò*),
1949, trans. Tim Parks (Penguin, 2021)
4 Pavese, *The Moon and the Bonfires*
5 Gilbert White, *The Natural History of Selborne*, ed. Richard
Mabey (Penguin, 1977)
6 White, *The Natural History of Selborne*

7 White, *The Natural History of Selborne*

8 Virginia Woolf, 'White's Selborne', 1939, in *Essays of Virginia Woolf*, 6, ed. Stuart N. Clarke (Chatto & Windus, 2012)

9 Dorothea Tanning (1910–2012), *Between Lives: An Artist and her World* (W.W. Norton, 2001)

10 Tanning, *Between Lives*

11 Tanning, *Between Lives*

12 Tanning, *Between Lives*

13 Georgia O'Keeffe to Alfred Stieglitz, 9 July 1929, in *My Faraway One: Selected Letters of Georgia O'Keeffe and Alfred Stieglitz*, ed. Sarah Greenough (Yale University Press, 2011)

Eye-catchers, furniture, peepshows

1 John Constable (1776–1837) cited in *The Life and Letters of John Constable*, ed. C. R. Leslie (Chapman and Hall, 1896)

2 Joshua Reynolds (1723–92) cited in Svetlana Alpers, *The Art of Describing: Dutch Art in the Seventeenth Century* (University of Chicago Press, 1983)

3 Soame Jenyns (1704–87), 1757, cited by John Barrell, *The Dark Side of the Landscape: The Rural Poor in English Painting 1730–1840* (Cambridge University Press, 1980)

4 Barrell, *The Dark Side of the Landscape*

5 Conversation with Paul Fletcher, 2014

6 Martin Creed, *Work No. 200 Half the Air in a Given Space*, Tate St Ives, 2011

7 Carsten Höller, *Test Site*, Tate Modern, 2006

8 Limits of Knowing with Chris Salter + TeZ, Mona el Gammal, Arrival of Time, among others

9 Director/composition Chris Salter + TeZ in collaboration with Ian Hattwick

10 Conversation with Paul Fletcher, 2014

11 Antony Gormley and Dr Priyamvada Natarajan, *Lunatick*, Acute Art, 180 The Strand, London, 2019

12 Peter Mundy (1596–1667), *The Travels of Peter Mundy in Europe*

and Asia, 1608–1667 (Cambridge University Press, 1925)

13 Mundy, *The Travels of Peter Mundy*

14 Jacob Appel (1690–1751), *Dolls' House of Petronella Oortman*, c.1710

15 'Hoogstraeten, die 't penseel verwisselt met de pen,' in
    Christopher Brown, David Bomford, Joyce Plesters and John
    Mills, 'Samuel van Hoogstraten: Perspective and Painting',
    National Gallery Technical Bulletin, 11 (1987)

16 Samuel van Hoogstraten, *Academy of Painting; or, The Visible
    World* (*Inleyding tot de Hooge Schoole de Schilderkonst*), 1678, ed.
    Celeste Brusati, trans. Jaap Jacobs (Getty Research Institute, 2021)

17 Samuel van Hoogstraten, *A Peepshow with Views of the Interior of
    a Dutch House*, c.1655–60

Unanchoring, sinking, at sea

1 John Constable to Maria Bicknell, 1814, *The Life and Letters of
   John Constable*, ed. C. R. Leslie (Chapman and Hall, 1896)

2 John Constable to Abram Constable, November 1838, in *Life and
   Letters*

3 John Constable, *Hadleigh Castle, The Mouth of the Thames:
   Morning after a Stormy Night, 1829*, Yale Center for British Art,
   Paul Mellon Collection

4 *Memoirs of the Life of John Constable Composed Chiefly of His
   Letters*, ed. C. R. Leslie (John Lehmann, 1949)

5 John Constable to John Dunthorne, 29 May 1802, in *Life and Letters*

6 Vija Celmins, in conversation with C. Close, in *Vija Celmins:
   Drawing as Thinking*, ed. W. S. Bartman (New York, 1992)

7 Hoogstraten, *Academy of Painting*

8 James Elkins, 'On Visual Desperation and the Bodies of Protozoa',
   Representations, 40: special issue, *Seeing Science* (Autumn 1992)

Curiosity, wonder, rupture

1 Thomas Kuhn (1922–96), 'Comment on the Relations of Science
   and Art', 1969, in *The Essential Tension: Selected Studies in
   Scientific Tradition and Change* (University of Chicago Press, 1977)

2 Epigraph added to a copy of Joris Hoefnagel's *Shells, Flowers, Insects and a Chick* (*Archetypa*), by his son Jacob

3 Plato (*c.*427–*c.*347 BC) *Theaetetus*, cited in Mark Kingwell, 'Husserl's Sense of Wonder', *Philosophical Forum*, 31/1 (Spring 2000)

4 Freya Stark (1893–1993), *The Valleys of the Assassins* (John Murray, 1944)

5 Albrecht Dürer (1471–1528), *A Rhinoceros*, 1515, Royal Collection Trust

6 Francis Bacon, *The Advancement of Learning*,1605, in *Francis Bacon: the Major Works*, ed. Brian Vickers (Oxford, 2008)

7 Plato, *Theaetetus*, trans. M.Cornford, cited in Krzysztof Pomian, 'Vision and Cognition', in *Pete Picturing Science, Producing Art*, ed. Peter Galison and Caroline A. Jones (Routledge, 1998)

8 Galileo Galilei (1564–1642), trans. Eileen Reeves in 'Galileo, Oracle: On the History of Early Modern Science', *I Tatti Studies in the Italian Renaissance*, 18/1 (Spring 2015)

9 Galileo, trans. Reeves, in 'Galileo, Oracle'

Disorder, slippage, glare

1 Elizabeth Bishop, 'In the Village', in *The Collected Prose* (Farrar, Straus & Giroux, 1984)

2 Bishop, 'In the Village'

3 Bishop, 'In the Village'

4 Elizabeth Bishop recalled by Frank Bidart in *Remembering Elizabeth Bishop: An Oral Biography*, ed. Gary Fountain and Peter Brazeau (University of Massachusetts Press, 1994)

5 Bishop, *The Complete Prose*

6 David Kalstone, *Becoming a Poet: Elizabeth Bishop with Marianne Moore and Robert Lowell* (Farrar Straus and Giroux, 1989)

7 Elizabeth Bishop, interview with Edward Lucie Smith, in *Conversations with Elizabeth Bishop*, ed. George Monteiro (University of Mississippi Press, 1996)

8 Elizabeth Bishop, 'Sleeping Standing Up', in *The Complete Poems 1927–1979* (Farrar, Straus & Giroux, 1979)

9 Bishop, interview with Lucie Smith, in *Conversations with Elizabeth Bishop*, ed. Monteiro, p. 13.

10 Elizabeth Bishop to Marianne Moore, 29 August 1946, in *One Art: The Selected Letters, Elizabeth Bishop*, ed. Robert Giroux (Farrar, Straus, Giroux, 1994)

11 Elizabeth Bishop, 'The Sandpiper', in *The Complete Poems*

12 From text on display during the eclipse at the National Museum of the Faroe Islands

13 *Maria Mitchell: A Life in Journals and Letters*, ed. Henry Albers (College Avenue Press, 2001)

14 Virginia Woolf, *A Writer's Diary: Being Extracts From the Diary of Virginia Woolf*, ed. Leonard Woolf (Harcourt, 1954)

Invisible, unseen

1 Fincelius, *Die Wunderseichen*, 1556, cited in Silvanus P. Thompson, *The Pied Piper of Hamelin* (Bedford Press, 1905)

2 Fincelius, *Die Wunderseichen*

3 Richard Verstegen (*c.*1550–1640), *A Restitution of Decayed Intelligence* (John Norton, 1634)

4 S. Erich, *Exodus Hamelensis*, 1655, cited in Thompson, *The Pied Piper of Hamelin*

5 Erich, *Exodus Hamelensis*

6 Erich, *Exodus Hamelensis*

7 Verstegen, *A Restitution of Decayed Intelligence*

8 Erich, *Exodus Hamelensis*

9 Virginia Woolf, 'Cornwall, 1905,' *A Passionate Apprentice: The Early Journals of Virginia Woolf*, ed. Mitchell A. Leaska (Hogarth Press, 1990)

10 Virginia Woolf, *To the Lighthouse*, 1927 (Vintage, 2004)

11 Amelia Earhart (1897–1937), source unknown

12 Julian Ross, 'The All-Seeing Drone's Gaze: An Interview with Jananne Al-Ani', Sonic Acts (11 November 2016)

13 Seamus Heaney (1939–2013), *Human Chain* (Faber, 2010)

14 Elizabeth Bishop, 'Over 2,000 Illustrations and a Complete

Concordance', in *The Complete Poems 1927–1979* (Farrar, Straus & Giroux, 1979)

The imagined image

1 'Why does the eye see a thing more clearly in dreams than with the imagination being awake?' Leonardo da Vinci (1452–1519), *Notebooks* (Oxford University Press, 2008)

2 'Studio Visit with Howardena Pindell' (video), Christies, 5 May 2022, youtube.com/watch?v=kICF9jrDYHs&t=14s)

3 Charles Babbage (1791–1871), *Passages from the Life of a Philosopher* (Longman, 1864)

4 Babbage, *Passages from the Life of a Philosopher*

5 Ada Lovelace's (1815–52) notes in her translation of L. F. Menabrea, *Sketch of the Analytical Engine invented by Charles Babbage* (*Notions sur la machine analytique de M. Charles Babbage*), 1842 (translation R & J. E. Taylor, 1843)

6 Ada Lovelace, notes in her translation of *Sketch of the Analytical Engine*

7 Ada Lovelace, notes in her translation of *Sketch of the Analytical Engine*

8 Dr Cayley et al., 'On Babbage's Analytical Machine', in *Report of the Forty-eighth Meeting of the British Association for the Advancement of Science* (John Murray, 1879)

9 Cayley et al., 'On Babbage's Analytical Machine'

10 Cayley et al., 'On Babbage's Analytical Machine'

11 Ana Maria Pacheco, *Remember*, Galway International Arts Festival, 2022

12 Christopher Marlowe, 'Hero and Leander', 1598, in *Complete Poems and Translations* (Penguin, 2007). Marlowe died before finishing the poem, which was completed by George Chapman

13 Marlowe, 'Hero and Leander'

Section one

page 1: (top) Marc Aźema, Ministry of Culture & Communication, France. Musée d'Archéologie nationale. Domaine national de Saint-Germain-en-Laye.

(bottom) Woodcut. Rosenwald Collection, National Gallery of Art Washington.

page 2: Lithograph on paper; dimensions (unconfirmed): 940 x 584 mm. © The Piper Estate / DACS 2023. Photo © Tate.

page 3: (top) Drawing; dimensions: 130 x 230 mm © Royal Meteorological Society / Science & Society Picture Library. All rights reserved.

(bottom) Drawing; dimensions: 96 x 180 mm © Royal Meteorological Society / Science & Society Picture Library. All rights reserved.

page 4: McKim, Mead & White. Museum of the City of New York / Art Resource, NY / Scala, Florence.

page 6: (top) Oil on canvas; dimensions: 2150 x 1300 mm. Uffizi Gallery, Florence.

(bottom) Aquatint on paper, dimensions: 162 x 241 mm. Photo © Tate.

page 8: Oil on canvas; dimensions: 908 x 1213 mm. Royal Academy of Arts, London. Yale Center for British Art, Paul Mellon Collection.

Section two

page 1: Watercolour, gold and silver paint, and ink; dimensions: 166 x 124 mm. J. Paul Getty Museum, Los Angeles.

page 2: (top) Dimensions: 128 x 183 mm. Rijksmuseum, Amsterdam.

(bottom) Ink, watercolour and gouache on paper; dimensions:
111 x 92 mm. Photo © Tate.

page 3: From wood engraving. Pallant House Gallery, Private
Collection.

page 4: Oil on beechwood; dimensions: 373 x 239 mm. Staatliche
Museen, Berlin. Artothek / Bridgeman Images.

page 5: Oil on canvas; dimensions: 929 x 727 mm. J. Paul Getty
Museum, Los Angeles.

page 6: © The Estate of Eva Hesse. Courtesy Hauser & Wirth.
Photo: Stefan Altenburger Photography Zurich.

page 7: Oil on wood; dimensions: 708 x 1089 mm. Museum of Fine
Arts, Houston; gift of the Enthoven Foundation. Bridgeman Images.

page 8: Drawing; dimensions: 142 x 196 mm. D. Franken Bequest,
Le Vésinet, Rijksmuseum, Amsterdam.

Section three
page 1: © Rachel Whiteread. Photo: Sue Omerod. Courtesy of the
artist and Gagosian.

page 2: Gelatin silver print; dimensions: 102 x 102 mm © 2023
Woodman Family Foundation / Artists Rights Society (ARS), New
York 2023. Image: Copyright Phillips Auctioneers LLC.

page 3: Dimensions: 1130 x 1460 mm. Saint-Quentin, Antoine
Lécuyer museum. RMN-Grand Palais / Dist. Photo SCALA,
Florence.

page 4: (top) Oil on canvas; dimensions: 1374 x 1677 mm © The
National Gallery, London.

(bottom) illumination from treatise on falconry, French translation
Frederick II (fol. 186), National Library of France, Department of
Manuscripts.

page 5: Oil on panel; dimensions: 308 x 242 mm. Mauritshuis
Museum, The Hague.

page 6: (bottom) Oil on canvas; dimensions: 510 x 600 mm. National Gallery of Art, Washington / Widener Collection, 1942.9.33.

page 7: Oil on canvas; dimensions: 1022 x 6480 mm. Philadelphia Museum of Art © ADAGP, Paris and DACS, London 2023.

page 8: Oil and egg on wood, 580 x 880 x 605 mm. Presented by Sir Robert and Lady Witt through the Art Fund, 1924. National Gallery, London.

Section four

page 1: Illumination on parchment. Condé Museum, Chantilly.

page 2: (top) The Sammlung Staedelmuseum, Frankfurt.

(bottom) Getty Research Institute, Los Angeles. Biodiversity Heritage Library.

page 3: Oil on paper laid on canvas; dimensions: 235 x 326 mm © Photo: Royal Academy of Arts, London. Photographer: John Hammond.

page 4: (top) From *Exchanging Hats: Paintings* by Elizabeth Bishop. Copyright © 1996, 1997, 2011 by Alice Helen Methfessel. Reprinted by permission of Farrar, Straus and Giroux and Carcanet Press. All Rights Reserved. Private Collection

(bottom) Schlossmuseum, Sondershausen, Germany.

page 5: © Jananne Al-Ani.

page 6: Acrylic, paper, powder, sequins and glitter on sewn canvas squares; dimensions 2197 x 2616 mm © Howardena Pindell. Courtesy the artist, Garth Greenan Gallery, and Victoria Miro.

page 7: Silverpoint, dimensions 290 x 215 mm. Private Collection. Photo © Pratt Contemporary / Bridgeman Images.

page 8: Cartridge paper, ink, pen; dimensions: 156 x 130 mm. Rijksmuseum, Amsterdam. D. Franken Bequest, Le Vésinet, 1898.

Acknowledgements

I would like to thank Joanna Woodall, Professor Emerita, Courtauld Institute, who taught me about seventeenth-century Netherlandish art, and the Wellcome Trust for the Engagement Fellowship (2013–2016) during which I began this work. Conversations with scientists in 2014 helped me formulate my first questions: Professor Colin Blakemore, Institute of Philosophy, University College London; Paul Fletcher, Bernard Wolfe Professor of Health Neuroscience, University of Cambridge; and Zoe Kourtzi, Professor of Experimental Psychology, University of Cambridge. I have also been helped by conversations with Sophie Scott, Professor of Cognitive Neuroscience, University College London.

Thank you, Ales Steger and Maja Petrovic-Steger for taking me into the Slovenian caves; Tim Dee for the solstice and equinox and Arctic journeys; Paul Dodgson for our time in Great Village, Nova Scotia, and Sandra Barry for her support while we were there; Richard Ayres for asking me to explore Peter Pan; Michael Rose for walking into the dark with me in Berlin; and Jürgen Ronthaler for explaining the glow in the distance in Leipzig; Aldeburgh Music, Artangel, BBC Radio 3 and 4, the Gulbenkian Foundation, the Faroe Islands Tourist Board, the *New Yorker*, the Poetry Foundation, *Granta*, *London Review of Books*, *Tate* magazine, Dundee Contemporary Arts, the Science Museum London, the archivists of the Philadelphia Art Museum, the Getty Foundation, Starlight Bus Tours LA, the Courtauld Institute, Jennifer Higgie and *Frieze*, the Rijksprentenkabinett at the Rijksmuseum in Amsterdam. I would also like to thank the Freie Universität Berlin for the Samuel Fischer guest professorship, which enabled me to give a seminar in 2017 on seeing and not seeing further. I am grateful to my students for our stimulating conversations.

Thank you to my agents, Sarah Chalfant and Jessica Bullock at the Wylie Agency, and to Alba Ziegler-Bailey for her guidance and encouragement in the early stages.

Thank you to my editor, Emmie Francis, who has helped me to bring thirty years of thinking into shape. Faber has given me a home for all those years, for which I am profoundly grateful. Thank you, Rachel Alexander, Alex Bowler, Kate Burton, Anne Owen and Sophie Harris, and also Kate Murray-Browne and Amanda Russell.

Thank you to my extended, far-flung, present and absent family for accompanying me on all these voyages, even when just waving me off.